# El Sistema

## Music for social change

OMNIBUS PRESS

London / New York / Paris / Sydney / Copenhagen / Berlin / Madrid / Tokyo

Exclusive Distributors
Music Sales Limited,
14/15 Berners Street,
London, W1T 3LJ.

Macmillan Distribution Services
56 Parkwest Drive,
Derrimut, Vic 3030,
Australia.

Every effort has been made to trace the copyright holders of the photographs in this book but one or two were unreachable. We would be grateful if the photographers concerned would contact us.

Printed in the EU

A catalogue record for this book is available from the British Library.

Visit Omnibus Press on the web at www.omnibuspress.com

# Table of Contents

*Proceeds from the sale of this book will support the students and families of Youth Orchestra Los Angeles (YOLA) at Heart of Los Angeles (HOLA).*

This book is dedicated to my first horn teacher, Joseph Buono, and to all music teachers who have changed the life trajectory of a student.

This book is also for my mother, a great advocate for music education.

# Acknowledgments

THIS book is a collaborative feat, so there are many individuals and organizations to thank. I would like to start by acknowledging the incredible time and energy of the book's contributors, who agreed to openly share their experiences, learning, ideas, and mistakes for others to see and consider. Persistence is clearly a characteristic of musicians and activists, and I am forever grateful that all continued with this project through many questions, conversations, and rounds of editing.

Also vitally important to the success of this book is the editor, Paul De Angelis of Paul De Angelis Book Development. Paul offered an articulateness, structure, and clarity to these pages without ever compromising the authors' voices or ideas. I have come to appreciate that editing is an artform dependent not only on significant language skill, but also critical questioning and considerate, patient collaboration. Like a great accompanist, a great editor offers egoless support to illuminate and deepen the intention of a soloist or writer. In this realm, Paul De Angelis is a true artist.

There are also several organizations and individuals to be acknowledged for their support of this book. In particular I wish to thank Robert Wise, Chris Charlesworth, and Nigel Gilroy of Music Sales Group; Eduardo Méndez, Romina Noviello, and Patricia Abdelnou of FundaMusical; Heart of Los Angeles (HOLA); The Los Angeles Philharmonic Association; The Longy School of Music of Bard College; Benjamin Rubinfeld and Ziffren Brittenham LLP; multiple El Sistema-inspired programs, including: The Baltimore Symphony Orchestra's OrchKids Program and Dan Trahey; Corona Youth Music Project; Crescendo Detroit and Damien Crutcher; Friends of El Sistema Japan; The Harmony Project; The Incredible Children's Art Network (iCAN), Adam Johnston, Xóchitl Tafoya, and Ilda Zavala; Juneau, Alaska Music Matters (JAMM); KidZNotes and Katie Wyatt; Núcleos Estaduais de Orquestras Juvenis e Infantis da Bahia (NEOJIBA), Ricardo Castro and Eduardo Torres; The

San Diego Youth Symphony Community Opus Project; El Sistema Colorado; Sistema Scotland; El Sistema Sweden; and Union City Music Project. I also must acknowledge and thank the past and present YOLA at HOLA and HOLA Music Faculty members: Jon Armstrong; Mani Baker; Claire Bergen; Dawn Bertani; Brandon Brack; Heather Breene; Leah Carter; Roxana Castro; Leslie Chinchilla; P. Blake Cooper; Scott Cummings; Jackie DesRosier; Michelle Elliot; Emily George; Rachel Hockenberry; Emma Joleen; Jessica Jones; Shabnam Kalbasi; Bruce Kiesling; Emily Kubitskey; Emma Kuzmanoff; Dorothy Micklea Valencia; Juan-Felipe Molano; Yuri Morelos; Nadene Rasmussen; Robert Reyes; Nikki Shorts; Megumi Smith; Mark Tyson; and Tim Winfield.

A special thank you to the children, parents, teachers, and staff of HOLA: I hope that in these pages others will also be inspired by the beauty and strength you hold because to me, it has been the most incredible gift possible; to The New England Conservatory, Mark Churchill and the 2009–2010 class of Abreu Fellows; and to my husband Dan, for bringing me tea and humor throughout this book's development.

Finally, I must extend my deepest and unending gratitude to José Antonio Abreu and the children, teachers, leaders, and communities of El Sistema in Venezuela. Thank you for continuing to teach the world through your incredible example and for inspiring a movement.

# Foreword

*By Deborah Borda, President, Los Angeles Philharmonic*

IN 2006, I took a trip to Caracas. Though I was searching for a music director, I discovered something that would change my life: El Sistema. There was one certainty after my ten days immersed in Maestro José Antonio Abreu's visionary program. Regardless of whether we could entice Gustavo Dudamel to become the music director of the Los Angeles Philharmonic, we would adapt El Sistema to Los Angeles. This was our responsibility. And this is precisely what we did, creating Youth Orchestra Los Angeles (YOLA) with the most exceptional community partners that our great city has to offer.

Of course, we were fortunate enough to bring Gustavo to Los Angeles as well. When he arrived, his very first concert as music director was not the traditional season-opening gala at Walt Disney Concert Hall. It was, instead, a free concert for 18,000 people at the Hollywood Bowl. We called it *Bienvenido Gustavo*. Gustavo's first downbeat as music director was conducting the new YOLA orchestra. I remember seeing the excitement in the student's faces – such an enormous stage for these young children! Their performance captured the imagination of the country.

*Bienvenido Gustavo* was an innovative launch to a music director's tenure, and one that pointed us in a new direction. YOLA's rendition of Beethoven's "Ode to Joy" was followed by the Los Angeles Philharmonic's performance of the full-length Ninth Symphony. From that moment forward, our community-based efforts and the artistry of our orchestra would be inextricably connected. YOLA students and their families sat just steps away from the Hollywood Bowl stage, seeing one of the world's greatest orchestras perform a piece that had become their own.

At our most recent Take a Stand Symposium in 2014, I had an opportunity to be interviewed by two of YOLA's first graduating seniors. These two students received full scholarships to college through the Posse

1

Foundation. To hear of their aspirations beyond the world of music reminded me of the power of our YOLA program to create a new generation of agents of change. This is very real progress, and we are only beginning.

I continue to be inspired by El Sistema, its founder, and the thousands of community leaders who share the Maestro's ambitious vision to use music as a vehicle for social change. And we know why this is successful: artistic excellence and social development carry equal weight in a program's construction. As you read the following pages, I hope that you feel empowered, inspired, and ultimately energized to take on Maestro Abreu's challenge and create a stronger future for this world through music.

*– May 2014*

# Foreword

*By Leon Botstein, President, Bard College*

THE historical context for the surge of interest in adapting and replicating the Venezuelan success of El Sistema, not only in the United States but also throughout the world, and particularly in Europe, is not arcane or difficult to construct. So called "classical music" – indeed the entire tradition of music-making in European and North American culture before 1945 – thrived primarily as a matter of amateur practice, much like a popular sport. However, during the second half of the twentieth century, the habits of active amateurism – singing and playing – declined precipitously. A palpable shift could be observed from active playing to passive listening, from studying instruments to buying records.

The prominence and stature once accorded music education in the schools and private instruction at home, and therefore to learning to play an instrument, likewise weakened as the generations changed, from adults for whom music-making and listening were parts of their memories and lives to those for whom they were not. The ultimate consequence of this historical trajectory was the apparent aging of the concert audience, the absence of interest in concert life among young people, and the perception of an overall decline in the significance of and interest in serious musical culture. Indeed any participatory musical life that involved a community or public space took on the aspect of irrelevancy. Only popular commercial music, bought, sold, and listened to, retained social and political prominence.

This should have come as no surprise. The huge interest in concert life, music journalism, music publishing, and instrument manufacture were all derivative of an active amateur population. Between the heyday of amateurism (consider the 1920s in Berlin, where in a city of about 4 million people there were over 250 registered amateur ensembles and choruses) and today's sparsely attended concert halls in Europe and the

3

United States was a brief period of enthusiasm for passive listening at home to the radio and to recordings. That too has passed into history.

Therefore the fascination in and enthusiasm for El Sistema are understandable. El Sistema represents a plausible hope that the power of the classical musical tradition and amateurism can be restored. Over a forty-year period, hundreds of thousands each year have been introduced to musical culture, learned to play, and learned to love listening to live music-making. Music has once again become central to cultural and public life. Not since the end of the Cold War have classical musicians and orchestras occupied such a prominence in shaping and representing national identity as they possess today in Venezuela.

However as we, particularly in the United States, look from the outside in and try to learn from El Sistema, we need to be self-critical and cautious. First, Maestro Abreu's charisma and genius cannot be replicated. Second, his insight that although a program of mass music education considered as a matter of arts education or the arts per se could not justify a national investment of public funds, it could be justified as an investment in social improvement, brilliant as it was, cannot be transferred easily to other nation states. In the United States, and in Europe – given the sustained deflationary economic crisis – there is no prospect of the sort of major national funding Abreu managed to get, even though from the start El Sistema was a program of social change, an instrument of social betterment for the least served in his country. Even as a social program, El Sistema, however adapted, will have to rely in the United States on private support, not taxpayer-based public funds. That prospect, despite the enormous growth in wealth among the most privileged and the widening gap in income between the rich and the poor, is dubious. With the decline in interest in music and music-making since 1945 has come a parallel erosion of patronage for classical music – or indeed any serious music education, whether in jazz or folk idioms. The young rich – whether in Silicon Valley or on Wall Street – are most interested in commercial popular music, not Beethoven, Mahler, or Stravinsky.

Third, the United States has been and will remain a heterogeneous place. In this country a single approach, whether by ethnicity, race, religion, or region, will not work. There is no centrally configured "silver" bullet in any sphere of education. For better or worse, primary and secondary education in the United States has remained under local control and is governed in small units, making the national map of education a patchwork quilt of jurisdictions.

Given that the growing network of El Sistema sites in the United States will lack a charismatic leader, national authority, and government support, what are the practical lessons we may nonetheless keep in mind that derive from the huge success of El Sistema in its original Venezuelan context? Here are just a few:

(1) Involve the entire community on a local level.
(2) From the start, give all participants, particularly beginners, a real public platform. Remember music is there to be performed in front of one's community, in public.
(3) Mix up the ages and generations. Avoid age segregation. Make the older teach the younger, and play with them.
(4) Do not privilege only one kind of music. Do not place "classical music" on a pedestal. Mix up genres and styles.
(5) Remember that the voice is the first and most important human instrument. Make sure everyone sings.
(6) Remember that being musical and making music is not about exceptional "talent." As Charles Ives observed, the most musical person in the community is not necessarily the one with perfect pitch or virtuoso skills, but the one who puts the most genuine emotion and effort into the experience. Music is a democratic participatory pastime, despite the wide range of skill that can be exhibited, much like a team sport.
(7) Involve everyone in the making of instruments and repairing them. Turn players into tinkerers who come to love their instruments.
(8) Music and music-making are not for the rich alone. In fact the wealthy are unlikely to possess the discipline and motivation to learn. Despite classical music's origins in the aristocratic habits of the eighteenth century, the notated Western tradition is open to everyone and is a universal art of all humanity, not a bastion of privilege or an exclusive aspect of European culture.

We can indeed learn from El Sistema's success. The most important thing to learn from its achievement is that music is not a peripheral and passive part of life. Rather it is an active pursuit, a gateway to hope where there is despair, to self-confidence where there is insecurity, to solidarity where there is competition and conflict, and to learning where there is boredom and ignorance. El Sistema has helped remind us of the centrality of music to life, its sacred place in that which we deem human. Music as an individual and social experience can play a role in building a world of collaboration, freedom, peace, and tolerance. That possibility has been made clearer by the impact of El Sistema on the Venezuelans who have benefited from it. It is that achievement which represents the major lesson to be learned beyond the borders of Venezuela.

*— November 2014*

# Preface

By Dr. José Antonio Abreu, Founder, El Sistema

WHEN I was a young boy growing up in Barquisimeto, I dreamed of becoming a musician. Through my teachers, my family, and my community, I had the necessary support to realize this dream. Since this time, I have aspired to see all Venezuelan children have the same opportunity. From that desire and from my heart stemmed the idea to make music a deep and global reality for my country. This was the inspiration for El Sistema.

El Sistema is first and foremost a social and community project. The essence of El Sistema's youth orchestras and choirs are much more than artistic structures; to play and to sing together means to intimately coexist toward perfection and excellence. Here, we strive collectively for a more perfect, more aware, more noble, and more just society.

Since its beginnings nearly forty years ago, El Sistema has grown exponentially, from eleven children in attendance at the first orchestra rehearsal to now 500,000 children in choirs and youth orchestras around Venezuela. This miracle has inspired a global movement, spreading to over fifty-five different countries across multiple continents. An international "Sistema" has begun.

This successful proliferation of El Sistema demonstrates the essential nature of its malleable structure. Our "system" is truly a "non-system" and we intentionally embrace controlled chaos, which demands constant reflection, change, and improvement. This flexibility permits adaptations for the specific features of each community. This is why El Sistema is relevant and viable in diverse towns and cities across Venezuela and around the world. The effect of the orchestra on each location is felt in real and palpable ways, transforming the child, the family, and the community.

Today, there is the potential for a worldwide social revolution through art, with an ever-growing number of children and young people overcoming material and spiritual poverty with music as the tool. To realize this potential, the revolution requires individuals – dedicated to art and social justice – to offer their commitment and passion. We invite those individuals to unite with us in this vision of peace through music. We do not wish to dictate this movement by sanctioning or authenticating certain projects and not others; rather, we wish to share our experiences and knowledge openly in hopes of receiving back knowledge and experiences.

Conceived in this same collaborative spirit and with the critical understanding of El Sistema as a non-system, this book intends to support the advancement of such an open, adaptable movement. My hope is that its readers will contribute in a full and meaningful way toward creating a new era of music education in other countries.

*– August 2014*

## Message from Gustavo Dudamel, Music Director, El Sistema

THE world is changing, and music no longer belongs to one single place or culture; gone is the time when there was a particular sensibility of "European music" or distinctly "American." Just as Euro-pop or Cuban-jazz are played and interpreted everywhere, so too are the European classics played around the world: Mozart, Tchaikovsky, Beethoven, and Mahler, the core of European traditional music is played and enjoyed almost universally.

That is precisely the foundation of our "El Sistema" project in order to expose as many young people to music education as we possibly can, from every economic class and ability. We have demonstrated that this process can also be effective with children who are visually or hearing impaired, living in the streets, in prison, or even for those without any significant degree of formal educational achievement. Access to music has been successfully democratized in the projects we continue to inspire around the world as a part of the El Sistema movement. It is worth noting that it isn't only music that can have this effect on young people, but I believe any of the art forms – painting, sculpture, theater, dance – any form which carries innately the capacity to transmit emotions and to transport the individual into a different place emotionally and intellectually, has the ability to change lives.

This technical process has been some forty years in the making, beginning, as the legend goes, in a parking garage in Caracas in 1975 when a small gathering of young, idealistic individuals dedicated themselves to creating something around the principles of collaboration, sharing, and creation, using the orchestra as the centerpiece.

The whole point is and has always been not about creating musicians, but about giving human beings the means to self-development as a way to achieve self-fulfillment. Our ambition is to accomplish something positive and is directed at a collective progress, a common purpose that teaches children and young people to make the most of their time, to work together, toward a common goal. It enables them to learn something that is worthwhile, something filled with emotion: at its core a quest for beauty.

When we teach a child to appreciate art and by extension to recognize and be moved by beauty, we are giving the greatest gift we have to the next generation. The genius of that gift is that it can never be taken away. It is for life. It is forever. This is why I have dedicated my life to providing as many people access to the arts as I possibly can.

Art is the most important part of our education, giving us a physical and temporal space in which to create beauty. Time is our greatest asset and our greatest challenge as educators is to use it to fine-tune our innate sensitivity and that of those around us, and to evolve into better human beings.

# Introduction

*By Christine Witkowski*

IN 2013, I gave Robert Wise, the managing director of the Music Sales Group, a tour of the El Sistema-inspired program I helped to found, Youth Orchestra LA at Heart of Los Angeles (YOLA at HOLA). We weaved through hallways and classrooms, greeting young musicians engaged in music learning and academic tutoring. The youngest students welcomed our guest with excitement, wielding the charm of their toothless grins and newly earned violin skills through a classroom mini-performance of the D-major scale. As the tour ended and we said our goodbyes, Mr. Wise told me that he hoped to find a way for the Music Sales Group to support El Sistema-inspired work.

A few months later, Robert Wise called to ask if I would write a book for teachers, musicians, and leaders of El Sistema programs outside of Venezuela. This would be the Music Sales Groups' charitable contribution to the field of Sistema-inspired work. Though wholly overwhelmed at the thought of such an undertaking, I was nevertheless compelled to take on the task.

Part of my apprehension came from the understanding that much of what makes El Sistema thrive is the very fact that it is not a written doctrine or manual – it is a living, breathing philosophy, capable of shifting form and shape to exist in entirely new environments. Conveying this truth throughout the contents of a book would be essential. Also, I knew that tackling this project would involve acute consideration of my having started as an outsider looking in. I am not Venezuelan, and did not grow up in El Sistema. My experiences and expertise involve adapting El Sistema to the United States. I believe such a vantage point brings with it both areas of illumination and areas of limitation; the outsider sees things that the insider takes for granted, and may be better suited to adapting the philosophy to a new community. At the same time, the El Sistema consciousness is not something I've been steeped in since birth; I acquired it as an adult. Though I fully believe in El Sistema's tenets and have immersed myself in the work, much of the philosophy differs drastically from my own formal musical experiences as a performer, student, and teacher. Not falling into these old habits of mind requires that I constantly reflect upon and evaluate El Sistema's ideals in my daily work. It is an intentional deviation from my experience rather than an innate understanding.

Despite these concerns, I knew that I could not pass up the opportunity to get a written resource into the hands of those desperately searching for guidance. Even in its earliest beginnings, YOLA at HOLA and I played host to hundreds of visitors looking for a muse for their El Sistema work in the United States. Often, these individuals were following similar lines of inquiry about how to implement El Sistema. They needed to see and experience it as a launching point for their own programs. I had been part of the inaugural class of Sistema Fellows (formerly the Abreu Fellows) at the New England Conservatory of Music in Boston. The program was created as a result of Dr. Abreu's 2009 TED prize. The yearlong fellowship had afforded me the luxury of time to examine and consider the philosophy of El Sistema and the opportunity for full immersion in núcleos around Venezuela. While in Venezuela, I identified promising practices and sketched out what an ideal program in the United States might look like. This sketch later became the framework for YOLA at HOLA, which I helped to begin after graduating the fellowship.

Many of the visitors coming to HOLA are in need of something experiential and concrete to hold on to as they adapt El Sistema – something more tangible than being told to "love the whole child" or "using music as a vehicle for social change." Therefore, I saw this book as an opportunity to share practical details of El Sistema's adaptations around the world with those seeking knowledge, inspiration, and/or guidance.

However, I did not feel comfortable writing a book entirely in my own voice, with my experiences and knowledge at its center. Besides possibly being misconstrued as a "how to" guide, such a book would necessarily offer a narrow view of adaptation. There are many ways to successfully adapt El Sistema and what works for one community and program will not work for another. Across the globe, programs may uphold the ideals of Sistema work, yet look vastly different. Therefore, in an effort to illustrate the variety of practices, programs, and communities involved in El Sistema work, I decided not to *write* the book, but rather to *curate* it. I invited a selection of individuals with relevant expertise to reflect upon and share their learning and practice. The contributors to this book are shaping the field of El Sistema outside of Venezuela as leaders, and advocates of the movement. Their voices are intentionally varied, with program directors, parents, board members, teachers, organizational leaders, and experts from outside fields all represented. Despite my best efforts to draw from the movement's leading experts, many programs and important voices who have inspired El Sistema work are not represented in these pages. Their absence is indicative of nothing more than the need to produce a focused manuscript in a timely manner. While I have made an effort to include voices from across the country and around the world, I have nonetheless relied heavily on El Sistema advocates based in Los Angeles. In part, this is the result of my connection to and work in Los Angeles, but it is also intentional. El Sistema has put down strong roots in southern California, with the development of YOLA and the presence of Gustavo Dudamel as catalysts. YOLA is a large, multifaceted operation that encompasses a variety of programs, points of views, and organizational partnerships. The team at YOLA offers within itself a wide array of experiences and expertise, and each essay by one of its members is distinctive and highlights areas in which her or his work stands out not only within LA, but in the El Sistema field at large.

Drawing expertise out of so many contributors has proved both challenging and rewarding. For many in the book, their day-in, day-out accomplishments were largely the result of intuition and experience. Articulating these successes in writing meant breaking them down to the core components and examining why things worked – a task many had not had the time to revisit since they began. The drafting and editing process thus involved considerable energy spent in reflection, evaluation, feedback, and multiple drafts. I hope these efforts have paid off and that the realizations, knowledge, and experiences my contributors impart here will positively influence the work of other musicians, teachers, directors, and community leaders.

## How to Use This Book

"Our 'sistema' is not a sistema . . . The day we define a system, it is already dead." Dr. José Antonio Abreu's 2010 words to the inaugural class of

Abreu Fellows at the start of our Venezuelan residency have echoed in my mind throughout the process of collecting, editing, and writing this compilation. El Sistema is a philosophy and a social movement, not a curriculum or dogma. Central to its success is adaptability. There is no prescribed way to "replicate" or "translate" El Sistema to new environments – especially since, from núcleo to núcleo around Venezuela, the philosophy of El Sistema manifests itself in such different ways. A folk ensemble filled with cuatros (a Venezuelan guitar) and lever harps is equally as valid as the multitiered system of orchestras, choirs, and special needs programs found at Barquisimeto (the núcleos where Gustavo Dudamel grew up). The philosophy and movement of El Sistema links these programs, not instruments or day-to-day logistics. So please do not expect to find in this volume a manual filled with instructions, agendas, and blueprints, or a comprehensive guidebook to the knowledge base and skills one needs to do El Sistema work. Prescriptive, definitive answers cannot be found in this book, or any book on El Sistema.

Rather, this book provides a focused lens on the quandary of adapting El Sistema outside Venezuela, and should be thought of as a supplement to the hundreds of materials written on non-profit management, teaching, learning, artistry, and community building. I have asked people out in the field and on the ground to articulate what they have learned so that others might find inspiration and adaptable approaches.

As Dr. Abreu explained it, El Sistema work is permanently "being, yet not being." An El Sistema program is constantly evolving and changing without ever being "finished." Thus the contributions in this book embody our thinking in the field today, and as time marches on, some lines of thinking will evolve, while others will remain unchanged. All of it can serve as a line of inquiry to follow back into your classroom, your program, your community, and your art. Question, practice, and amend the writings in this book as you need to serve best your students, families, teachers, audiences, and colleagues. The information is yours to adapt.

This book is created by a community of learners for a community of learners. There is room for all interested parties; whether you are a performing musician seeking ways to make your art relevant to a wider audience or a veteran community leader curious about El Sistema, I hope there are many lessons here for you to extract. If only one idea resonates as something to try or consider, then we have done our job. While a genuine

14

attempt has been made to set appropriate context and foundation for those new to the work, I expect that some of the content will provoke even the most seasoned of leaders and community minded-musicians.

On a practical note, the term "El Sistema" used throughout this book is meant to indicate the philosophy and core values of music for social change as founded and modeled by Venezuela and adapted to the global movement. In the field today, the adaptation of El Sistema is commonly referred to as being "El Sistema-inspired" as a way of distinguishing between the original Venezuelan program and its subsequent development in other countries. For simplicity's sake, in this book we use "El Sistema" more broadly to encompass the philosophy and ideals both inside and outside of Venezuela, and "El Sistema in Venezuela" when specifically referring to the original.

## About the Content

*Music for Social Change* has four main parts. "Why El Sistema?" gives a historical and philosophical overview of El Sistema in Venezuela and evidence of its value in arts education and advocacy in the twenty-first century. The first chapter of "Understanding Communities" offers brief portraits of five El Sistema programs in widely varying contexts in the United States, Europe, and Asia, while the other two offer caveats to consider when working within communities in crisis. "Teaching and Learning" describes practices and attitudes that empower and engage students, teachers, and musicians in the El Sistema classroom; and the chapters in "Groundwork" provide sketches of practical and administrative solutions that support a program's development, growth, and connection to the movement.

These four subject areas were selected because they enhance the discussion of El Sistema's adaptation outside of Venezuela. Many issues addressed in the essays answer questions frequently brought to me by aspiring programs. Equally critical was the need for any individual 5,000-word essay to contribute meaningfully to a given topic within these subject areas.

This last condition meant that not every question could be answered. One subject that was not explicitly addressed – although it is alluded to in several essays – is fundraising. We've heard many times from Sistema's founders that funding is secondary to exceptional work, and these pages will focus on that work. The fundraising question is not El Sistema-specific but common to all nonprofit arts organizations. Each country, state, and city is unique in its development needs and opportunities – a fact that has led me to defer to the multiple books and other channels of information that already exist on the topic. That said, strategies for raising awareness that may ultimately generate funds and help provide program sustainability are discussed in the "Groundwork" section of the book.

Editing and compiling these essays gave me the opportunity to reach out to other musicians, teachers, leaders, and advocates in a way that I had not done since beginning my work at HOLA. The daily work of a large El Sistema program requires complete dedication. Often it feels as though I'm just keeping my head above water in managing the diverse interests of the students, parents, teachers, organizations, and partnerships. The idea of spending extra energy to stay connected to the movement and the larger arts and youth development worlds can be daunting – but it's essential. We have much to learn from one another, and we are all in the fight together. It's heartening to know that, all over the world, other leaders, teachers, students, and parents share the same struggles and the same joys.

During this editing process of the contributions, I had one particularly late night preparing for a large production the following day. While in the midst of making orchestra stage plots and copying running orders, I received an email from Malin Aghed of El Sistema Sweden, one of the authors in this book. She was also going through a particularly challenging period, but she wrote to me: "You know me and the gang, we won't give up! We share the core of El Sistema with all you guys, with Venezuela, and the rest of the world. That's what keeps us going when times get rough."

As El Sistema spreads around the globe, there is a broadening of individuals who find themselves drawn to or involved in the work. This ever-expanding network brings a diversity of experience, knowledge, and skill that strengthens the movement. It is my hope that these essays incite actions, both large and small, that advance the social mission of art in communities, classrooms, and concert halls around the world.

– *Christine Witkowski, June 2014*

# PART I

# WHY EL SISTEMA?

While in Caracas during the spring of 2010, I heard the following story many times: In 1970s Venezuela, there were very few professional opportunities for an orchestral musician. The limited positions that did exist were filled almost exclusively by European musicians, lured to Venezuela by large salaries, thanks to the oil boom. A young Venezuelan bassoonist graduating from the Caracas Conservatory inquired with his teacher about finding work, to which he was regretfully told, "You will have to wait until someone dies to have a job." Discouraged, the young musician called his conservatory colleagues into an outdoor courtyard and announced, "I will never be able to play in a symphony orchestra in my country. I cannot play merengue with this bassoon. There is no use for this instrument." He then proceeded to pour kerosene on his bassoon, light a match, and set it on fire. José Antonio Abreu was a part of the crowd that watched this bassoon burn.

The details of this legend are murky, as stories passed down from person to person over many years so often become. However, the idea of this bassoon, engulfed in flames, was seared into Dr. Abreu's mind. He became determined to change the status quo of "art for the minority by the minority" into "art for the majority by the majority." He vowed to create an orchestra where Venezuelan musicians could play. Over four decades and 1 million children later, Dr. Abreu has achieved this dream in Venezuela through El Sistema. Every person in Venezuela knows a friend, family member, or neighbor who has been in an El Sistema orchestra. Bootlegged classical music CDs are as commonplace in markets around the country as their popular music counterparts. By making the orchestra inclusive, it has also become relevant.

Today in the United States, arts education has been stripped from many public schools. This hurts all children, but proves especially detrimental to those growing up in poverty with access to fewer learning opportunities and attendancee at overburdened schools. Most of these same children are without the resources necessary to supplement their education with the arts outside of school. Further, students, players, and audiences seeking involvement with orchestras have traditionally encountered multiple barriers, so that typically only a small, privileged group ends up participating. These circumstances are the byproducts of inequity on a much larger scale. Underserved communities not only lack access to formal arts education, but also to health care, housing, food security, unbiased policing and judicial processing, transportation, and safety.

El Sistema begins to bridge this opportunity gap for the most vulnerable children. By providing a path to ensemble music learning while simultaneously fostering positive youth and community development, El Sistema programs reach those who otherwise might never have the chance to join an orchestra. The potential outcomes of these efforts are exemplified by program successes in Venezuela, where communities have found new life and hope centered around their local orchestras. The world-famous Simón Bolívar Symphony Orchestra of Venezuela is a particularly vivid image of what can be accomplished artistically and socially. Given the imperative need to level the playing field for students living in poverty and the positive results demonstrated in Venezuela, it is easy to understand why so many have turned to El Sistema.

There are many steps in between first partnering with a community in need and then producing an impressive outcome like the Simón Bolívar Symphony Orchestra. The majority of this book tackles different versions of these in between steps – the *how*, if you will. This opening section, however, largely explores the value of El Sistema through its history, philosophy, and outcomes. It explores the *why*.

Internationally acclaimed conductor Gustavo Dudamel reminds us that the "quest for beauty" is innately linked to our humanity. Teaching a child to appreciate and create beauty translates into that child being more aware of and sensitive to himself and others.

As the most famous pupil of El Sistema, Gustavo Dudamel is defined by his dedication to reach all children with access to art. When he works with young musicians, whether they are in Venezuela, Scotland, or Japan, his aesthetics remain perfectly intact. I once watched Gustavo, with great charm and a warm smile, resolutely insist that a children's orchestra repeat the single opening note of Mozart's *Eine Kleine Nachtmusik* over and over. This was not a demand for perfection, but rather for a state of transcendence; he only allowed the group to move on when every child demonstrated a connection to the music, to him, and to one another. In that instance, the students had sculpted a moment of beauty.

In the United States, a narrative centered on funding often necessitates a focus on the tangible and practical outcomes of El Sistema. Therefore, the profound and emotional experience of creating and recognizing great art is often left out of the "why" conversation, as its inherent value and purpose is impossible to fully measure.

All musicians understand the divine nature of art. Gustavo Dudamel's message, as the starting point for the journey of this book, compels us to relentlessly pursue beauty for our students and ourselves as the elevating principal of the work.

In Chapter 1, Tricia Tunstall rolls out a tapestry of El Sistema, past and present, through an overview of its history in Venezuela and subsequent proliferation around the globe, especially in the United States. Tricia is uniquely qualified for this task, being a celebrated advocate for El Sistema and author of *Changing Lives: Gustavo Dudamel, El Sistema and the Transformative Power of Music*, the first major book to tell the story of El Sistema, Dr. José Antonio Abreu, and Gustavo Dudamel. Today, she and Eric Booth (author of the article that follows Tricia's) put out *The Ensemble*, a monthly newsletter for the US and Canadian El Sistema movement.

With all the energy concentrating around El Sistema today, many fear that it may just be another "fad" that will fade over time, that the attention of the public is short-lived and fickle. Tricia's essay reminds us, however, that El Sistema in Venezuela was built over many years of dedication, experimentation, and refinement. The work has been ongoing now for over forty years in Venezuela and for several decades in larger Latin America, receiving wider international attention only in the last decade. This fame has allowed El Sistema to reach an entirely new swath of children from around the globe. It is wise for us newcomers to ride the coattails of El Sistema in Venezuela as we gain our footing, and to remember that educational trends lose steam because they lack substance and outcomes. The history of El Sistema's growth around the globe is still being written, but it is rooted in a tested, proven program. In Venezuela, the movement has withstood many storms (several far greater than the dwindling of public attention) and continues to succeed today.

El Sistema's success in delivering social change is rooted in its philosophy, which Eric Booth explores in his essay. Eric is an international arts consultant and a key figure in El Sistema's rise across the globe. As the author of *The Music Teaching Artist's Bible: Becoming a Virtuoso Educator*, Eric has been enthralled for decades by the question of what makes for quality in arts education.

Ideally, the essence of El Sistema is felt and experienced as a whole. This makes expressing its core in writing particularly challenging, as intellectual understanding requires that the components be segmented and categorized. It proves limiting and quite artificial to construct an organized list of fundamentals for a philosophy that thrives on its organic nature of "being yet not being." Dr. Abreu himself has not written a clear set of fundamentals. In many respects, this type of neatly packaged explanation defies El Sistema's very spirit.

However, the El Sistema field abroad – and especially in the United States – desperately needs an articulation of El Sistema's key concepts if it is to grasp the scope of the work and how it differs from other forms of music education or youth development. Eric has risen to this task beautifully and graciously, outlining the essential ideals that comprise El Sistema work in real, attainable ways while also conveying the organic spirit of the movement. The essentials listed here are meant to be referred to as points of inspiration, not places of limitation, and should continue to evolve along with their users and creators.

From this historical and philosophical context, we can begin to imagine what El Sistema may yield in the new programs sprouting up across the world. Of course, the most marketable story is that of the student on a path towards self-destruction who is "saved" by music and never turns back. These heroic, neatly tied-up "turnaround" tales do exist, but they are the outliers. More often than not, progress with a family, student, and community is two steps forward, one step back. It requires diligence, patience, and an ability to play the long game. In El Sistema, success is more process than product. Paloma Udovic Ramos does not shy away from the complexity of this topic in "What Is Student Success?" – the first part of a chapter devoted to "inspiration from on the ground." Paloma has been working for the Harmony Project in Los Angeles since 2008 and is the program director who runs the organization's Youth Orchestra Los Angeles at EXPO venture. With a background in ethnomusicology and anthropology, Paloma looks at her work with honesty and healthy skepticism. An essay on student success could have yielded a series of self-congratulatory, feel-good stories, but instead, Paloma chose to openly share the challenges she faces in defining and acknowledging success for her students and program.

Discussions with parents offer another important look at the outcomes of an El Sistema program. Parents know how, when, and why a program affects their children and communities. This feedback can be sought out regularly and leveraged to strengthen the educational process. Ines Williams and Ariadna Sanchez are El Sistema parents located respectively on the East and West coasts, and their testimony makes up the second part of our "inspiration" chapter. Both of their statements make evident that El Sistema work is not only influencing children, but also their parents.

The final chapter of this first section of the book deals with the measurable outcomes of El Sistema-inspired work. Shirley Brice Heath came to study the world of arts education through her research as a linguistic anthropologist. In 1987, she examined 120 community-based organizations in low-income areas that provided three types of afterschool programming in three areas: athletic-academic, community service, and arts-based. The results were rather unexpected; Shirley found that kids involved in arts-based organizations exhibited the highest intensity of motivation, persistence, critical analysis, and planning. Compared to the other groups, they were more satisfied with themselves, twice as likely to win an award for academic achievement, and more likely to feel capable of making and executing plans. She published these findings with Elisabeth Soep in a paper titled "Youth Development and the Arts in Nonschool Hours."* Shirley will quickly explain that she is a scientific researcher and not an advocate for arts education or El Sistema programs; that she has no agenda or emotional attachment to arts education.

In the essay Shirley publishes here, she examines the benefits of

---

* *Grant Makers in the Arts* Newsletter, Vol 9, No. 1 (Spring 1998),
   http://www.giarts.org/article/youth-development-and-arts-nonschool-hours

ensemble-based learning and points out why this learning is of particular importance to students from poorly served communities. Shirley's research provides us with new language and metrics for describing and measuring our outcomes, a critical tool for programs that require quantitative results, research, and assessment to demonstrate value to funders and partners. She calls for the El Sistema field to invest more seriously in research to prove its validity. Few new programs can afford the cost of research that goes beyond the simple reaffirmation of the most basic assumptions, but other studies in progress today are doing so.

In 2012, the University of Southern California Brain and Creativity Institute, the LA Philharmonic, and Heart of Los Angeles announced a five-year longitudinal research collaboration to investigate the emotional, social, and cognitive effects of early musical training on childhood brain development. Led by acclaimed neuroscientists Hanna and Antonio Damasio, the study uses standard psychological assessments and advanced brain imaging techniques to track brain, emotional, and social development; the results are compared to a control group of children. Similarly, Harmony Project in LA is collaborating with Northwestern University to study learning, communication abilities, and biological development in grade-school children and a University of California San Diego study of the impact of music training on the brain and behavior development is looking at students of the San Diego Youth Symphony's Community Opus Project. Moving beyond anecdotal proof of El Sistema's value is a daunting task, but ultimately one that will sustain the work.

The field of El Sistema will inevitably have its critics; traditionalists may scoff at the methodology and idea of open access, while those entrenched in the work of reducing poverty and crime may see a social program activated through music as a romanticized notion. Of course, "the proof of the pudding is in the eating." Even the staunchest cynics are hard pressed not to sense the value of El Sistema when they experience it firsthand.

– C.W.

# CHAPTER 1

# El Sistema: A History

## *Tricia Tunstall*

MANY social and historical movements have a well-known founding story: Boston patriots dumping tea into the harbor, for example, or Rosa Parks sitting down in the front of the bus. The founding story of El Sistema is famous enough that even among those who know little about it, this is one of the things they know: in 1975, the Venezuelan economist, government official, and accomplished musician José Antonio Abreu gathered eleven young people in an abandoned parking garage in Caracas. He told them they would one day become a great symphony orchestra. The rest is history.

It's a splendid story, a Pygmalion tale for musicians. And it is even largely true, although the whole truth is, as usual, more complex and more interesting. But in fact there is a foundation story that predates this one by several decades, a story containing all the essential seeds of the extraordinary experiment in artistic and empathic imagination that is El Sistema today.

When José Antonio Abreu was a child in Barquisimeto, Venezuela, in the 1940s, he took piano lessons with a distinguished pianist and teacher, Doralisa Jiménez de Medina. Senora de Medina's musical standards were high, as befitted her orthodox musical training in Paris, but her studio was unconventional in several ways: she taught numerous poor children free of charge, as well as children of middle-class families who could pay, and she sometimes taught as many as seven children at the same time. Lessons took place at the seven grand pianos ranged around her home's inner courtyard, and students were encouraged to help one another. So that they could experience the joy of playing orchestral masterworks together, she made arrangements of the symphonies of Beethoven and Mozart and Haydn, creating parts of varying degrees of difficulty so that students at all skill levels could participate. Family members and friends of her students were welcomed into her studio many times a year to hear them perform.

This experience made an indelible impression upon the young Abreu. When he left Barquisimeto in 1957 to study piano, organ, harpsichord, and composition at a Caracas conservatory, he took with him the internalized idea of music as a sphere of inclusion, cooperation, and joy.

In the years after completing his conservatory studies, Abreu studied economics in Caracas and at the University of Michigan, eventually earning his doctorate, and went on to serve as a deputy to the Congress of Venezuela. At the same time, he maintained an active musical life, often playing with music students and teachers in Caracas   and in so doing, he became ever more acutely aware of the fact that the country's few professional symphony orchestras were populated almost entirely by musicians from North America and Europe, who were drawn there by large salaries made possible by the oil boom. It was nearly impossible for Venezuelan musicians, even those with conservatory degrees, to find an orchestral job.

It's here that the famous founding story comes in. Deciding that the young musicians of Caracas needed a way to play together, Abreu rounded up fifty music stands and put out a call to his musical friends and acquaintances to join him in an abandoned garage.

When Abreu recollects this moment in speeches and interviews, he confesses that he had felt deeply disappointed to see only eleven music students show up. The thought crossed his mind that perhaps he should send them home. Instead, in one of those prescient leaps of imagination that the universe grants only to true visionaries, he told the eleven teenagers that if they committed themselves to becoming an orchestra, they would one day change the musical culture of their entire country, and become one of the best symphony orchestras in the world.

To a man, they thought perhaps he was crazy. But to a man, they stayed. Something about the clarity of his vision and his passionate certainty led them to decide in that moment not to walk away.

They came back the next night, and the next; they brought friends, who brought more friends. One of the first eleven, Abreu's lifelong friend Frank di Polo, drove around Caracas in his dilapidated Chevrolet. "Hey," he yelled out of the window, "we're starting an orchestra, do you want to join?" Within a month, there were seventy members coming to nightly rehearsals, and a youth orchestra was born.

There were no auditions and no entrance fees. As in Doralisa de Medina's piano studio, anyone was welcomed who wanted to play and was willing to work hard. They met and rehearsed every day for many hours, often long into the night. Four months after they began, they gave their first public performance, playing works by Bach, Vivaldi, Mozart, and Tchaikovsky for a large audience that included several government officials. They received a standing ovation.

And less than a year later, Maestro Abreu brought his orchestra – now officially named the Simón Bolívar Youth Orchestra of Venezuela – to an international festival of youth orchestras in Aberdeen, Scotland. They were the only Latin American orchestra in attendance, and a completely unknown quantity, but they left triumphant, with more Venezuelans chosen to be in the festival orchestra than musicians of any other nationality.

Members of the musical establishment of Caracas, from conservatory professors to symphony orchestra patrons, were astounded; they could not understand how such a radically unorthodox ensemble could possibly achieve international success. In fact, the key to their success lay in a few simple principles, all born of necessity.

The first principle was the idea of performance as a deeply motivating goal. With scheduled performances on the near horizon, the orchestra members threw themselves into the process of pursuing excellence. This disparate group of musical novices were propelled and unified by their intense desire to prove themselves worthy of public esteem.

To accomplish this goal, there was an urgent need to bring the less skilled players up to the level of the more accomplished ones. And since Abreu himself could only work with them during the evenings after his official workday was over, the task of pursuing collective excellence fell largely to the players themselves. Thus evolved the second great principle of their success: peer teaching and learning. The peer-to-peer teaching ethos that developed during this process has been elegantly explained by David Ascanio, one of the founders: "Even if you only know A, B, and C, you have the capacity to teach A, B, and C. And not only the capacity, but also the responsibility!"

A third principle was the concept of learning music through ensemble work. Certainly the youngsters of the Simón Bolívar Youth Orchestra, intent upon a fast learning curve, did some solitary practicing. But the great majority of their learning happened through rehearsing together. They honed their skills and shaped their music within the vibrant sound and feel of the orchestra itself, constantly listening to one another, adjusting, refining. "To play and sing together," Abreu has written, "is to intimately co-exist toward perfection." These young players' intimate co-existence inside music allowed them to cohere and make swift progress together.

Frequent performance, peer teaching, ensemble learning – we can see the seeds of these principles in Abreu's childhood experience with Doralisa de Medina. And one other element came from that experience, less a principle than a way of life: the new youth orchestra was joyful. With Abreu as their model, they never forgot to take passionate pleasure in the splendor of the music and the sheer fun of working and playing together.

In 1977, the Venezuelan government was eager to support the new ensemble that had so surprisingly boosted the country's musical reputation. A government support foundation was established, not within the Cultural Ministry but as a youth development program; Abreu requested this distinction, because he knew that whenever regimes change and programs are cut, the arts are always the first to go. As a social program, the orchestra project would have somewhat more protection against political vicissitudes.

Over the next few years, as Abreu's youth orchestra grew in size, proficiency, and ambition, so did his vision. And he arrived at another, and overarching, big idea. He saw that the process of radical orchestral immersion, which made it possible for his young protégés to get better fast, was also having a remarkable effect on another level entirely. They were not only better musicians; they were more confident, secure people. They were more self-disciplined, more empathic, better equipped to cooperate and forge community.

Maestro Abreu understood that he had found the great work of his life. He vowed to bring the same opportunity to every Venezuelan child – especially the children of poverty and deprivation. "When you put a violin into the hands of a child," he has famously said, "that child will not pick up a gun."

The process of evolving from a single youth orchestra to "El Sistema" was gradual and organic, spanning the next several decades. Abreu traveled the country tirelessly, setting up a new youth or children's orchestra initiative anywhere he could find an available space and an adventurous teacher or two. Members of the orchestra joined his musical mission, and set up orchestra programs in Caracas and throughout the countryside, in their own towns and provinces – programs based on the same principles of inclusion, peer teaching, ensemble learning, and joy that characterized the spirit of their own orchestra. Programs were launched sometimes in school buildings after school hours but often in unused "found" spaces like that original Caracas parking garage: an abandoned bus terminal, a deserted warehouse, a racetrack empty on weekdays. In some cases, children played under the largest mango tree in town.

Over the years, these "núcleos," as the youth orchestra programs were called, engaged younger and younger children. Ensembles for different age and skill levels evolved, and choral activities began to develop; a typical núcleo would include a beginner-level string orchestra, a mid-level orchestra, an advanced student orchestra, a teacher's orchestra, and several choirs, so that every student had the chance to belong to a musical ensemble at every age and skill level. At the same time, master teachers such as Susan Siman and Josbel Pulce began to focus on pedagogy for very young, pre-school age children that would prepare them for entering ensembles as they grew.

Without conscious intent, the young people of that first Simón Bolívar Youth Orchestra were developing a new model for what it means to be a musician: as they continued to rehearse and perform with their orchestra a number of times a year, they also worked as leaders and teachers in núcleos, fostering children's social and musical development. The paradigm of musician as performer, teacher, and citizen was so compelling to the first generation of núcleo students that many aspired to become precisely such a musician; and so a second generation of núcleo founders and teachers began leading the ongoing growth of El Sistema.

At every juncture during that growth when Abreu could have chosen between ambitious expansion and high musical standards, he invariably chose both. During the early 1980s, the Sistema expanded rapidly to include over fifty núcleos across the country, providing access for thousands more children. Choral programs were developed in every núcleo, parallel to the orchestral ensembles. At the same time, master instrumental and vocal teachers were regularly brought to the provinces to give master classes for advanced students, and in Caracas, the Simón Bolívar Conservatory was founded to provide rigorous musical training for aspiring professionals. Abreu became minister of culture in 1983, and among his first initiatives was the establishment of a university-level institute of music, so that for the first time in Venezuela's history, gifted young musicians could complete their musical education without going abroad.

In the early 1990s, Abreu asked famed Mexican conductor Eduardo Mata, longtime leader of the Dallas Symphony Orchestra, to rehearse and conduct the Simón Bolívar Youth Orchestra in a series of recordings on the Dorian label, featuring Latin American composers such as Villa-Lobos, Ginastera, Estevez, Revueltas, Chávez, Orbón, and de Falla. It was the orchestra's professional recording debut, and marked the first time that Abreu passed the baton to another conductor so that he could devote all his energies to developing El Sistema as a whole. Maestro Mata was thrilled at the ease and precision with which the orchestra executed the highly complex rhythms of Latin American orchestral music, and amazed at the young musicians' eagerness to rehearse for long hours to achieve perfection. Several of the recorded pieces featured the choral group Scola Cantorum, an esteemed Venezuelan choir, founded by Alberto Grau and led by Maria Guinand, that was developing parallel to El Sistema and in accord with many of its ideals.

By the mid-1990s, with the Simón Bolívar ensemble fully mature both artistically and personally, and with hundreds of núcleos across Venezuela producing another new musical generation, Abreu decided it was time to launch a new national children's orchestra. He and his orchestral comrades sought out the most skilled young musicians in the country, some as young as nine or ten, for the new ensemble. Among the recruits was fourteen-year-old violinist and aspiring conductor, Gustavo Dudamel.

As he had done with his original orchestra, Maestro Abreu poured his abundant energy into shaping and nurturing this one. And as before, he catalyzed their musical growth with an outsized performance goal: in 1996 he took the group, called the National Children's Orchestra, to play at the Kennedy Center in Washington, D.C. Several years later, when most of the children had become teenagers, this group evolved into the new Simón Bolívar Youth Orchestra of Venezuela; the older group retained the name but was designated "Simón Bolívar A," while the new one was "Simón Bolívar B." In 1999, at the age of eighteen, Gustavo Dudamel became the conductor of the "B."

At the dawn of the 2000s, El Sistema had become a vast, mature, and complex interrelated network of children's and youth orchestras. National academies and festivals were developed for each orchestral instrument, with the aim of continually raising the musical standards of the Sistema. The range of orchestral repertoire widened to include other genres, with particular emphasis on the rich Venezuelan folk music traditions.

Simultaneously, there was a steady intensification of focus on social goals; núcleos began expanding their programs to welcome children with all kinds of special needs. The núcleo at Barquisimeto inaugurated this process in the late 1990s, and in the twenty-first century has become a model for comprehensive, in-depth inclusion. Many núcleos now serve students with hearing, sight, physical, and cognitive special needs through percussion ensembles, bell choirs, and "white hand choirs" in which hearing-impaired children use their gloved hands to express the meaning of words simultaneously sung by children with other special needs. In addition, children with special needs are integrated with non-special needs children in choral and orchestral ensembles. For sight-impaired students, there is a program to translate all written musical parts into Braille.

And with each passing year, new núcleos continue to be founded in ever more remote parts of the country. By 2013, El Sistema comprised 400,000 children and young people playing and singing together every day.

In the continual process of expansion and development, El Sistema has never lost its core principles. At the heart of every núcleo is the principle of ensemble learning: the orchestra and the choir are at once pedagogical context, artistic goal, and social world. The ensemble is the emotional landscape in which learning takes place, a landscape of beauty and belonging. It is an environment where needing help is never wrong, and empathy and compassion are always rewarded. Crucially, it is an environment of contribution: everyone in the orchestra is responsible for everything about the orchestra. "We are not trying to create musicians," nucléo leaders will invariably say. "We are trying to create citizens."

During the 1990s, awareness of El Sistema spread in Latin America; a number of countries, most prominently Colombia, Brazil, and Mexico, developed their own Sistema-inspired programs. But the Sistema remained under the radar in the rest of the world until late in the first decade of the twenty-first century, when the Simón Bolívar Youth Orchestra "B," playing at ever higher levels of technical and artistic brilliance with Dudamel at the helm, began to tour internationally. They performed in the great European cultural capitals, including London, Paris, Berlin, Vienna, and Lucerne; in Scandinavia, Russia, and Japan; in the United States at the Kennedy Center and Carnegie Hall. Audiences everywhere were transported by the young Venezuelans' precocious virtuosity and unbridled passion. For the first time, the international musical community began to sit up and take notice of El Sistema.

In 2007, the Simón Bolívar Youth Orchestra delivered a particularly sensational performance at the London Proms. A video clip of one of their encores, the three-minute "Mambo!" from Leonard Bernstein's *West Side Story Suite*, went viral on YouTube as musicians around the world circulated the link, amazed to discover that classical music was alive and well in an unlikely corner of Latin America, where young people were reimagining what a symphony orchestra could be.

The prestigious German label Deutsche Grammophon signed the Simón Bolívar for a series of recordings. And world-renowned musicians – including conductors Sir Simon Rattle, Daniel Barenboim, and Claudio Abbado; violinist Itzhak Perlman; pianist Martha Argerich; and tenor Placido Domingo – came to Venezuela to observe the Sistema firsthand and to work with its ensembles. Maestro Rattle, the conductor of the Berlin Philharmonic, said of El Sistema, "If anyone asked me where there is something really important going on now for the future of classical music, I would simply have to say – in Venezuela. It is an emotional force of such power that it may take some time to assimilate what we're seeing and hearing."

The growing international awareness of El Sistema brought widespread recognition to its founder. After being awarded the title of UNESCO Ambassador for Peace in 1998, Abreu was honored in the following years with prizes and testimonials from countries across the world: Sweden's Right Livelihood Award; Italy's Life and Music prize; Germany's Frankfurt Music Prize; Sweden's Polar Prize; Holland's Erasmus Prize; and the Seoul Peace Prize. From Toronto came the Glenn Gould Prize; the Latin Grammys awarded a Doctorate Honoris Causa. Spain awarded its prestigious Prince of Asturias Award to the entire Sistema, "for having combined, within a single project, the highest artistic quality and a profound ethical conviction applied for the improvement of our social reality." Lincoln Center awarded the World Culture Open Peace Prize to Maestro Abreu, celebrating him as "a beacon of hope in a troubled world."

---

There is a strand of music education history in the United States that resonates with El Sistema's ideal of social engagement and inclusion. In particular, the settlement house movement, which began in the 1880s with Chicago's Hull House and reached a peak in the 1920s with 400 settlement houses across the country, embraced a social agenda for the arts, using arts education as a means to improve the lives of poor and marginalized populations. Settlement houses were located in poverty-stricken areas and offered a broad variety of cultural and artistic learning experiences; the activist teachers and leaders who led this movement viewed the arts, particularly practical arts such as craft-making and singing, as a vital means of improving lives and fostering community through creative engagement and expression.

The Works Progress Administration continued to develop this tradition. Launched during the Great Depression as a job creation initiative, the WPA employed over 40,000 artists in the fields of visual arts, music, theater, and writing. These artists' charter was to connect with communities and engage in a wide range of public art projects, from making posters to producing plays to forming choruses and other musical ensembles. Their work, like the settlement house movement, challenged the elitist traditions of "high art" and celebrated the spirit of art-making in community.

Even as this tradition began to wane after World War II, there was still a strong ideal of arts learning as essential to civic life, as arts education retained a generally robust presence in the public education system during the latter half of the twentieth century. Many, if not most, urban and suburban public schools had at least one music teacher, and children at every socio-economic level were taught music fundamentals and rudimentary choral and instrumental skills. This began to change, however, in the early 2000s, as one school system after another reduced or eliminated music education in an effort to dedicate all resources in severely straitened budgets to "core" subjects such as science, math, and reading. The 2008 Survey for Public Participation in the Arts published by the National Endowment for the Arts cited a "decline in school-based arts education offerings, particularly since 2001–2002 . . . Declines were greatest in music and visual arts."* A study commissioned by the Wallace Foundation in the same year found that the decline dated from the early 1990s, asserting that "arts education has been a low priority in the nation's public schools for more than thirty years."†

Inevitably, arts education cuts have been most drastic in impoverished urban areas. In the words of the Wallace Foundation study: "More recently, the arts have had difficulty keeping even a tenuous foothold in many urban schools because of general education reforms, such as the No Child Left Behind Act, that holds schools accountable for standardized test scores in mathematics and reading."‡ Musicians and music teachers across the country have been dismayed by this trend toward the diminishment of music learning as a vital part of cultural life and an entitlement of every child.

The discovery of El Sistema, therefore, has been nothing short of electrifying for many musicians and educators. Awareness came slowly at first, through the viral Proms YouTube clip and a *Sixty Minutes* program about Gustavo Dudamel. A few intrepid music educators who saw these videos, including Dan Trahey of Baltimore, Anne Fitzgibbon of New York, and Leonard Bernstein's daughter Jamie Bernstein, immediately boarded planes to Venezuela in order to immerse themselves in the Sistema philosophy and bring it home.

Then, in 2009, two seminal events caused a sharp uptick of awareness and interest in El Sistema. The first was Dudamel's appointment as conductor of the Los Angeles Philharmonic at the age of 27 – and along

---

* Rabkin, Nick, and E.C. Hedberg, "Arts Education in America: What the Declines Mean for Arts Participation," Research Report #52, National Endowment for the Arts, 2011, p.14.
† Bodilly, Susan, and Catherine Augustine, with Laura Zakaras, "Revitalizing Arts Education Through Community-wide Coordination," Rand Research in the Arts, commissioned by the Wallace Foundation, 2008, p.11.
‡ Bodilly, p.11.

with that appointment, the launch of Youth Orchestra Los Angeles (YOLA), a Sistema-inspired initiative of the LA Philharmonic and its community partners, Harmony Project, the Expo Center, and Heart of Los Angeles. The other seminal event was the award given to Maestro Abreu by TED, a non-profit organization devoted to "ideas worth spreading." (TED conferences present and live-stream talks by thought leaders in a wide variety of fields.) Abreu was among the 2009 winners of the TED Prize for the year's most inspirational speakers; he was invited to make a wish that the TED organization would help to make a reality. His wish, stated at the end of his indelibly moving TED talk (another YouTube viewing essential, entitled "José Antonio Abreu: The El Sistema Music Revolution"), was that a program be established to train "fifty gifted young musicians, passionate about art and social justice," in how to develop and sustain El Sistema programs in the United States and around the world. An Abreu Fellowship program dedicated to this goal was established six months later at the New England Conservatory of Music in Boston.

All of a sudden, the United States had, on the West Coast, an active model for what an El Sistema-inspired program might look like in the United States, and on the East Coast, a training center for potential program leaders. On both coasts and across the country in between, the imaginations of music educators and social activists were galvanized around the idea that we needed El Sistema here, and right away. There were over 100 applications for the ten Fellowships offered in the Abreu Fellowship's first class, which began in October 2009 in Boston. At precisely the same time in Los Angeles, Gustavo Dudamel inaugurated his tenure at the LA Philharmonic by donning a tee shirt that said "Youth Orchestra Los Angeles" and conducting the very young fledgling musicians of the YOLA program in the "Ode to Joy" at a packed Hollywood Bowl. It was the first official downbeat of his new career in Los Angeles. The thousands of musicians and music teachers in cities and towns across the United States who watched that live-streamed event knew that something important was happening – something that indicated a seismic shift back toward the tradition of music as social engagement and music education as deeply important in the lives of children and communities.

In short order, programs inspired by El Sistema began to spring up in cities across the country. Pioneering programs like YOLA, the Baltimore Symphony's OrchKids, and the Harmony Program in New York were quickly joined by new initiatives in San Antonio, Boston, Atlanta, Philadelphia, Newport News, San Diego, and many other places. During the next few years, the tally of Sistema-inspired programs in the United States rose to over 100. The Sistema idea was spreading equally fast in Canada, with programs emerging in Ottawa, Toronto, New Brunswick, and elsewhere.

In some ways, the growth of El Sistema in North America has been the opposite of the Venezuelan story. In Venezuela, things began with a national youth orchestra created with no model, beginning with Venezuelan student musicians and developing into an ensemble of the highest quality. The members of that orchestra were then able to carry their vision across their country and establish núcleos that reached younger and younger students.

In contrast, North America has a robust tradition of high-level youth orchestras but no precedent or mechanism for support on a national level. Programs have therefore been launched in a very local way, almost always because one or two or three people catch the inspiration of the El Sistema idea and resolve to bring it to their towns or cities. They find a source of funds (usually modest), a space, some gifted teachers, some interested partners, and then, as long on optimism as they are often short on resources, they begin.

The great majority of North American programs have chosen to start their work with young children, on the assumption that early intervention will be most effective in reaching both social and musical goals. Almost all programs follow a famous piece of advice from Maestro Abreu: "Start small; dream big." Each one develops according to its own local circumstances, and there's no template for finding support. Some programs are funded by foundation grants, some by philanthropists; some partner with youth symphonies, and a few are supported by major symphony orchestras. Others are sponsored by community service organizations or churches.

In 2011, the directors of some local programs began experimenting with regional gatherings, or *seminarios* as they are called in Venezuela, in which the students, teachers, and parents of several programs come together for a day of intense collective music-making and learning, ending with a mega-concert in which all the students, and sometimes even the parents, perform together. These events create powerful feelings of interconnection and solidarity that last long after the day is over. There have also been several attempts at creating national structures: the "Take A Stand" partnership, created by the Los Angeles Philharmonic, Bard College, and Longy Conservatory, sponsors yearly national symposia; a "National Alliance" has undergone the process of incorporation and begun speculating about ways to serve the field. But there is no organizational connection between the hundred-plus programs doing Sistema-inspired work.

Despite the lack of centralized organization so far (or perhaps, this being America, because of it), communication between programs is fluid and frequent, and on the few occasions so far of national convening, the energy of interrelation is powerful. Unquestionably, people involved in this work feel they are part of an authentic movement, one both social and artistic in nature – a movement many feel is the most important experience of their professional lives.

That movement has even more recently exploded on the international scene. Some of the first global programs to launch include Big Noise in Scotland, which was powerfully championed by Richard Holloway, the head of the National Arts Council and a fervent Sistema advocate; and El Sistema Sweden, in Gothenburg, where Dudamel brought his missionary zeal as principal conductor for six years. In 2014, these programs are in their fifth year; most programs in Europe and elsewhere in the world, however, have begun in the past three years.

They are making up in rapid reproduction, however, what they lack in longevity. As of this writing, there are Sistema-inspired programs in fifty-six countries across the world, located on every continent except Antarctica . . . and perhaps that isn't far behind. There are Sistema programs in Korea, the Philippines, Australia, and New Zealand; there's a program in Palestine and one in Israel. Programs in Eastern European countries are forming a pan-national Sistema program called Superar, bringing children of different nationalities and languages to sing and play together. A communications portal on the LinkedIn Network called Sistema Global is beginning to provide a channel for informal dialogue and exchange between practitioners and interested parties around the world.

While the ideal of helping children in need to change their lives through musical ensemble is the bedrock of all Sistema programs, it's interesting that various countries are finding the program valuable in meeting needs other than poverty. In Colombia, for example, a Sistema program launched two decades ago has focused on helping the children stranded as refugees of the protracted civil war. In Korea, where educators find that many children have difficulty with verbal expression, Sistema leaders find that the programs help children to engage expressively with one another. A Sistema program that began in Japan last year aims to help children traumatized by the great tsunami of 2011 to regain psychic and social wholeness. Whatever their particular emphases, however, Sistema practitioners across the world, just as in the United States, feel an intense sense of solidarity with one another, and a conviction that they are part of a worldwide movement that holds the promise of true social and artistic change.

Why now? What is it about El Sistema that at this particular historical moment elicits such a powerful surge of interest in social engagement among musicians and music educators across the globe? And why has the El Sistema phenomenon suddenly caught the imagination of so many social workers, philanthropists, government officials, and thought leaders who believe in this movement and support it?

It may be conjectured that musicians and other artists around the world are hungry for new paradigms of professionalism and artistic life. The classical performing tradition in which they were so rigorously trained feels increasingly marginal in the wider culture, and sometimes joyless within its own circles. Many musicians are looking for ways to make music that connect them meaningfully with the vital life of their societies.

Social activists, for their part, are confronting the failure of conventional ways to meet the challenges of childhood poverty and need. Many are becoming newly aware of the power of artistic expression and artistic models to help change lives. So these two great spheres of human endeavor, and artistry and social engagement, are perhaps beginning to intersect as never before.

It's noteworthy that as El Sistema becomes an international movement, El Sistema Venezuela has scrupulously foregone any kind of direct leadership role. Rather, it has remained the acknowledged beacon of the movement simply by virtue of the sheer positivity, wisdom, and ethical imagination with which it continues to develop in Venezuela – and by virtue, too, of its immense generosity in welcoming visitors and providing help and mentorship across the world.

There are now four national orchestras that tour internationally: in addition to the Simón Bolívar Orchestra "B" (now no longer designated "youth," since its members are in their twenties and early thirties); the Teresa Carreno Orchestra, most in their early twenties and conducted by Christian Vasquez; the Youth Orchestra of Caracas, many still in their teens, conducted by Dietrich Paredes; and the new National Children's Orchestra, some 350 members strong and including children as young as eight. The tours of these ensembles form a kind of ongoing ambassadorship in action; wherever they go, they engage with children's orchestras – mentoring, coaching, and playing side-by-side concerts. Almost always, Maestro Abreu goes along on the tours. He has a near-miraculous gift for forming relationships with musicians and cultural leaders wherever he goes – and a quiet dedication to occupying a prominent seat at every concert, cheering on the young performers as though every concert was the very first.

"There is one simple reason the Sistema is so successful," says Gustavo Dudamel. "It is the Maestro. He is the soul of it – not only the creator, but the soul."

Maestro Abreu remains the most eloquent advocate of his singular vision; his axioms are quoted in Sistema programs everywhere, and they have the force of artistic truth as well as social vision. "Let us reveal to our children the beauty of music," he has said, "and music shall reveal to our children the beauty of life."

# CHAPTER 2

# What Is El Sistema?
# The Fundamentals That Comprise the Venezuelan Beacon

*Eric Booth*

THOUSANDS of dedicated, smart leaders and hundreds of well-funded social service organizations, NGOs, and government programs have devoted themselves to disrupting the cycles of poverty and giving children of poverty a different chance in life. Decades of heroic effort have provided scattered positive results, but many more disappointments. We have to admit that our best and brightest don't know how to redirect the trajectory of young lives born in poverty in other than individual or small-scale ways. Exactly the *last* place one would turn for an effective, proven method for improving lives on a large scale is a classical music orchestra. Meet El Sistema, and allow me to introduce the fundamental elements that enable it to succeed where other programs have largely failed. Let me point to the filaments of the beacon that shines so brightly we all can follow, each in our own way.

I went to Venezuela in 2007 to check out El Sistema. I was dubious, pretty sure the talk about it was hype. The clips on YouTube were thrilling, and the reports from those who had visited were breathless in excitement – so I had to see it. But I am old enough to have seen a lot of "education marvels" prove to be more salesmanship than substance, more glitz than substantive learning. Humans have been refining arts education for the past forty thousand years; there's not much new under this beautiful sun. Interest and skepticism got me on the plane. What I encountered on the ground was the single most astonishing accomplishment in arts education, in youth development, in activating sheer human potential, that I had ever seen. I have devoted much of my time since then to learning more and to helping it grow.

That learning has included three visits to Venezuela and the study of its growth in other countries, particularly in the United States. I helped design and teach the five years of the Sistema Fellowship (originally called the Abreu Fellowship) at New England Conservatory – which embodies José Antonio Abreu's TED Prize wish to train fifty young leaders to carry the El Sistema movement deeper into the United States and beyond. I publish the monthly newsletter *The Ensemble* about the growth of the movement in the United States and Canada, and have served as consultant with dozens of programs in their start-up phase and growth.

This chapter emerges from many kinds of experience in the deep dive into El Sistema. I hope to provide the reader with a broad foundation of partial answers to the natural questions: What *is* El Sistema? How does it work? How should we think about it in the very different culture of the United States? How is it the same and different than the good music education programs we already have in the United States? The chapter introduces the key question answered in the other chapters of this book: Why is El Sistema important for us in the United States?

I can promise only "partial" answers. This is the nature of El Sistema – it is not a program; it's an inquiry. Its very nature defies codified answers and categorical conclusions. If you fight this reality, you find yourself frustrated, in a way that academic and institutionally minded U.S. professionals can get. If you relax a little and explore, if you get interested in the processes and experiments, and most of all, if you *see* the work and talk to those who are dedicated to developing it, you lose that frustration and find the same excitement that fills the pages of this book and the historically unprecedented growth of this movement.

Founder José Antonio Abreu doesn't like the term "El Sistema." He finds it misleading because it suggests a kind of organizational settledness and programmatic certainty that belies the nature of the work. He says El Sistema is "*ser no ser todavia*" – permanently being and not yet being at the same time. It is both a national program with over 280 sites, some 400,000 young people currently active, and over a million people involved over its history; and at the same time it is a living, breathing, growing *something* that has no name or settled identity. The foundation basics I share below are *"ser no ser"* in practice, real and powerful when embodied but not finite and tidily named. Join the inquiry.

What is the best metaphor to describe the relationship between the development of El Sistema in Venezuela and its growth to the rest of the world? It isn't *translating* El Sistema to new cultures – because cultures are so different that practices developed in Venezuela have to be different in other lands, not merely the same with different words. It isn't *adopting* or *transferring* for the same reason. It isn't *re-creating* because success requires that the Venezuelan core be embraced, not reinvented. *Adapting* feels close, because it captures the balance of respecting the core truths while adjusting to fit different circumstances. Perhaps the right metaphor is *planting the seeds* from the bloom of Venezuela's success to grow in new soil. Except that seeds produce almost identical plants, whatever the new soil that receives them. No, I default to the metaphor that hit me as I got on the plane to come home in 2007: Venezuela's El Sistema has established *a beacon*; and all of us, Venezuelans included, who helpfully lead us, are finding our way toward it. We hope practitioners of all kinds will be drawn toward it too, in their own way – El Sistema has much to contribute to more traditional music education practices, to school music programs, to conservatories and orchestras. This chapter describes the key attributes of that beacon, and this volume describes the movement toward it.

El Sistema is a set of inspiring ideals that inform an intensive youth music program that seeks to effect social change through the ambitious pursuit of musical excellence. El Sistema focuses primarily on children with the fewest resources and greatest need and is delivered at no cost to participants. It holds a set of core values:

- Every human being has the right to a life of dignity, contribution, and rich personal access (to the experience of beauty).
- Every child can learn to experience and express music and art deeply, can receive its many benefits, and can make different critical life choices as a result of this learning.
- Overcoming the damages of poverty and adversity is best accomplished by first creating a deep personal sense of inclusion and value, and thus strengthening the spirit, creating, as Dr. Abreu puts it: "an affluence of the spirit." This affluence is then invested as a valued asset in a

40

community endeavor to create excellence and beauty in music. This process, over time, builds the personal strengths that allow for positive life choices.

- Effective education is based on love, approval, joy, and experience within a high-functioning, ambitiously aspiring, nurturing community. Every child has limitless possibilities and the ability to strive for excellence. "Trust the young" informs every aspect of the work.

- Learning organizations never arrive but are always becoming – striving to include: more students, deeper impact, greater musical excellence, better teaching, improved tools, more widespread community connectedness. Thus flexibility, experimentation, risk-taking, and collegial exchange are inherent aspects of every El Sistema-inspired program.

The following ten fundamental guidelines from El Sistema are a scheme that somewhat artificially teases apart elements that in practice function together. Other writers offer different organizational schemes, and I encourage readers to explore them too – we are in the early stages of using words to tease out some of the knowledge contained in the abundance of El Sistema. What makes the beacon of El Sistema powerful and demanding is that the Venezuelans and leaders in the United States and elsewhere strive to succeed in all ten areas. They don't pick and choose, emphasizing the ones that are easier or more like the way we currently do things in youth orchestras, and avoiding the more challenging provocations. El Sistema programs experiment and invest wholeheartedly in *all of them* at the same time. That makes this work a commitment, not for the faint of heart. El Sistema-inspired work is not great music education; it is holistic youth development through great music education. And if you don't have a visceral feel for the difference between those two goals by the end of this book, we have failed to clarify the beacon, and have not helped you see the illuminating marvel and potential of El Sistema.

As I introduce these ten "fundamentals," let me add two notes. First, I will suggest some ways in which the privileged learning laboratories of El Sistema-inspired programs – replete with a luxury of more time with children and freedom to experiment with fewer institutional constraints – may produce new practices that can be shared widely to benefit music education in all settings. Second, the version of the fundamentals presented here is neither completely new nor entirely my own. The first version I wrote, in 2010, was a synthesis of my observations, with feedback from colleagues in the U.S. movement, especially Mark Churchill and the 2009–2010 class of Sistema Fellows at New England Conservatory. I have continued to revise this thesis with my own continued learning in ongoing dialogue with many.

## 1. Mission of Social Change (*Tocar y Luchar*; To Play and to Strive)

El Sistema uses ensemble music to enable every child to experience being an asset within her or his community, inside and outside the "núcleo." Rather than merely complying with instructors and curriculum, students feel an ownership of the music-making process, taking responsibility for both individual and group improvement. For example, they often take on teaching roles themselves starting at an early age – peer-to-peer instruction is omnipresent as an organic part of the ensemble process. There is a saying in El Sistema: "If you know how to play four notes, it is your responsibility to teach your friend who only knows three. And in teaching it, you become better prepared to learn your fifth note." The social learning environment includes vertical integration, with interaction between age groups, as opposed to rigid age or skill level layering; and may, over time, include socio-economic vertical integration of children from different social strata. One teacher has said, "The simple secret of our work is to place the child who plays better next to the child who is not so good."

The "feel" of the social mission is captured in the slogan "to play and to strive." As intensive and driven as the process may feel, the work is neither effortful nor discipline-driven; it is the serious play of an artist naturally pouring herself into the "flow experience." Research on flow, proposed as the psychology of optimal engagement by researcher Mihaly Csikzentmihalyi, affirms that this state of fully absorbed attention enhances learning and maximizes performance. The moment a person totally commits herself to something, everything changes; spending lots of time in the playful striving of flow leads young people toward such commitment and to the social change that is the goal of El Sistema work.

Social change, for the individual, for the group, for the community and beyond, is the *purpose* of El Sistema work, not a hopefully reliable byproduct as we view it in more traditional programs. Thus, all substantive music education questions (from how to seat children in practice, through what music gets played) must be filtered through the lens of what will best serve the social development of those involved.

If you peered at a good youth orchestra practicing in Chicago and one in Caracas, they wouldn't look much different. Also, leaders of both sites are equally committed to changing kids' lives for the better. Having a mission of social change as the true north, the guiding purpose, is only a few degrees of difference than the goals of more traditional youth orchestras; but those few degrees, when pursued over decades of developing teaching practices and creating the learning culture children grow up within, leads to essential differences. Few phrases chill me more than a dismissal of what El Sistema offers with the words, "Oh, we already do all that. If we just had the kind of hours they do, we would be El Sistema." No, traditional programs do *not* do what El Sistema does, and if they had more hours, they would not end up with the youth development accomplishments of El Sistema. A close reading of these ten fundamentals will identify dozens of elements that differ from our current music education practice. For example, we do not foster organic an omnipresent peer-to-peer instruction.

## 2. Access and Excellence

El Sistema includes as many children as it can, bringing young people into its communities whenever possible, as young as possible, for as long as possible, whatever their background or abilities. All are welcome, regardless of talent or progress, including the disabled. The work targets children of poverty, núcleos are usually housed in poor neighborhoods and welcome all. El Sistema strives singlemindedly toward musical excellence, which is the only way to fulfill the social development aspirations. Unlike our jumble of music education offerings, especially for children in poorer communities, El Sistema provides a consistently engaging continuum from age two through high school and beyond, fulfilling its promise to be a second home for all students' growing years, regardless of skill.

The experiences within this continuum develop a yearning for, a raging hunger for, the sound of great and greater music – not for the few who get excited to follow a musical track as we know it, but for majorities of the youngsters involved, who will take their healthy sense of potency and possibility in life and pursue many other paths. In El Sistema, young learners work with and play with more advanced players, listen to more advanced orchestras (often playing the same pieces), hear the top El

Sistema orchestras comprised of their more advanced peers (which are now among the world's best orchestras), to develop that personal sense of "true north" in musical excellence with which they guide their own rapid improvement.

The wide access to all learners, and using all ten of these fundamental points, provides both: youth development for *all* participants, and *also* a self-selected funneling of the most dedicated and talented individuals to go further. This higher-commitment pathway provides intensive, accelerated training at "academies," preparing them for the highest-level national orchestras and cultivating them as teacher-leaders in their own communities and beyond. In this way and others, the ideals of access and excellence are maintained in a productive balance that maximizes both the fullest success for all and the highest accomplishment for some. Those who go the furthest, with the most celebrated accomplishments, feed new energy and expertise back into the system for wider access and greater excellence. "Giving back" is an unquestioned article of faith and universal practice within El Sistema. When their highly celebrated orchestras tour, the players often spend time with young learners, giving back, generously and instinctively sharing widely from the benefits they have received.

## 3. The Núcleo Environment

The núcleo is a physical location within the neighborhood where students live that embodies the values and goals of El Sistema. It is a haven of safety, fun, joy, and friendship, with an ethos of positive aspiration, where all students are encouraged relentlessly to explore their potential. Visitors from traditional youth music cultures recognize that the quality of the learning environment is not like those at home; it is a learning culture so rich and charged that even less skillful students know they are valuable assets and grow well musically and personally, and even mediocre teachers get extraordinary results. One often finds a thriving atmosphere of "coopetition" in the núcleo – a healthy mix of cooperative competition as a spice to add playful fun to the rehearsal mix. Visitors describe it as the "good kind" of competition, as opposed to the "bad kind" they see adding tension and anxiety, a sense of separation, to their students. Everyone who works in a núcleo, from the top conductor to a security guard, embraces the purpose of the place. I would ask random workers, from a young teacher to a janitor, about their work, and without exception they would articulate how their work contributed toward these fundamental goals, in their own words and in total alignment with others.

The núcleo's doors are always open to the community – community members often volunteer, and use the facility to support other community needs. Creating the distinctive quality of the learning environment, and the teachers' personal ownership of and committed alignment toward the fundamental goals, is more significant in achieving El Sistema-inspired success than any particular pedagogical practices used within it. As a result, the highest priority for a successful program is not "teachers of the highest skill" but a cohesive faculty with a visceral understanding, shared intention, and frequent open communication about the values, experiments, and ways of creating the best possible learning environment.

I have noticed a developmental pattern in new programs in the United States and other Western nations. In start-up, they take several years to find confidence in the kind of learning atmosphere that feels right – their work leans a bit more toward the social than the musical in the early years as they solve the deep and unpredictable challenges of creating a distinctively El Sistema-esque learning environment. As they start to find their footing in an environment that feels right, there is an increase in the focus on musical achievement. This sequence feels normal and right, because the drive behind the musical achievement must come from a rich and confident El Sistema-esque environment, or it misses the youth development impact that is the whole point of the work.

## 4. Intensity and Performance Frequency

Students typically spend a large amount of time at a Venezuelan núcleo, often over four hours per day, six days per week – with extra time for special opportunities like festivals (in which players of one instrument in a region gather to study, perform, learn together), seminarios (several orchestras from different sites coming together), and camps (an intensive retreat for an orchestra). And this doesn't count additional practice time at home. The intensity derives from more than mere hours; rehearsals are fast paced and rigorous, demanding a durable commitment, personal responsibility, well-developed skills of attending, and the grit of a strong work ethic.

No programs outside of Venezuela have been able to involve students in the twenty plus hours a week that is typical in Venezuela, but some have reached twelve to fifteen, and all aspire to add time as they can. I also note that a year or two after start-up, some programs in the United States have felt the need to add instructional hours to the week, and not once has there been a resistance by students or families to expanded hours; they recognize the value of more time playing.

Rather than building to a few key performance highlights a year, frequent performance takes advantage of the benefits of performing, which include a learning boost as musicians challenge themselves to excel, reduced anxiety (there is much less fear of making mistakes than in traditional programs), and community connectedness of sharing their accomplishments with their peers, family, and the community. KidZNotes, an El Sistema-inspired program in Durham, North Carolina, presents about 100 student performances in the community in a given year.

El Sistema intensity is an expression of aspiration and intention more than a sense of discipline or of any specific elements of curriculum. It is not imposed; it is born of each individual's hunger to create the greatest possible beauty, and an unspoken agreement between everyone to achieve it together. El Sistema nurtures powerful intrinsic motivation in young musicians – this might be identified as the crucial feature of its success; it certainly explains the work ethic and years of intense investment. Even more, the El Sistema process concurrently develops a potent *group* motivation, within which the ensemble gathers the individuals' aspirations into a collective drive that invigorates and elevates them all. Maestro Abreu believes it is the balance of these two – personal and group motivation – that over time leads to youth development in the exemplary community of a healthy orchestra.

The personal motivation and intensity of commitment comes from students' passionate personal investment in the music, so that every piece offers and extends relevance and personal meaning. El Sistema conductors and teachers invest significant instructional time in verbal descriptions, story lines, and vivid images in order to provoke and enhance a visceral connection. To see how Gustavo Dudamel works with Youth Orchestra of Los Angeles students, look up one of the video clips on YouTube.* By evoking characters and plot within the music, Dudamel enables the young

---

* For example, go to http://www.youtube.com/watch?v=SiWPn1pKBTw.

musicians to make strong emotional and physical connections to the music. This investment in emotional connection fuels the Sistema teaching truth that "passion provokes precision" – meaning that over the long haul a young artist's emotional investment leads to mastery more reliably than does technical drill; indeed, the hunger to express fully drives the improvement and creates motivation for technical solutions more than compliance or a generalized hunger for improvement. It is not just Gustavo Dudamel who dedicates orchestral rehearsal time to telling stories of what is going on in a musical section, or using metaphors and analogies to draw sections toward a better sound – prioritizing emotional connection to draw forth better music. All conductors in El Sistema conduct from their heart connection, which encourages musicians to pour their hearts into their playing, and to experience every performance as a personal connection with those who attend.

Let me add a note here about the kinds of music played in El Sistema. Indeed, the music played *is* the curriculum of El Sistema, more than any preferred set of teaching tools. The fundamental genre is classical, with a general plan of particular works (Marche Slave, William Tell Overture, Tchaikovsky, Beethoven) usually included in the progression. In students' early years, the music fundamentals are introduced through games, play, and chorus, with many kinds of music. Children move into instruments around ages four and five, with classical music in a mix with folk and world music. As children settle into orchestras, each núcleo fills out the repertoire in their own ways, always including Venezuelan folk music, but playing a wide repertoire of orchestral music from around the world, with a special appreciation for Latin American composers. In recent years a national project called Alma Llanera invests in a more intensive exploration of traditional music from Venezuelan cultures as a part of the learning progression. Since intrinsic motivation drives El Sistema, opportunities for others kinds of music emerge from the interest of students, teachers, and communities. Thus, some areas will develop orchestras of cuatros (the cuatro is a traditional Venezuelan instrument), or a flute orchestra, or jazz bands; even rock music groups emerge. The range of music in El Sistema is far broader than most people suppose. I think of a progression that begins musically wide and leading to a learning spine in classical (perhaps because it develops skills and heart most effectively), which then opens into an ever-wider array of genres.

## 5. The Use of Ensemble

The learning in El Sistema is based predominantly in ensemble, with group learning and practice, sectional learning, frequent performance, and consistent (but strategic) individualized attention within and beyond the group setting. Individual lessons are prized and do contribute (especially as students develop into more accomplished orchestras and in the Academy), but the ensemble is the main learning setting. El Sistema invests a lot of time in sectional rehearsal; some say sectional identity and the detail work a smaller group allows is a unique structural part of their work. Much of the "group musical instruction" that drives improvement happens in the sectional work. (Let me note that "group teaching" is one of the biggest challenges for start-up U.S. faculties. Not only have they little such instruction in their own personal background, but they have not seen the Venezuelan style of driving a group hard – using repetition, but with refined steps of challenge, keeping the work playful even as it is demanding and driving.)

I was able to learn from a group of top Colombian youth musicians who had just spent intensive weeks with first a team of top U.S. conservatory teachers (gathered for their expertise and wish to work with young Colombians), and then with a team from Venezuela's El Sistema. The students compared them. They found the U.S. teachers to be lovely people and better players, to have incredible tips and insights into technique, but they weren't very demanding, didn't know how to advance a whole group sectional, were inconsistent in how they taught student to student, and tired quickly. They said the Venezuelans didn't play as well personally and didn't have technical insights or musical ideas as remarkable as the U.S. teachers, but they were demanding, consistent, drove them hard, and could keep the whole group moving forward. The ideal, they said, would be to get both kinds of instruction, but on balance, they learned more from the Venezuelans.

The orchestra acts as a model society in which an atmosphere of competition between individuals is replaced by shared aspiration and invest-ment. (Dr. Abreu: "The orchestra is the only group that comes together with the sole purpose of agreement.") Young El Sistema musicians spend most of their discretionary time while growing up creating beauty together, striving to hear one another more intimately and blend more exquisitely, developing a feel for taking risks and succeeding as a group.

Smaller ensembles and choruses thrive in the same ethos. When I have asked Venezuelan youth why they come to the núcleo for so many hours, they almost always give me the same two answers: "This is where my friends are," and (spoken a little uncertainly) "It's the sound of the music." When I ask them to tell me about themselves as players, they almost always answer first with how long they have been playing with this particular orchestra, and then when they began to play their instrument. Group identity before individual story.

## 6. The CATS Teacher Model: Citizen/Artist/Teacher/Scholar

Those who work at the núcleo take on many tasks and multiple roles in relationship to the students. By acting as citizens, artists, teachers, and scholars (this CATS model was a suggestion from the first cohort of Sistema Fellows), these adults model their encouragement for students to develop holistically: as active musicians, helpful educators, inquisitive learners, and responsible civic contributors. We know from life that our actions teach more deeply than our words, and CATS teachers embody a fierce proclamation about what it means to be a musician and a teacher.

Students see their teachers proactively working in their communities to advance the work of the núcleo and for other social improvements. Students see their teachers perform, frequently in classroom demonstration, and as often as possible in orchestras performing for the community. Students see their teachers as learners, experimenters, as curious students, and thus we might call them scholars. If my adage "80 percent of what you teach is who you are" is valid, then the visible embodiment of these roles instructs young musicians about how to participate fully in life. Becoming a music teacher is seen as a great life accomplishment. Certainly, much of the cohesion and alignment of núcleo faculty derives from the fact that over 75 percent have grown up in El Sistema, so they think and make choices in the software of CATS. I believe that the biggest challenge in U.S. El Sistema faculties is "the gig mentality." It is natural enough for music teaching artists to develop this short-term, limited-commitment attitude to their work – it is the way the field works. But since "80 percent of what you teach is who you are," El Sistema programs require wholehearted, unconditional commitment, an essential model to achieve the youth development goals. There is often turnover in the first year of faculty development as gig-minded teachers transition out, and gut-fired teachers become the core. When núcleo faculties are working well, they create a community of practice among like-minded educators and musicians who learn how to deepen the work together. Faculty groups that achieve this cohesion report deep satisfaction in their experiences of collaborative inquiry.

I should also note that El Sistema teachers pour out high energy, all the time, with a drive that at first exhausts more traditional musicians from the Western conservatory tradition. There is a fast and insistent motor underneath every minute; time is never wasted. Also, repetition is the dominant rehearsal strategy (nothing innovative in that!) and often seems to be relentless. But it is finely tuned, so that each repetition adds a challenge, a nuance, something new to aspire toward. It is the opposite of the rote practice it first appears; it is a delicately scaffolded development of skills, using every moment toward evident improvement. This is even used in practicing scales, eliciting high quality attention for twenty minutes on the D scale because of the fun in the challenges.

## 7. The Multi-year Continuum

El Sistema provides a "conveyor belt" of services, supporting its students from early childhood into adulthood. Despite variation in resources and practices, all núcleos work toward a full program of this kind. Starting with students as young as possible (with family present for those as young as two), they start with musical play ensembles (and many fewer on-site hours per week). They move into choral work, where the immediacy of the learning within the body develops ensemble and musical understandings and prepares students for playing an instrument. There is a transition period in which beginning string players (almost all students start on a string instrument) sing and play at the same time. There are opportunities for students to change instruments along the way, but those occasions are taken seriously by everyone. Students start in string orchestra ensembles from the beginning, and move up to more skilled orchestras with skill and age, in a kind of laddering. Larger núcleos tend to have three levels of orchestra, and then there are citywide, regional, and national level orchestras ascending above those. Along the way, there are opportunities for branching off into additional groups that respond to availability and interest, such as creating a percussion ensemble, or joining a jazz band, or delving into Venezuelan folk music traditions. The developmental continuum is exquisitely attuned to maximize the learning at each stage of growth. Since faculties continually refine their practices, the learning tends to accelerate. I recall visiting a Venezuelan núcleo with a host who had studied there ten years prior; she noted that the students were now able to play Mahler's First Symphony two years earlier than when she was there.

Leaders of "academies" and other national teams have formed lists of sequential repertoire, orchestral levels, and pedagogical practices that create a through-line for every child's learning, even though customization is expected at every local site. (And they never become rigid, routinely adjusting their own system for the benefit of any individual child's growth.) Although each núcleo is encouraged to develop programs that suit its community, a shared teaching and learning-community set of practices and unified vision allow El Sistema to provide its students with a continuous, seamless, consistent, and developmentally coherent musical experience across their years and stages of development. The consistency of much repertoire allows for students whose families relocate to slip right into a new núcleo and continue their learning momentum.

This longitudinal commitment recognizes something all educators know but rarely have the luxury to enact – it takes time and consistency to foster deep understanding, develop character and habits of mind, change lives. I met a thirty-something teacher at Sistema Colorado who together with four best friends had grown up in a Mexico City barrio within Sistema Mexico. I asked him about the whereabouts of his friends. He thought for a moment and tallied that one was a lawyer, two were businessmen, and one was a priest. He was the only one who had made music his career, and had just completed his doctorate. The five had lived in El Sistema for ten crucial years of their barrio upbringing, and their changed lives led to those different destinations. But all had escaped the all-too-common dangers of their childhood environment.

## 8. Family and Community Inclusion
Family participation is an essential aspiration of El Sistema. Siblings often go to the same núcleo, parents attend classes with the youngest students, family members are taught ways to support student learning, and families form an eager and enthusiastic core audience at all concerts. Many sites have parent musical ensembles, and all actively work to involve the community at large through outreach concerts. The núcleos often have

strong walls for security reasons, but these membranes are highly porous, and there is a constant flow and exchange between inside work and outside relevance, value, and acknowledgement.

El Sistema aspires to change communities, and they accomplish this through a kind of ripple effect. When the energy and effectiveness of the núcleo is strong, each child brings that energy home and uplifts the spirits and personal connections in the home. Each member of that enriched home deals with neighbors and extended family and beyond. It sounds idealized, but the ripple effect is real. I visited Sistema Scotland's núcleo in Raploch, which was just six years old at the time. It is a particularly concentrated program, with most of the kids in this poorer, public housing area involved with the núcleo. The taxi driver who brought me there started telling me (in a dialect I could barely follow) about the local music program before he knew I was involved with them; he credited it with "turning this community around," and even attributed (whether accurately or not) the government's decision to build a new community college in the Raploch neighborhood to the reknown of the music program.

## 9. Connections and Network

Although núcleos run independently and customize their programs, they are strongly connected to the national leadership organization, which provides financial resources, and, as importantly, gives the network a unified vision and tools that can be used consistently. Additionally, each núcleo is indispensably tied to the many other núcleos that form local and regional networks. These lateral networks are highly responsive to needs and opportunities, and actively support one another. The interdependent relationships are manifested through events such as "festivals" and "seminarios," which are intensive, project-based musical retreats where orchestras share repertoire, streamline technique, and build personal and institutional relationships. A region may discover that a respected bassoonist is going to be in the area, and they will arrange a bassoon festival, drawing every bassoon player in the region to a three-day intensive with the teacher, culminating in a public performance featuring an all-bassoon orchestra. By uniting students and teachers in isolated parts of the country, the núcleo network embodies the El Sistema ideals of sharing and learning; together it adds up to more than the sum of its parts.

While few countries are likely to enjoy the strong vertical support that a national center like FundaMusical provides for Venezuela (the South Korean model is similar), all countries would be wise to aspire to some such structure. Such a set-up would include a national entity providing functions best provided by those with dedicated overview, balanced with active regional and local cooperation that supports and accelerates local growth. Sistema Canada is a strong example of such national balance. One clear message from Venezuela's model is that núcleos should not be left to fend for themselves on their own; such isolation undermines success.

The local stakeholder networks that U.S. sites are developing are another version of the community support of Venezuela's El Sistema. U.S. sites are increasingly partnering with social service agencies, businesses, schools, government entities, and volunteers to widen their foundation of support, and create a community network that "owns" the success of the program.

## 10. Ambition and Achievement

El Sistema work is more than merely good for young people. It aspires to transform young lives and widely succeeds in setting a healthier, fuller, vision and trajectory for the lives they can create. What makes the crucial difference? What changes a music program's impact from being *positive* (which all good music education programs are) to being *life-transformative*? The *positive* social development happens because of the music-making practices described above. However, the catalyst that makes for a *life-transformative* impact is not just the aspiration for excellence, but something more – the degree of hunger driving the aspiration for excellence, that drive inside children not normally expected to achieve great things. The núcleo faculty believes in these students, even before they believe in themselves, and holds high expectations of their achievement. Their self-esteem and ambition grow as they discover they do indeed accomplish at high levels, and are capable of yearning for and achieving even more.

Compared to the norms of Western music education, El Sistema work always leans toward the highly ambitious end of every opportunity, some-times bordering on the outrageous. Seminarios commit to performing a piece that is nearly impossible for them to master in their time together, to give the urgency that maximizes learning. Leaders know how to set just the right target – reaching higher than anyone expected, but just within grasp. I saw this principle in practice when Sistema Scotland students performed Beethoven's *Egmont* side by side with the Simón Bolívar Symphony Orchestra. The Scottish kids were using simplified scores to match their skill level. Without telling their teachers, several kids found the full Beethoven score on the internet, printed it out, practiced like mad on their own, and brought their full scores in to set up on the music stand beside their Venezuelan partners (to their strong approval). They hungered to take on the full challenge, reaching higher than their teachers had aspired, to be as great as the colleagues from overseas beside them.

What changes young lives is being a valued, responsible member of an aligned community (teachers, students, community included) that reaches unreasonably high together, regularly, taking risks to achieve excellence that matters to them and to others. This cycle of ambitious yearning and achievement, repeated consistently for the sake of beauty and contribution to community, changes, over time, an individual's belief in what is possible for him or her. This belief guides the thousands of small and larger choices a young person makes in creating a life. This is the changed internalized pattern that disrupts the entrenched cycles of damaging life choices by a child in the struggling sector of whom little is expected. This enables a boy to believe he can make choices that no one else in the family or neighborhood has made, and that he can succeed.

The renowned twentieth-century physicist David Bohm addressed the complexity we face in many modern scientific and social systems, saying, "Any time you see seeming opposites, look for the greater truth that contains them both." El Sistema is so powerful on the global scale because it is so powerful on the smallest scale – the minuscule skills it takes to refine the intonation of a note on the violin proves to be exactly the skillset needed to disrupt the cycles of poverty that have defied the best efforts of humans' best organizations. The invisible task of improving one's own performance while concurrently listening hard to what others are doing, in order to create something more beautiful together, proves to be the habit that builds a contributing citizen and a healthier community. The "elitist" entity of an orchestra proves to be the endeavor that leads children out of material poverty and into lives of material sufficiency and spiritual abundance. And the fuel that drives these historically intractable individual and community changes proves to be joy.

# CHAPTER 3

# Inspiration From on the Ground

## I.

## What Is Student Success?

*Paloma Udovic Ramos*

WHEN I first met Claudia she would sit herself in the very back of the orchestra, slouching, and always with more than a healthy dose of attitude. She was a natural leader. Of course back then she was leading in a bit of an unhelpful direction, but I immediately liked her regardless.

For years, she has led both in positive and negative ways, and hardly ever in the middle. When she's positive, she is one of the most motivating team players I've ever met. She often posts on Facebook, tagging as many people as she can think of, congratulating the whole orchestra on a great concert. When she's negative, a single look of hers can make her whole class think an activity is stupid.

She's one of those kids that can't wait to be older. One day I waited with her outside for her mom. I asked her what she was going to do with her weekend. She replied by saying she was going to go to a party with her sister that night: "It's called a rave, you've probably never heard of one of them Ms. Paloma, but they're really cool." I wondered . . . Should I mention to her something about my early twenties? . . . I don't think so. Instead: "Nope, never heard of that."

Claudia clearly has immense talent, and it's easy to see that she practices at home. But she doesn't like to admit it. She plays her passages better than anyone else in class, but during auditions? Forget about it. She can't get through them without shaking her head and muttering, "Whatever, I can't even play this thing, I never even practice." Too cool for school, this one.

All of the teachers have always had a soft spot for her though. I can't remember the exact reason she decided to switch to viola, but I do remember her last concert as a violinist. She was on a good run, and had been practicing and showing up with a great attitude, encouraging her peers and giving us ideas on how to motivate others. We held seating auditions for a big concert, a side-by-side with the Los Angeles Philharmonic. It was a close call in the auditions, and we decided to have Claudia take concertmaster for her last concert. It was beautiful. She sat tall, smiled, moved with the music. I could hardly remember her slouching in the back of the section.

Just a few days ago she posted her latest on Facebook: "I know for a FACT that a musician is what I wish to become in the near future." One of our teachers posted the best response: "You ARE a musician."

**What is Success?**
Dominant American culture defines success as stability, money, home ownership, and higher education. It is a car, a job, and upward mobility. In the classical music world it is acceptance into top conservatories, owning valuable instruments, and playing perfectly executed orchestral excerpts. This type of success assumes a universal value system and equal opportunity.

In fact, success is complicated, and has many definitions. It can be momentary or it can be long term. It can be happiness or it can be a balance of emotions. It can be spending a lot of time working and providing for loved ones, or it can mean having actual time to spend with your loved ones. Perhaps the only things that can be agreed upon are that success is personal, and it can be fleeting.

My personal definition of success includes living a life with meaning, finding a job you enjoy, and meeting your own personal standard of excellence. It is this definition I take with me to work, and this definition I will use to discuss our students and their multiple successes.

I have not always had such a clear and balanced definition of success. In fact, I consider myself to be critical to a fault, unwilling to accept and celebrate success. When Christine asked me to write about "student successes," I pretty much panicked. All I could think of was the failures. How could I write about any success stories when they all came with such major challenges and we all still had such a long road ahead of us?

As it turns out, the process of writing about student successes is the best kind of therapy for someone who has worked in this field for several years. We live in a beautifully imperfect world, and any job that works toward social justice will never be done. Working on the ground with students and community is wonderful and messy. Any time it seems like real progress is made we are faced with a new set of unexpected challenges. With an ever-present daily set of small emergencies, it often feels near impossible to see that the big picture actually looks pretty good.

Working for an El Sistema-inspired program like Harmony Project offers its own set of challenges in defining success. In such a new field we applaud even the smallest successes: Yay!! This nine-year-old can play "Twinkle Twinkle"! And with only a handful of wrong notes!

To be honest, I still have a hard time enjoying small successes and not frantically considering how I can make sure that child improves her reading skills and helps her father get a better job and her older sister a car so she can get to school. . . . But momentary successes coupled with small failures may be what really leads to long-term success, and each and every one should be celebrated.

## In the Beginning

Seven years ago, Harmony Project – a Los Angeles nonprofit organization that promotes positive youth development through music education (of which I am program director) – started a flute and a cello class at the EXPO Center, the largest recreational facility of the City of Los Angeles. The LA Philharmonic soon joined the effort in anticipation of the arrival of Gustavo Dudamel as the new artistic director. I started managing the program a few months before Dudamel's official arrival. There were 120 students – except that once I started counting there were really only about ninety, and attendance was not stellar. We were in the process of hiring a new conductor, and students and their families had no idea what they were working toward. In one parent meeting, I was asked at what point in the program a couple's child would audition for a job with the LA Philharmonic.

Our first challenge was Dudamel's inaugural concert at the Hollywood Bowl, *Bienvenido Gustavo*. Our students would perform the simplest possible arrangement of Beethoven's "Ode to Joy" right before the LA Philharmonic would perform the entire Ninth Symphony. It was a mess.

Too hard for the strings, and the arrangement felt weird. The students were far from grasping the concept of intonation. And yet somehow, it was a success. Our students made it through the arrangement. Their families, sitting at the very front of the audience, cried. Fireworks went off at the end of the concert, and I'm not sure anyone had ever felt so happy as our community.

The next few years have been filled with highs and lows. Harmony Project Youth Orchestra Los Angeles EXPO is now at its maximum capacity of 300 students. We have three full orchestras, several chamber music groups, a mentorship program, college support, parent classes, social service support, and a private lesson program. Our most advanced students are learning a full Tchaikovsky symphony.

Every day there are challenges. Children we care about come and go, family crises feel like the end of the world and then subside, and even our most stable students have moments of distraction that make us feel that we've failed at keeping them constantly engaged. But when most of them come back more motivated than before, we remember that success is a long journey. We stay true to ourselves and to our mission; and we do our absolute best to be patient with everyone, including ourselves.

## Equality and Personal Success

The core principle of Harmony Project's mission statement is positive youth development. Music, of course, is merely the vehicle. If one of our students ends up in the Berlin Philharmonic, that's an added bonus. But it's by no means the ultimate success story. Success looks different for everyone, and our goal is to help each student meet his or her own excellence.

Within the day-to-day of our program, success has a clear definition. You come on time to all of your classes with your instrument, a stand, a pencil, and a good attitude. You practice at home. You progress at a pace that is good for you. Once you are able, you help students who are less advanced than you. You dress appropriately for performances, and you take on new challenges with enthusiasm and confidence. This type of success looks fairly similar to most other types of early musical instruction.

For some of our families, it seems life gets in the way of this typical version of success. They aren't set up for it. Their families operate on a playing field with more obstacles than most. How can you be on time in

58

LA with no car? How can you practice at home when you live in a one-bedroom apartment with four siblings and both parents? And your siblings are supposed to practice too? How can you dress appropriately when your mom can't find the money to replace your ratty red Converse shoes with nice black dress shoes?

In 2010, 39.1 percent of black children in the United States lived in poverty, while 35 percent of Latino children and 12.4 percent of white children lived in poverty (www.pewhispanic.org). The effects of poverty are great. Poorer children are at greater risk of poor academic achievement, school dropout, abuse and neglect, behavioral and socioemotional problems, physical health problems, and developmental delays. These facts beg the question, what does success look like for a child in poverty? Is it different than for a child not in poverty?

It is important for our program to have the same high expectations as any music school, and it is equally as important for our program to make lots of exceptions to our own rules. This does not mean to lower the expectations, but rather to acknowledge and respect the limited resources of our families and help them find ways to succeed in a culture that may not always give them that same acknowledgement or respect.

Providing a space to fail is an important part of how we approach our teaching. When you are already at the bottom of society, space to fail does not exist. One parking ticket can lead quickly to eviction and homelessness. Multiple instances of car trouble can lead to schoolteachers not believing in a student's intentions.

It is our job to become acquainted with all of our families and their circumstances, so we can measure a student's success based on their circumstances. We deal with each transgression individually, and yes, it is exhausting. We make sure that we are doing everything we can at least to give them the opportunity to succeed, and this usually means witnessing some failure and staying by their side. In that way, we try to achieve a slice of the social justice we strive for.

**Small Successes**
Small successes happen every day at our program. Students learn concrete skills, and they get better every day. Older students help younger students, somebody plays a passage correctly for the first time. Sometimes we rejoice just because a student shows up. Sebastian recently moved into the

intermediate orchestra after five years in our program. Relative to other students this is a long time, but I am incredibly proud of him.

Sebastian lives with his grandparents, and sometimes visits his mom in Oregon, where she works as a seasonal farm worker. He is often late or misses class. If we held Sebastian to every attendance rule in our program, he would have had to leave long ago. But his grandparents both work a lot, and I know it's not out of disrespect or lack of care that he has poor attendance.

Sebastian's grandparents don't speak English, and in trying to raise a young boy in Los Angeles they already have several strikes against them: language, culture, and generation. It's difficult for them to know how to help him succeed. I asked his grandmother to sit in on lessons so she could know what he was supposed to practice and help him at home, but almost every time she was there she would fall asleep. I didn't take it personally; I really do think she was just tired.

I started meeting with Sebastian every week before his regular class because both he and his grandmother were frustrated with his progress. I didn't really have time to do this, and sometimes I would have to cancel because I was too busy putting out a different fire. But I couldn't say no to his grandmother: "He is still in the beginning orchestra, with the little kids!" his grandmother would complain, "I know he's short, but he's older than them, and he's been in the program for so long, Ms. Paloma, can you help us?!" Sebastian also expressed a desire to improve. He told me he really enjoyed the violin, and he just didn't know why he couldn't find the motivation to practice.

Sebastian is a perfect example of a student who can get lost without private instruction or attention. In group class and orchestra, he hides behind his peers. He is a sweet kid, and he makes jokes whenever the attention comes to him. He qualifies every attempt at playing in front of classmates or anyone else with a funny statement about how he probably won't be able to do it. And then he allows himself to make a mistake, without really trying to play it well.

After a few private lessons, Sebastian was able to play through a good portion of a piece of music without stopping every time he made a mistake. Maybe he even believed my sincere encouragement that he plays really well, he just needs to allow himself to. He finally made it into the intermediate orchestra. We don't have lessons anymore, and it seems they were only a temporary kick in the pants. He's not really progressed since then.

However, I know the seemingly small success of him advancing to the intermediate orchestra had a big impact. Sebastian and his family now have proof that change is possible, and Sebastian has a basis on which to believe he is capable. He may never be a musician, or maybe he will. But hopefully that moment of achievement will stay with him wherever he goes.

One of our most dedicated students recently came to talk to me about switching to a new high school. Hugo, a talented clarinet player, complained that his current school was too strict, and too academic. He attends a fairly new charter school that prides itself on academic performance, and Hugo wanted more time to pursue music. Attending the charter school has been frustrating for him, as his prior education did not adequately prepare him. During his freshman year he told me how shocked he was that teachers wouldn't accept late homework: he had never experienced such strict and high expectations. Though the school often keeps students late after school for additional tutoring, Hugo's grades have continued to be very low. He is unmotivated and often down on himself. It seems that the only thing he is sure of is that he is not cut out to be an academic, and that he would rather be playing music.

Hugo's parents are unsure of how to help. Both are from Oaxaca, Mexico, and have limited education themselves. They just had another baby, and his father is working an extra job while his mother cares for the newborn.

As we discussed his options, I wondered whether I should push Hugo to succeed at his current school or encourage him to find his own path. Knowing Hugo for some time already, I knew him to be fairly self-assured, with a good understanding of where he wanted to be in a group. A few years prior, he had made a decision to stop hanging out with the wrong crowd (kids who were already partying and skipping school). He credited our music program with giving him something to focus on, something to keep him motivated and happy.

Without seeing his current report card, I told him about an audition-only public arts school, where students played music for more than half their school day. His mood perked up. "Do you think I could get in?" he asked. I assured him he had a good chance, and I'd try to set up an audition. I momentarily had a vision of Hugo's life changing dramatically after attending such a prestigious school that has close ties to top conservatories.

Only after the audition was scheduled did I realize his GPA (just below 2.0) might prevent him from being accepted. Not only that, but as I researched more, I found out that the arts school's academics were known to be even more difficult than his current school. It seemed that most students relied on their parents or paid tutors to help them with academics. I knew Hugo did not have this option. I found out that some of our other students who attended the school were struggling to keep up and were being offered little support. As I started to see the whole picture, it started to feel like it was not the right fit, and I felt guilty for getting his hopes up.

I spoke with his family about the changes that would have to happen were he to attend the school. He would have to get up much earlier to catch the bus. He would still have to spend an enormous amount of time keeping up his grades. Still, I encouraged him to take the audition and to submit his grades.

Hugo's audition impressed the music director and his GPA turned out to be just above the limit. He was accepted to the arts school. After thinking about it for a few days, he decided not to attend. He called to thank me for getting him the opportunity. I was impressed with his difficult decision. He seemed to be genuinely interested in pursuing the things that he felt good at, and not interested in fitting in somewhere that wasn't ready to support him.

Some people may think that Hugo gave up on a dream he should have pursued. Perhaps it seems like he lacks the "grit" that is so often talked about in terms of success. I think it's a bit more complicated than that, but I suppose only time will tell. Hugo's current priorities are his family, friends, and music. He has a great relationship with his parents, filled with mutual respect and trust. He is a responsible and loving older brother to two younger siblings. He is a loyal friend. He is a dedicated musician, and has commitments not only to our program but also to a banda in the community that plays several times a week. (Banda is both a brass-based form of traditional Mexican music and the ensemble that plays it.) Hugo is resourceful, and I have no doubt that he will find success. It just might not look like the status quo.

## A Traditional El Sistema Success

Kayla is a student who could be seen as a poster child for her commitment to our program as well as for her artistic success. She has been in the program for six years, and is an excellent flute player. She has three siblings in the program, one of whom is also excelling as a violist. She has superb attendance, and attends the program five days a week, with up to fifteen hours of direct instrumental instruction. She is often at our site several more hours of the week; doing homework, mentoring younger students, or just hanging out.

Kayla and her family have benefited from almost every other aspect of our program; our social services team has intervened a few times because of domestic violence, we found a tutor for her when her grades were slipping, and she is part of our private lesson program, which rounds out a high-quality music education. She is musical, motivated, punctual, and committed. She wants to be a professional classical flautist, and she has what it takes. Two years ago, Kayla auditioned and was accepted into the most competitive arts high school in Los Angeles with our encouragement. No doubt, she is a true success story.

Kayla's story appeals to many who are looking for a fix to music education. It appeals to many who want to show the proof that young people like her – ones who come from low-income, single-parent households with no classical music in the home – can grow up to be part of a world that seems inaccessible unless you can pay for hours of private lessons, summer music institutes, and competitive youth orchestras.

Time will tell if Kayla continues on the path toward becoming a professional musician. Success stories are never simple, and the complexity of Kayla's story perhaps is yet to be written. As I write this, she considers transferring out of the arts high school she worked so hard to get into because, as she tells me, her classmates are "different," and she's tired of not being a good student. It's a rigorous school, and the academics are just as difficult as the music. Attending a public school prior to this did not prepare her for the advanced courses they offer at her new school. Her grades are improving, but it will be hard for her to be the star student, as she was at her old school. The adjustment seems to be taking a toll on her self-esteem, and the "difference" between her and her classmates seems only to exacerbate the situation. It's not easy to be one of the few students at your school who takes the bus for more than an hour, especially when you are also one of the only students of color.

We will continue to encourage Kayla to excel at her current high school and beyond, and will provide a safe space for her to come to express her feelings as she goes through different and challenging life experiences. Yet it is hard not to get frustrated that, outside our walls, we may not always be able to help her.

## And the True El Sistema Success . . .

This year we will graduate our first class of students. Among those students is Ayana. Ayana's family is from Ethiopia. Her father walked for a week over the border into Sudan in order to escape the Ethiopian Civil War. Her parents both work as card dealers at the same casino, although they are no longer together. Ayana's family has been through some difficult times over the past few years.

Ayana is a good violinist, but she's not the best. She loves classical music, and she takes her practice very seriously. But I doubt she will become a professional musician.

A few years ago, Ayana's violin teacher of four years left her position to pursue a master's degree in psychology. Ayana wrote a beautiful letter telling of the impact that Irina had on her. The challenge and discipline of her class had given Ayana structure that she deeply enjoyed, taking her away from troubles at home and the stress of school. The friends she had created in her class were the closest of any in her life, and she valued their bond and trust. She had made a great friend in her teacher, and she had found a space in which she felt safe to learn and grow and make mistakes. Even though she may not take that learned skill to a profession, these relationships and the learning process will support her through her life.

In turn, Ayana has given back to the program, and I hope she'll do so for a long time. As a mentor, Ayana has helped the same younger student once a week for the past three years. She encourages her student toward her own success, and prepares her twice a year to perform at a recital. To watch Ayana look on as her student performs is a great thing; she stands nervously offstage knowing exactly the points in the piece where her student might make a mistake. We have several great mentors, but few take such care in what they do.

Ayana has taken part in student leadership committees, and has interned at both the LA Philharmonic and earned a paid position at Harmony Project last summer. Ayana's success must be attributed to many things: hard-working parents who scraped enough together to hire a tutor, among other things. But the model of her success is an inspiration as I think of what we hope to see from all of our students. Positive youth development needs to be balanced, and unfortunately, music cannot do it alone.

Last summer, I nominated Ayana and a few of her classmates for the Posse Scholarship, a four-year, full-tuition leadership scholarship to college. Ayana called me a few nights ago around 10 p.m. to tell me that she had received the scholarship. She is attending Grinnell University this coming fall, with another student from our program who also received the scholarship. They happen also to be best friends.

## Conclusion

An important part of finding sustainable personal success may be enduring failure. Perhaps Claudia's periodic moments of attitude, followed by our corrections, are important to her development. Maybe I should have continued teaching Sebastian privately, but perhaps he will learn more from having to learn to practice on his own. We could have called Hugo another several times to remind him to complete his arts school application, but then what would have happened if he didn't turn in complete assignments at that same school?

Our job is to build capacity within our students, and to help them help themselves. When we achieve this, we will have well-rounded students who have made a set of personal decisions that fits their circumstances and value systems. Along the way we will have taught them to love music, mentorship, and community. We will have helped them to be proud of where they are from and to always hold their head high. And we will call that success.

# II.

# Letters From Two Parents

*Located just 6.8 miles from New York City, Union City occupies a mere 1.3 square miles, but with a population of 66,455, it is the most densely populated city in the United States and has 18,000 children under the age of eighteen.*

*In 2012, recognizing that orchestral music education could have a transformative effect on her community, Melina Garcia, a native of Venezuela and a nine-year resident of Union City, created the Union City Music Project (UCMP), the first El Sistema afterschool program in New Jersey. Ines Williams is the mother of Shiloh, Breanna, and Ashley. Mrs. Williams was born in the Dominican Republic and has lived in Union City for seven years. This is their story.*

# Great Opportunities From the Union City Music Project
## *Ines Williams*

I first learned about the Union City Music Project (UCMP) and El Sistema de Orquestas at the Eugenio Maria de Hostos Center for Early Childhood Education (ECC), which my two youngest daughters attended. It was during back-to-school night, in the fall of 2011, when Mrs. Melina Garcia, UCMP's founder, made a presentation. I had never heard of El Sistema before but that night, I simply became fascinated about the possibility that my two younger daughters would have the chance to apply and, I hope, be accepted into the UCMP.

I was very impressed with Mrs. Garcia's presentation and intrigued to find out how they would implement this music model in Union City. When Mrs. Garcia explained that the program had been successful in many other cities around the United States, I felt confident about it.

I love music and have loved to sing since I was young. When I became a mother I decided that my children would be exposed to music so they could reap all the proven benefits that it brings to children in academics. For this reason I wanted my daughters to be admitted into this program.

Mrs. Garcia explained that because she was launching UCMP with very limited funding, therefore, it would only be available to a small group of children who attended the ECC. I was sad because my oldest daughter Ashley, who was nine at the time, would not be able to enroll. But I was extremely excited when I found out that my daughters Breanna and Shiloh had been chosen.

The UCMP began classes in March 2012 with fifty three- to six-year-old students in the Paper Orchestra, a three-month pre-orchestral session. During the first few weeks my daughters and I were delighted by the process of creating their own cardboard violins. We designed and manually decorated them with their favorite colors and accessories, and we had a lot of fun.

I had been very concerned about how such young children would be able to handle real instruments without damage. I knew that good-quality violins are expensive and I was afraid that I would not be able to afford replacing them if the girls accidentally broke them. Much to my surprise, I now realized that my girls had become gradually initiated to love their cardboard string instruments, how to properly care for them and the importance of storing them in a safe place. They would explain to me that once they were given their real instruments, they had to make sure that they were kept in cool room temperature at home so they would stay tuned for a longer period of time, and that they had to ensure they were kept in a safe place. I was very impressed. Breanna and Shiloh graduated from the paper orchestra and transitioned to real instruments in October 2013. My oldest daughter, Ashley, who is now ten, was eventually admitted to the program in January 2013. She was very happy to join her sisters.

I love the UCMP because it is a multicultural music program that brings people from different social economic status, ethnicities, and religions together to learn the universal language of music. The teaching staff is highly qualified and very professional. Children receive classes in voice, music theory, string and percussion, and music immersion.

My youngest daughter, Shiloh, who is now six and in kindergarten, took the percussion classes, which enabled her to learn how to read in a fun and musical way. Before the UCMP I was teaching her phonics with an electronic toy that I had placed on the refrigerator. I would try to teach her the ABCs to the best of my ability, but it was difficult for me as Spanish is my native language. I did not want to confuse her. She never showed any interest in learning the sounds from the toy. After taking percussion classes however, I noticed that she was really into recognizing all the sounds that this toy produced. The class had developed her hearing ability and given her faster sound recognition. Now when Shiloh is trying to learn a new word for her class, she sounds it out by clapping with rhythms she has learned in her class. I am fascinated by her progress and how she uses music to her benefit.

There are many anecdotes I can share about how my children have grown since joining the program and how it has affected my family. My daughters have learned how to work and interact with children from different ages, schools, and grades. This gives them the opportunity to create new friendships and help build a greater sense of community. Now when we walk around the neighborhood or at church, we encounter people from the program who we did not know before. During concerts and family events, we get to not only enjoy watching our children perform, but these are also opportunities where as parents and members of this community we get to engage in conversations and share experiences with one another.

I have been impressed at how my daughters use music as a way to focus when they do their homework or get inspired to do their art while they listen to classical music. For me, this is fascinating; when I study or read, I need to have complete silence in order to focus!

At the UCMP, my girls have not only learned about music-making. The founder and teachers in the program instill in them good manners and proper behavior. If children misbehave, the teachers talk to them and also communicate with us parents. I have seen how children are disciplined in a caring and loving way. As a mother, this makes me feel extremely happy.

Another opportunity: We have been able to go on field trips with our children and watch professional musicians play for us in our own community. As a parent, I see Mrs. Garcia as a great community leader who cares not just about the needs of the UCMP, but about the families, taking time to develop relationships with all the parents. The UCMP has given me a sense of belonging and made me realize that as parents we are part of the UCMP as much as our children are.

On a personal level, I must say that the UCMP has had a big impact in my own life as well. I recently went through a difficult health-related problem and Mrs. Garcia was constantly calling me to make sure how I was doing. She was very respectful and considerate of my situation. Additionally, last year I went through some personal problems and I thought I would have to take the girls out of the program. I told Mrs. Garcia about my plans and she made me realize that this was an exceptional opportunity and that I should reconsider my decision, especially because my daughters would be negatively affected if I took them out. They truly love the program. I listened to Mrs. Garcia and kept the girls in the UCMP. I can say unequivocally that I made the right choice. Breanna plays the cello while Shiloh and Ashley play the violin. They all get percussion classes as well. I am very happy that I changed my mind.

Through the UCMP I have been able to fulfill all the aspirations I had for the proper development and education of my three daughters. Mrs. Garcia told me that Ashley had asked her if she would be taken out of the program when she was twenty-four years old. Surprised at her question, Mrs. Garcia told Ashley that she had no plans to kick anyone out of the program to which Ashley replied, "Well, good thing, because I don't ever want to leave this program. I want to grow old at the UCMP."

★   ★   ★

*Since 1989, Heart of Los Angeles (HOLA) has been providing underserved youth in the Rampart District with exceptional afterschool programming in arts, athletics, and academics. In 2010, HOLA and the Los Angeles Philharmonic partnered to create YOLA at HOLA, an El Sistema-inspired, free, afterschool music program. Living only one block away from HOLA, Ariadna Sanchez, her husband José Jarquin, and their two boys Carlos and Mateo were among the first to sign up for the orchestra program. Today, while the boys are in class learning violin, Ariadna champions literacy among other families – she and José support the HOLA parent book club and Ariadna recently wrote an alphabet book entitled H is for HOLA to encourage parents to read to their children. Ariadna and her family have made HOLA a central part of their lives. This is Ariadna's story.*

## YOLA at HOLA: A Soothing Sound for Our Community

### *Ariadna Sanchez*

I still remember the morning of September 13, 2010, when Ms. Christine, the YOLA at HOLA music director, gave a presentation at my son Carlos's school. The presentation was for parents of children in first and fourth grades. Ms. Christine explained that it was the first year that the program would operate in our neighborhood, the Rampart District in Los Angeles, California. She said that this music program would allow children to improve their academic skills while discovering the magical world of music. YOLA at HOLA, she explained, is directly inspired by LA Philharmonic Music Director Gustavo Dudamel's enriching experience with Venezuela's youth orchestra movement, "El Sistema."

Ms. Christine emphasized that the goal of the program was to motivate children and youth to develop their full potential. In addition, the program would keep them safe and away from the negative activities taking place in our neighborhood. But best of all was that YOLA at HOLA was a free musical training program with top quality staff and academic support. Of course, as a mother hearing all this I was extremely interested, but space was limited and the selection of students would be done using a lottery system. Still, my mind did not waver. Instead I said, "He who dares, wins," and I put my son's name on the list. When a YOLA at HOLA member called me to notify me that Carlos had been selected, the news brought joy to my heart. September 20, 2010 was the first day of programming. Carlos was nervous, yet eager to discover what it was all about. It was the beginning of an unstoppable metamorphosis.

As an immigrant mother, I am very fortunate to have YOLA at HOLA in the community. I was born in a rural town called Ejutla de Crespo in the state of Oaxaca, Mexico. Ejutla de Crespo is a place where huge, green mountains adorn the outskirts of the valley during the day and shiny stars light the sky at night. While I was growing up my father had to immigrate to this country so that my family could have a better life. My heart experienced long periods of time without my dad's presence. With sadness, I also remember the time when my mother immigrated to the United States to join my dad, leaving us behind under my grandparents' care.

My parents sacrificed their time and savings so that I could receive the best education possible. When I married my husband José A. Jarquín, I faced my own challenges. The first was immigration. I came to Los Angeles when I was twenty-three years old, but my husband had been in Los Angeles for twelve years when we married. When my first son, Carlos Manuel, was born, I considered myself a timid, discreet, and reserved woman. I spent most of my time taking care of my son and truly enjoyed it. Three years later, Mateo came into this world so I spent a lot of time being a mom. When Carlos started to attend school, I began to discover some of my hidden talents.

Life has been very rewarding to me and one of the things I never imagined is that my two sons were going to be part of the YOLA at HOLA family, that they were going to participate in concerts at such an early age, and that they were going to have professional music teachers as role models. In Oaxaca, I was not exposed to classical music at all. However, I grew up listening to the melodic pieces played by the town's wind ensemble, which I thought was ordinary music. When I came to Los Angeles, the variety of music available on the radio made me realize that each type of music has its own beauty. Thanks to this awakening, I also began to appreciate the type of music I listened to as a child in my hometown. As Carlos began to play his violin, I tried to listen to classical music on the radio, but I did not like it much. I thought of classical music as boring and only for wealthy individuals.

When Carlos had his first concert at Walt Disney Concert Hall, I experienced a radical change in thinking about classical music. Classical music sees no color, gender, economic status, or ethnic background. As illustration of my statement, think about a concert where sponsors, teachers, parents, and children come together as one big family to listen to a musical piece. I have also learned that participation in the program requires a huge commitment, but every family has made an effort to develop a solid foundation of discipline in each of our children.

Our children are like flowers. We parents provide the water, and the leadership team at YOLA at HOLA provides the sunlight. The results are children and families equipped with the tools to be successful members of the community. Although it is not as easy as it sounds, parents, students, and teachers have all made it possible thanks to the inner voices that say "we are a community and need to work together." We – the leadership team and parents – are now partners in this musical journey full of surprises.

In my opinion, YOLA at HOLA is a successful program because of the respect, reciprocity, and equality that exists between the leadership team and the parents. Since day one, the leadership team opened a new world for the parents and children, but they did not leave us alone. Every member of the leadership team has served as a guide for us, and what I like most is that they have showed respect for our culture, language, and way of thinking. This respect has flourished into a relationship with a strong foundation.

Four years have passed since Carlos started at YOLA at HOLA program. As a mother, I feel very fortunate that music instruction is expanding in the community and among families. And my joy doubles now that my second son Mateo, who is six years old, is a new member of the YOLA at HOLA family, and I know that both my children have music as an ally in their educational journey. Thanks to the YOLA at HOLA program, their future emerges as a beautiful sunrise: music in our community is opening doors toward success for our children.

I remember when Ms. Christine said, "Together, we can work to strengthen our community. By interacting with other families, the community of the Rampart District will function like an orchestra." I now understand the meaning of those words. Each family in our neighborhood plays an important role, inspiring other families in Los Angeles and the rest of the nation. I now realize that in order to resemble an orchestra that plays beautiful music, we must believe that our community is special and deserves the very best. When that happens, we begin to discover our talents and share them with community.

For instance, some of us are discovering that we have a dormant volcano inside us waiting to erupt with new ideas and energy. Spending time with families and YOLA at HOLA personnel has motivated me to further my education. I am very proud to say that thanks to YOLA at HOLA, I am currently attending college and plan to attend a four-year university. I also like to encourage other mothers to do the same. I want them to know that they deserve the best, just like our children. I know this is only the beginning of a lifelong journey full of success, music, and long-lasting relationships. ¡Qué viva YOLA at HOLA!

# CHAPTER 4

# The Benefits of Ensemble Music Experience

## (and why These Benefits Matter so Much in Underserved Communities)

*Shirley Brice Heath, Stanford University*

*To an alien scientist, music – and the desire to create it – might be one of the most puzzling aspects of humanity.* – Gary Marcus, *Guitar Zero*, p.5

IF this epigraph holds any truth, then we want to know more about the puzzles surrounding what happens to those who create music. Specifically, how does learning music hold particular effects for those children who live in communities with few learning resources beyond their regular academic classes? Of particular significance for these questions is the emphasis of our alien scientist on the desire to *create* music and not on the effects of passive listening to music.

This chapter takes up implications of the epigraph in three parts. The opening section gives a brief historical overview of how beliefs about qualities of mind for those who create music came about during the European Enlightenment. Views about what learning music does for individuals encircled notions of what being "educated," "cultured," or "refined" meant. Music and other fine arts were believed to separate those with good tastes and financial means from those lacking in education and opportunities for wealth accumulation and pursuits of leisure. However, since the last decades of the twentieth century, this attitude has shifted to favor the democratic view that opportunities to learn ensemble music can and should be available for *all* children, including those living in impoverished communities around the globe (Higgins, 2012).

Following this opening section is the heart of the chapter. Here we consider the interdisciplinary research on what happens as individuals learn to create music within ensemble groups. What are the cognitive and social effects of sustained practice and group rehearsals? Research that addresses this question helps explain the neuronal, visual, and aesthetic effects of creating music.

The chapter closes with a brief consideration of what is gained through *research* into what happens within music learning as distinct from *evaluation* that attempts to prove functional school-related outcomes of learning music.

## Artful Science

For more than two centuries after the Enlightenment, the view prevailed that creating and appreciating ensemble music (particularly instrumental music) marks individuals as financially secure and "well rounded." During the Enlightenment, the view that auditory and visual experience contributed to knowledge formation accompanied the swell of emphasis on pedagogy for children and the public alike (Stafford, 1999). A leisure industry burst onto the scene in the late seventeenth century only to become widely accepted as normative by the mid-eighteenth century. What came to be known as a "middle class" developed rapidly as people traveled and sought out theaters, lectures, museums, and sites of musical performance. Literacy spread through these forms of public pedagogy, as well as through the broadening introduction of children's literature and music books for children. Members of the merchant class as well as the intelligentsia and those of landed wealth ventured out to learn what travelers to faraway places had observed and collected.

Public pedagogies of these types seeped into the ideologies of middle-class parents. Handbooks of child-rearing, as well as the writings of pedagogues and philosophers that repeated and expanded the ideas of John Locke, Jean-Jacques Rousseau, and Johann Pestalozzi entered libraries and influenced parents wishing to amplify their children's worlds of knowing. Pestalozzi planted the idea of learning by "head, hand, and heart." Edification began at home with orientations to visual arts as well as through music lessons for girls and boys alike. Parents and the public prized work with the fingers and hands that resulted in products and performances that left no doubt of long hours of practice toward perfection. Proper posture

74

disciplined the body during these pursuits, so that public performances or presentations would be offered with a modest, albeit "proper," bearing. Tools of arts production, ranging from easels and paint boxes to musical instruments, became normative household display items, along with artifacts attesting to literacy, such as bookstands, bookcases, and ceramic figures and paintings that portrayed individuals reading, painting, and playing music.

To take home the learning of music, whether in singing or playing musical instruments, became expected within middle-class families. Sales of instruments soared, as did demand for private lessons, especially for girls. Ensemble orchestras, including percussion, string, and brass sections, developed in eighteenth-century Europe, and chamber music groups proliferated. Behind this emergence lay the view that while churches had been primary sites for the performance of music during the Baroque period, such should not be the case looking forward. Composers such as Beethoven, Mozart, and Haydn became increasingly widely known to those whose weekly schedules did not include either church attendance or attention to the scheduling of musical performances taking place in churches beyond worship service hours.

Recognition of the legitimacy of individual interpretational powers in music paralleled the eighteenth-century Protestant culture of reading and writing on "one's own." For musical interpretation, the idea of individual access and interpretation contributed to the distinctiveness of styles of interpretation claimed not only by individual performers but also by ensembles.

Beliefs surrounding the artful science of creating music that became normative during the Enlightenment held firmly into subsequent centuries and also among many upper- and middle-class families in modern economies today. This collective ideology embraces musical learning for its powers to further children's learning of specific qualities of mind: individual interpretive creativity, development of mental and physical discipline, competence in reading into and beyond literate sources, acquisition and care of material objects, and practice and instruction leading to mastery. Those of the upper and middle classes holding these beliefs then and now look ahead to individual success for their children. They know that learning to play an instrument or to sing well enough to be included in a group requires many hours of practice as well as years of lessons. Much valued is the belief that such learning within groups instills the value of working together to produce something beautiful and creative that audiences will appreciate.

Yet since the final decades of the twentieth century these opportunities, long cherished by those of substantial financial means, have become available for children living in some under-resourced communities in nations around the world. Democracy as an international ideal for all people and all nations led many to embrace goals of social justice and equity for children living in poverty around the world. As a consequence, the idea spread that music, and indeed all arts, should be available to all children, regardless of class background. This view accelerated along with the conviction that the arts, especially music, can change lives for the better (Tunstall, this volume, and Tunstall, 2012).

The United States is a modern economy that has no exemplary history of equitable distribution of non-school enrichment learning opportunities in music except to those involved in religious institutions. Moreover, the costs in time and financial outlay for under-resourced families as well as schools and communities have long seemed prohibitive. Music lessons, along with purchase or rental of instruments (and their storage and use in at-home practice sessions), have generally exceeded the discretionary incomes and spatial resources of working-class or working-poor families in the United States. Furthermore, as migratory labor patterns for immigrant families accelerated with agribusiness development, transport of large and fragile musical instruments for these families was entirely unrealistic.

Societal changes within churches also worked against the spread of opportunities to learn music. Particularly since the turn of the twenty-first century, sustained and professionally led choral or instrumental music pro-visions in churches and other religious institutions have declined along with decreasing church attendance across the United States. In the hope of retaining adolescents and young adults, some churches have "modernized" church music and introduced new instruments. However, professional leadership and sustained practice rarely characterize these changes.

Furthermore, as budgets for public education faced increasing cuts with the turn of the new century, access to music teachers or ensemble groups remained available primarily to students enrolled in private or independent schools. The only public schools able to retain the arts were those located in upper-income residential areas where parents formed foundations to support art in their schools. Moreover, in these communities, parents car-pooled to ensure additional practice and rehearsal time for their children's participation in arts programs.

Families living in communities of more limited means had no such opportunities. Moreover, even when public transport was available, working-poor parents were often reluctant to send their children across town to unfamiliar sites for long hours of practice and rehearsal. These parents often worked two jobs and only rarely in positions that offered flexible hours for transporting children to lessons or rehearsals or for attending afternoon or weekend concerts. Community centers, when present in under-resourced communities, tended to support sports opportunities, occasional short-term visual or dramatic arts programs, but more often homework "clubs" and volunteer tutoring. In short, especially since the turn of the twenty-first century, youngsters living in locations that could not offer music education either during or beyond school hours had little hope of growing up with sustained participatory experience in music ensembles.

When news of Venezuela's phenomenal success with its El Sistema programs reached the United States about this time, musicians and educators who had previously served primarily upper- and middle-class families wondered, "Why can't the Venezuelan phenomenon happen here in this country?" Debates and deliberations followed, with ample recognition of the many differences between the culture, geography, and economic patterning of leisure time in the United States and Venezuela. Yet as individual programs of what was initially termed "El Sistema USA" emerged in different parts of the United States, means of resourcing and promoting these opportunities arose through the efforts and resources of individuals from middle- and upper-income families, many of whom held the democratic and social justice views noted above. Moreover, as the realization of the declining effectiveness of US public education for children living in poverty became more widely recognized, enthusiasts for arts programs, including ensemble instrumental music programs, found motivation in the longstanding view that arts learning positively affects all learning. Moreover, many individuals felt that ensemble music could uniquely promote high learning demands for children and adolescents living in under-resourced communities unlikely to provide such arts learning for local children during afterschool hours.

## Creating Music: How Does Learning Happen?

With the spread of El Sistema-inspired programs, both within and after school in the United States, researchers increased attention to the question of how ensemble music participation advances learning. Simultaneously, more researchers gave their attention to the learning contexts – studios and rehearsal zones, for example – for the arts. Moreover, some researchers addressed the issue of voluntary expertise development (sometimes termed "informal learning") by young and old. In these instances, individuals or small groups determined the need or desire to learn something and set about finding combinations of ways to learn and work together. Some researchers wanted to know, in particular, the effects of voluntary expertise development opportunities for children living in communities with few resources of time, space, material goods, or local experts in highly specialized art forms.\*

What follows are brief summaries of five primary features of the learning environment of ensemble music that have increasingly drawn the attention of researchers in the learning sciences. These contexts seem to account for the depth and retention of learning that lie at the center of creating music for mastery. The affordances offered by such contexts are generally invisible and lie outside the awareness of accomplished musicians. Working within an ensemble environment forces individuals to hone their memory for details. The context demands as a matter of course visual attentiveness, mental quickness, and collaborative skills. Such skills are the same as those required in an information-based and technology-driven world where academic advancement, employment, medical care, and other critical aspects of daily life rely on quick and ready use of them.

Research on voluntary expertise development points repeatedly to the effectiveness of learning contexts devised by local individuals in collaboration with experts in the targeted field. In some afterschool clubs and community centers, small groups pursue interests from choral music to wild flowers that motivate them to practice and to seek out information

---

\* Community arts organizations and local arts advocates, as well as the National Science Foundation in the United States and the Crafts Council in the United Kingdom, stepped forward to support and spread information about what some termed the "pro-am" (or professional amateur) movement and its potential for local learning. See, for example, journals such as *Community Literacy* and works such as Crawford, 2009; Leadbetter & Miller, 2004.

in order to improve skills and to gain knowledge. Working with others in a common pursuit fosters self-directed learning that benefits the full group as well as the individual (Heath, 2012).

Within the actual work of groups dedicated to music, the need to learn structured symbol systems such as musical notation means some private study and practice as well as focused attentiveness within group practices. Such is certainly the case for both choral and instrumental ensembles. Noted below are some of the key features of learning that pertain in general to *both* types of music ensembles.

(1) Rehearsal zones that support kinesthetic and haptic exploration (exploration through movement and touch) as well as accumulation of information and skills that encourage self-monitoring.
(2) Consistent need and call for visual attentiveness to multiple cues and sources of cues within the immediate environment, plus development of the ability to tune out visual distractions.
(3) Evidenced need to develop tolerance and understanding of the need for repetition and redundancy, both in the music itself and in routines of practice.
(4) Consistent need to pay attention simultaneously to several structured symbol systems.
(5) Acceleration of empathy and a sense of caring – for others within the ensemble, as well as for instruments and about relations between the music and the audience.

## 1. Rehearsal zones

One of the first vehicles for learning to create music is space – rehearsal zones and studios in particular (Heath, Paul-Boehncke, & Wolf, 2007; Hetland, Winner, Veenema, & Sheridan, 2007). Close examination of these spaces brings to our attention not only the visual and auditory nature of rehearsals, but also two distinctive forms of learning: the kinesthetic and the haptic.

In *kinesthetic learning*, individuals observe the body in motion – their own and others'. Alignment of the individual body as well as positioning in relation to others in the group conveys critical information in ensemble music. This information indicates whether or not individuals are mutually attending to the same stimulus, working in rhythm and with synchrony when called for, and anticipating future moves of either specific members or sections of the full group.

*Haptic learning* is generally thought of as learning that derives from touching or gaining information through the "eyes of the skin," particularly with the hands and forearms, as well as the fingers. In some art forms, such as dance, haptic learning involves several portions of the body at once. Architects consider in their designs the haptic learning that derives from the "feel" of the entire body within particular spaces, where walls or divisions differ in their exterior surfaces (Pallasmaa, 2009, 2012). Musicians echo this sentiment when they speak of the "feel" of certain concert spaces as well as the acoustics of these venues.

But beyond this general sense of "feel" in a space are the minute aspects of haptic understanding (see especially Chapter 11 of Wilson, 1998, on the hands of musicians). Advances in fMRI (functional magnetic resonance imaging) technologies now permit neuroscientists to see what happens to internal visual images in the brain when individuals grip, hold, or touch what they see. The haptic or hand-guided feedback that young musicians gain when they grip an instrument such as a bow, drum stick, or the neck of a violin, viola, or cello enhances the act of mentally visualizing, of envisioning what lies beyond the current moment. Gripping with the hand sends what neurologists call "force patterns" to those portions of the brain that enable individuals to envision what lies ahead (Reiner, 2000, 2008). As children learn to verbalize this sense of "nextness" when gripping objects in their hand, they learn to think before they act. The question: "What am I to do now that I have this object in my grip?" becomes operative as children mature beyond their own initial assumptions about possible actions to take with gripped objects. With maturity and linguistic abilities comes the verbal exploration of "What should I do with this?"

With such maturation, children move into more complex powers of seeing and interpreting. Guided practice is essential, however, for individuals to continue to improve visual (as well as auditory) perception of multi-layered details; all of this often in the midst of seeming chaos – messages and signals to different sections of the ensemble, and demonstration by the conductor that may seemingly be directed toward only one section. Visual discernment by young learners reduces the number of struggles the cognitive system faces in attempting to sort out irrelevant cues from those pertaining directly to one section or another, one portion of a page of music, or one part of an instrument. Being attentive and alert comes not only through practice but also maturity.

Researchers who examine rehearsal zones give particular attention to how spaces become "instrumental" to the creative work of musicians as well as dancers and actors. The acoustics of spaces enhance the listening possibilities for members seated in various parts of the ensemble (as well as audience members). However, musicians also need to have within their spaces of rehearsal a sense of the mutual tuning in by others to the sounds in the immediate space. Joint attention of the group has to grow for individuals to achieve mastery. Thus, no individual player or singer can "zone out" or lose focus, for if they do so, the sense of togetherness is lost for others.* This attentiveness to space receives considerable practice in different settings, since travel for performances in various kinds of spaces comes about for groups as they develop mastery.

The importance of space to learning goes largely unnoted for many sites other than those in which the arts take place. Similarly, when assessing resources for young children's growth, developmentalists rarely note the importance of spaces – both indoor and outdoor. Young learners living in crowded housing conditions and neighborhoods without either open spaces or buildings suitable for music rehearsals have few opportunities to learn how to "listen to space." Families without discretionary income or time to learn within dedicated spaces (in either their homes or local neighborhoods) can rarely attend to their children's interpretive skills for either spatial knowledge or awareness of tactile, haptic, or kinesthetic cues.

## 2. Visual attentiveness

Perhaps the most obvious fact about ensemble music is that learners who want to become members must develop habits of sustained attentiveness and observational awareness to what seems to be *everything*. Observers of youth working in ensemble music sometimes ask: Does holding visual gaze on matters of detail to be found in pages of sheet music aid the mental attentiveness of young people who live in a world of constant distractions? The unequivocal answer is a resounding "yes." Much of the work of

---

* For further understanding of how relationships of listening and observing work in music, see Black, 2008 as well as Schutz, 1964. Turino, 2008 illustrates the extent to which creativity in music around the world relies very much on norms of interaction and interplay that are rarely voiced but rather attended to through listening and looking.

learning in music comes through imitation. As musicians new to an ensemble settle in, they spend much of their time observing and watching others around them look and pay attention. Novices want to do what others do, and they need to do as others do in many ways. Highly critical, however, is learning which players to imitate and when.

To the experienced musician, it is obvious, for example, that reading a sheet of music differs for those who play different instruments. This distinction is learned as novice musicians sense their own belonging within a section or as an alto or tenor within a choral group. Timing, interpretation, and much else about performance relies then on imitation as a starting principle. Yet mastery relies on depth of understanding of distinctive roles, parts, and styles. As individuals gain mastery, they also grow more sensitive to nuances of coordination of these differentiated contributions from various parts of the ensemble (Levitin, 2006; Zbikowski, 2005, 2006). Thus, individuals within the string section must attend to what others in this section do with specific parts of the body, but they must also pay attention to notes, rhythm, pace, and the conductor's movements and detect these as cues that must be met with action in order to bring about desired outcomes for their section. Both direct and peripheral vision matters for beginners as well as for the most accomplished musician. Cues to be followed seem to be everywhere all at once.

With maturity and experience, young musicians gain in their ability to "think" with and through the complementarity of being visually attentive to what goes on around them and also controlling their own hands and body for purposeful actions. Cognition becomes grounded as children gain practice in motor-dependent production from what they see, anticipate, or envision. They also learn to assess their own actions as they do so. Cognitive neuroscientists use the term "grounded cognition" to refer to the extent to which the brain's modal systems ground internal representations of what others refer to as "concepts" (Barsalou, 2008). In ensemble music, this grounding or conceptual understanding comes about through simultaneous input from the environment, body, situational emotive stimuli, as well as through the work of the brain's modal systems.[*]

---

[*] See Barsalou, 2010. Such ideas have been around among neuroscientists and others since 2001, though specified in different terminology; see Schlaug, 2001 and the "speculations" of Benzon, 2001.

For example, the combination of visual perception, spatial sensing, and the work of the hand and forearm creates what some have termed "the thinking hand" (Pallasmaa, 2009).

### 3. Habituated tolerance of redundancy

Within instrumental and choral ensembles, learners repeat, repeat, repeat. They see within their music an order that is created by repeated patterns within particular segments of a set of lyrics or stretch of notes or portions of a fugue or sonata. With practice comes repetition of these patterns in multiple attempts to improve and to "get it right." Individuals become accustomed to hours and hours during which they must tolerate repetition. They thereby become habituated, albeit subconsciously, to the practice it takes to improve and move toward mastery and the fact that this practice is vital.

As young learners gain familiarity with hearing and foreshadowing in their heads repetition of notes as well as bars and stretches of musical scores, they internalize stretches of this patterning. Only through hearing and taking part in stretches of music again and again will this habituation enable learners to move to a level of automaticity in recall, as well as recognition of how one repetition differs from another. Such is the case in many fields of intellectual mastery. Learners move into an unfamiliar space with dissimilar language uses, material items, and individuals playing roles that seem highly disparate. With practice, the environment becomes familiar. Habituation must be achieved in order to master the skills needed to compare these dissimilar items and roles, identify patterns, grasp the meaning of metaphors, understand particulars in relation to a whole, and figure out order and system (Rothstein, 2006).

As noted above, this kind of mastery applies in any type of engagement with the worlds of information or technology. For example scientists in all fields, just like musicians, rely on sorting out patterns and order as they carry out their work (Heath, Paul-Boehncke, & Wolf, 2007). Repetitive movements of any phenomena studied by scientists carry meaning (whether of celestial beings or geophysical structures). But to know these phenomena, both scientists and musicians look repeatedly, try to work out patterns, and determine how trying again may bring new results. The frequent question as to why so many scientists have also studied music has numerous answers. One certainty is that those who have participated in the sustained work of ensemble music as youngsters know the meaning of repetition and patterning. They also understand the value of looking and listening closely to detect segments of phenomena that differ from time to time or under varying circumstances in only one element or detail (such as the vitality of one note or the shaping of a single molecule).

*4. The layering of structured symbol systems*

Learning the vital role of repetition enables even very young musicians to identify parts and to grasp the ways in which parts contribute to the whole. The arrangement of the many parts or elements involved in the production of music, whether choral or instrumental, amounts to layers of structured symbol systems, with notes, sounds, and numerals being only the most obvious of these. A page of music presents several systems (arrangement of lines and spaces along with musical notes, indications of time through both words and numbers, and, for choral groups, the words to be sung).

The structuring of symbol systems, and that alone, allows humans to detect meaning. As infants and toddlers learn to recognize and produce language(s), they do so only because the symbols (sounds) of every language make meaning through their structuring. Later children learn to read and count because they come to understand the structuring within their particular script system, whether alphabetic or otherwise. Each language of the world differs in its patterns of structuring. Though different languages contain many shared sounds (consider, for example, Spanish and Portuguese), nearly every language includes sounds that may not appear in other languages (for example, the five clicks of Xhosa, a South African language). The same is true for the musical systems of different cultures of the world. In learning to read the different script systems or alphabets of the worlds' languages, individuals must recognize how the lines, circles, and other segments of marks used relate to the sounds of the language. The same is true in reading the musical notation of cultures around the world. It is therefore no surprise that research in music learning continues to emphasize the extent to which the "language" areas of the brain work during the creation of music (Levitin and Menon, 2003).

Youngsters involved in ensemble music must learn to read the several layered structured symbol systems simultaneously – a stronger cognitive demand than when reading only alphabetic letters or the written script system of any language. Beyond the page, children must also learn to interpret the movements of the conductor's baton. Musicians must read, encode, and translate all of these symbol systems to produce sounds that reflect timing, pace, emotional interpretation, and physical and musical coordination with the conductor's wishes, as well as with the actions of others in one's section and the ensemble group as a whole.

A further point is often overlooked when researchers talk about the layering of different symbol systems in music. Young musicians must learn to grasp the meaning of highly abstract terms that conductors use to refer to aspects of interpretation that cannot be rendered directly in symbol systems or literal language. This demand has been termed "cross-domain" learning.* For example, characterizations of musical pitch as "falling" or "rising" have no necessary relation to the actual vertical placement of notes on the printed page or the vertical orientation of the page. Essentially, much that happens in music relies on metaphorical interpretation and the suspension of belief in the literal. Other domains must then be called up to interpret music. Musicians have to "map" what they know about the real world onto specific usages in music of words and phrases and learn to act accordingly. "Text painting," or mapping the semantic meaning of words of lyrics onto notes, is familiar to those in choral groups as well as to instrumentalists who play such music. In such "painting," melodies "ascend" and "descend" often in relation to semantic meanings of accompanying words of the lyrics. In particular, musicians have to translate into specific actions metaphors reflecting concepts used in music such as "beauty," "mystery," and other "emblems" of what some have termed the "inner life" of music.

This "inner life" of music is often expressed by conductors and aficionados alike in terms of emotion or aesthetic quality using verbs such as *ascend, descend,* and *lift* as well as nouns such as *texture, integrity, truth,* etc. Moreover, conductors sometimes urge young musicians to create an aesthetic effect by providing analogies or metaphors, asking them to "play that feeling you get when you run in the wind" or "show here the release you get when you achieve something you struggle hard to do." Again, just

---

* Zbikowski (2005, 2006) developed this term to account for the fact that musicians must map meaning across many domains. On related points, see Halwani, Rüber, & Schlaug, 2001.

as scientists must sometimes use words or phrases that rely on metaphorical interpretation, so must musicians.

*5. Empathy and caring work*

This environmental feature often seems too obvious to merit mention in treatises on the life and meaning of learning music. Yet being within a space that becomes familiar over time and involves the same group of people in the act of creating music brings a sensual reality to the meaning of words such as *collaboration* or *cooperation*. Staying attuned to others through having to be mindful of their movements and actions at all times brings about a sense of cohesion over time. Being in a group where one person's error, absence, or lapse of attention has consequences for specific others, as well as for the group as a whole, builds empathetic responsiveness.

Children who participate within ensemble groups must learn to care not only for their instruments, but also for others within the group. This type of caring refers to attention-giving, as when coordinating movements of bows in the string section. *Caring* in this sense refers to "being alert." This meaning is the same as that we convey in the caution to "take care." The further sense of "care about" also applies in ensemble music. The need for continuous care that comes with *playing* musical instruments is unique. Some musicians speak of their particular instrument in animate terms and see life stories revealed – especially within instruments made of wood.

Key aspects of sociodramatic play are found in the learning ecology of instrumental music ensembles. Individuals who are fully engaged also care about what and how others express meaning and respond to one another (Damasio 1999, 2005). Those who spend time simply observing others work out a portion of a score identify with the meaning or emotion the singers or players wish to convey. Picking up cues, interpreting emotion through sounds and action, and responding appropriately constitute core aspects of singing a part as well as playing an instrument. These skills cannot come through solitary practice. They can evolve only through observing and being with other singers or players whose expertise grows through years of practice in "taking care" and "caring about." Both uses of *care* point to the potential to make a difference in the state or condition of something or of someone else.

Moreover, the need to care for an instrument conveys special meaning for children of families living in small spaces, communities with high crime rates, or in neighborhoods without reliable public transport. Each time a youngster picks up his or her musical instrument, that instrument requires attentive care – whether tuning and adjusting or checking on alignment of components. The interdependence between player and instrument is established at the moment a child is given responsibility for an instrument. Learning to care about it comes along with learning to play.

Families who move their households often and live in temporary or small spaces rarely accumulate expensive material items that require constant care. Therefore, when children from these families enter the study of instrumental music within a group, being entrusted with a material item that requires care may be a unique experience. Learners must:

- tune the instrument
- maintain its components
- pack it within a case for transport
- ensure that it is not damaged as they carry it about
- learn to distinguish one particular instrument from others similar in appearance.

Without this care, the instrument will fail them, and they, in turn, will fail both *to take care* and *to care about* the instrument as well as the ensemble.

## Conclusion: Reflections on Research and Evaluation

Education reforms after the opening of the twenty-first century intensified the need for schools to take responsibility for student and teacher performance as measured through standardized tests of academic achievement. Moreover, within the United States, "learning" in the public's mind slimmed down in definition to refer primarily to scores on academic achievement tests. Justification for expenditure in support of supplementary learning opportunities for children living in under-resourced communities needed to include evidence of gains on standardized test scores, particularly in reading and mathematics. From 2000 forward, learning of skills linked with science, technology, engineering, and mathematics (STEM) became a national focus, along with improved rates of growth in language and reading achievement.

Federal and national bureaucracies, as well as private funding sources, called increasingly for "evaluation" of any learning opportunity offered to children both within and after school. Consulting firms and evaluation teams collected school scores and attendance records, surveyed parents and educators, and often asked children for self-reports of satisfaction with their learning experiences. Priorities in funding centered on programs of tutoring to eliminate deficiencies and raise standardized test performance. As a consequence, afterschool programs that promoted pursuits in the arts fell out of favor. Ensemble music programs suffered in particular ways when urban centers (such as Syracuse, New York) saw major arts centers close or symphony orchestras disband for lack of funding.

Thus, ensemble music programs faced increasing pressure to provide evidence that learning music benefits performance on academic tests and grades in school. This emphasis came to overshadow attention to the numerous specific fundamentals of learning gained by children who take part in sustained, professionally led ensemble music throughout their youth. Most of the features of learning environments of music and other arts easily pass unnoted by evaluators (as well as artists and musicians). The former generally know little about child development and the need, for example, to provide guidance and extensive practice in the "head, hand, and heart" work available only through the arts. Musicians and artists typically come to think of what they do as they create art or sing and play as being "only natural" or "just the way we do it." However, these fundamentals of behavioral, visual, auditory, haptic, and interpretive practices that learning ensemble music demands give youngsters much more than an ability to create and make art.

Research carried out by scholars in several disciplines of the learning sciences, such as cognitive psychology, anthropology, and the neurosciences, continues to identify the complex ways in which practices central to the arts make differences in learning. The general goal of these scientists is to understand what happens in different types of learning environments that reinforce behaviors possible at certain maturational levels. At what age, for example, can young children translate into action highly abstract metaphors or read the intention of a conductor? This area of research by learning scientists tends to center on contexts of voluntary expertise development in which participants must meet high demand, take risks in performance, and undergo regimens of practice in order to acquire even mid-level mastery. Researchers in the learning sciences do not offer judgments on conditions or claim causal factors that figure in certain patterns of behavior unrelated to the learning context studied. To be sure, they compare learning environments, but they do so primarily to identify specifics of certain environments that occur together with patterns of observed behaviors. They also compare the extent and nature of learning by individuals as behavioral changes take place over time. These changes are, in many instances, compared with data on maturational changes. In other words, learning science researchers can indicate the extent to which patterns of behavior *differ* in pace for children working in ensemble situations from the developmental trajectory human developmentalists regard as "normal" for children who have no ensemble experience.

In fact, learning scientists have pointed out that much of what happens in these learning environments promotes lifelong habits beneficial for gaining skills and acquiring information in any field. Moreover, the interdisciplinary research of learning scientists leaves no doubt that claims of specific functional outcomes, such as performance on standardized academic tests, tell us very little about what actually happens in the brains, bodies, and emotions of youngsters involved in ensemble music or any of the other arts so long as professional guidance and sustained practice are provided.

Creating music reaches much deeper into the lives of young musicians than the scores on their next set of reading or mathematics tests. As indicated above, young musicians gain, among other vital skills, visual and auditory perception, interpretive skills, and practice vital to processing multiple sources of information simultaneously. As we study rehearsal zones in which ensemble music is created, we deepen our understanding of how much practice it takes for young people to automate the cognitive processes necessary to read and respond to messages that come from the layered symbol systems that characterize ensemble music. In addition to these particular cognitive and linguistic abilities, young musicians also gain practice essential to the automaticity necessary for response to simultaneous and fast-moving visual, kinesthetic, haptic, and auditory cues. Social growth in empathy and various modes of caring become deeply embedded within the interactions of music ensembles. Cognitive, linguistic, and social learning support numerous other types of learning, from self-regulation to facility in interpreting abstractions and metaphors through cross–domain mapping.

Evaluations that rely primarily on standardized test scores cannot capture what learning sciences researchers are rapidly documenting and analyzing about the differential effects on learning of various types of environments. When evaluators and educators go after only functional, surface-level, often temporary and contingent kinds of learning gains, they short-change what happens in any deep learning, such as that of ensemble music. To be sure, this learning takes place subconsciously and only with professional guidance and sustained practice over years. Yet changes in levels of mastery can be observed, noted, and analyzed together with shifting development of musical knowledge and skill. These research findings are supported through annual administration of specific tests that measure growth in visual perception, detection and memory of patterns, categorization and language processing skills, and interpretation of metaphors and abstractions related to emotional responses. In time, ensemble music groups and their financial supporters will come to value the research that documents growth in musical mastery as well as changes in the above-noted abilities. Validation will come for the expanding research on music learning from all the disciplines included in the learning sciences.

The learning that results from participation in ensemble music brings life-long and life-wide consequences (Young, 1999). The skills and concepts acquired through sustained music practice and rehearsal carry value in academic and career-preparation settings. Moreover, these skills increasingly appear at the top of lists of characteristics predicted to be essential to successful participation in the twenty-first century economy. Such skills have been identified by employers and researchers working in the worlds of wellness and health, as well as industries linked with information technologies. In list form, the skills sound so simple as to be unworthy of notice in the everyday world. Yet the cumulative effects are what matters: seeing and hearing patterning of parts in relation to the whole, reliable interpreting of multiple symbol systems as well as metaphors and abstract references, maintaining interpersonal and intrapersonal behavior in accordance with situational circumstances, and developing and sustaining mentally challenging activities that call for visual and auditory perception as well as long-term memory for details and patterning.

In short, the very skills and concepts that become manifest with extended participation in the learning ecology of ensemble music are central to effective learning, now and into the future, not only for children living in under-resourced communities but for *all* young learners. However, those from poorly endowed communities are less likely than their wealthier counterparts to live in symbol-rich environments with regular intense cognitive and linguistic demands that call for highly specific listening, interpretive, and motor skills. Moreover, impoverished families can rarely provide their children close supportive sustained association with experts and other learners working toward the same goal of mastery in performance.

If El Sistema as it plays out in communities across the world survives as more than a passing fad among the current approaches to social justice, its supporters must invest in research. Moreover, a first step to giving more attention to ensemble music is the need to re-socialize parents across all social classes as well as educators and public and private funders. They need to be made aware of what happens as their children work and learn within ensemble music. Knowing that, they will know more of what lies within creating music that makes it an eternally valued – and ever puzzling – aspect of humanity.

## References

Barsalou, L. W. "Grounded Cognition." *Annual Review of Psychology* 59 (2008): 617–645.

Barsalou, L. W. "Grounded Cognition: Past, Present and Future." *Topics in Cognitive Science* 2.4 (2010): 716–724.

Benzon, William. *Beethoven's Anvil: Music in Mind and Culture*. New York: Basic Books, 2001.

Black, Steven P. "Creativity and Learning Jazz: The Practice of 'Listening.'" *Mind, Culture, and Activity: An International Journal* 15/4 (2008): 279–295.

Crawford, Matthew. *Shop Class as Soulcraft*. New York: Penguin, 2009.

Damasio, Antonio. *The Feeling of What Happens: Body and Emotion in the Making of Consciousness*. New York: Harcourt, 1999.

Damasio, Antonio. *Descartes' Error*. 2nd edition. New York: Penguin, 2005.

Halwani, Gus, Psyche Loui, T. Rüber, and Gottfried Schlaug. "Effects of Practice and Experience on the Arcuate Fasciculus: Comparing Singers, Instrumentalists, and Non-musicians." *Frontiers in Psychology* 2.156 (2001): 1–9.

Heath, Shirley Brice. *Words at Work and Play: Three Decades in Families and Communities.* Cambridge, UK: Cambridge University Press, 2012.

Heath, Shirley Brice, Elke Paul-Boehncke, and Shelby Wolf. *Made for Each Other: Creative Sciences and Arts in the Secondary School.* London: Creative Partnerships, 2007.

Hetland, Lois, Ellen Winner, Shirley Veenema, Kimberly M. Sheridan. *Studio Thinking: The Real Benefits of Visual Arts Education.* New York: Teachers College Press, 2007.

Higgins, Kathleen Marie. *The Music Between Us: Is Music a Universal Language?* Chicago: University of Chicago Press, 2012.

Leadbetter, C. and P. Miller. *The Pro-Am Revolution.* London: Demos, 2004.

Levitin, Daniel J. *This Is Your Brain on Music: The Science of a Human Obsession.* New York: Penguin, 2006.

Levitin, Daniel J. and V. Menon. "Musical Structure is Processed in 'Language' Areas of the Brain: A Possible Role for Brodmann Area 47 in Temporal Coherence." *Neuroimage* 20 (2003): 2142–2152.

Marcus, Gary. *Guitar Zero: The New Musician and the Science of Learning.* New York: Penguin Press, 2012.

Pallasmaa, Juhani. *The Thinking Hand.* New York: Wiley, 2009.

Pallasmaa, Juhani. *The Eyes of the Skin: Architecture and the Senses.* New York: Wiley, 2012.

Reiner, M. "The Validity and Consistency of Force Feedback Interfaces in Telesurgery." *Journal of Computer-aided Surgery* 9 (2008): 69–74.

Reiner, M. "The Nature and Development of Visualization: A Review of What is Known." In *Visualization: Theory and Practice in Science Education*, J. K. Gilbert, M. Reiner, and M. Nakhleh, eds., 25–29. Surrey, UK: Springer, 2000.

Rothstein, Edward. *Emblems of Mind: The Inner Life of Music and Mathematics.* Chicago: University of Chicago Press, 2006.

Schlaug, Gottfried. "The Brain of Musicians: A Model for Functional and Structural Adaptation." *Annals of the New York Academy of Sciences* 930 (2001): 281–299.

Schutz, Alfred. "Making Music Together: A Study in Social Relationship." In *Alfred Schutz, Collected Papers*, A. Broderson, ed., vol. 2, 159–178. The Hague, the Netherlands: Martinus Nijhoff, 1964.

Stafford, Barbara Maria. *Artful Science: Enlightenment Entertainment and the Eclipse of Visual Education.* Cambridge, MA: The MIT Press, 1999.

Tunstall, Tricia. *Changing Lives: Gustavo Dudamel, El Sistema, and the Transformative Power of Music.* New York: W. W. Norton, 2012.

Turino, Thomas. *Music as Social Life: The Politics of Participation.* Chicago: University of Chicago Press, 2008.

Wilson, Frank. *The Hand: How its Use Shapes the Brain, Language, and Human Culture.* New York: Random House, 1998.

Young, James O. "The Cognitive Value of Music." *The Journal of Aesthetics and Art Criticism* 57, no. 1 (1999): 41–54.

Zbikowski, Lawrence. *Conceptualizing Music: Cognitive Structure, Theory, and Analysis.* New York: Oxford University Press, 2005.

Zbikowski, Lawrence. "The Cognitive Tango." In *The Artful Mind: Cognitive Science and the Riddle of Human Creativity*, Mark Turner, ed., 115–132. New York: Oxford University Press, 2006.

# PART II

# UNDERSTANDING COMMUNITIES

At a magnitude of 9.0, the Tohoku earthquake of 2011 was the most powerful to ever hit Japan. It triggered a violent tsunami that tore many miles inland, causing reactor meltdowns at the Fukushima Daiichi Nuclear Power Plant. In the tragic aftermath, 15,000 people lost their lives and hundreds of thousands were displaced. After such a disaster, many children were left homeless and orphaned.

Hammarkullen, Sweden, is in a particularly transitional and culturally stimulating period: over half of its residents are immigrants, representative of hundreds of diverse nationalities and spoken languages. In addition to the challenges of high unemployment, gang activity, and drug abuse, there has been concern over the increasing segregation of age, class, and ethnicity.

A young man in Bahia, Brazil, learned to play the viola through his parochial school. He was drawn to music but had no place to further his education beyond high school – there was no youth orchestra in the entire state. With limited prospects for employment or educational opportunities in his impoverished hometown after graduation, he regretfully packed up his viola and moved away to live with relatives. He found work as a street vendor, but continued to long for his viola.

Despite these diverse different circumstances, leaders and musicians from each of the communities mentioned above found the same promising solution: music as a vehicle for healing, bringing people together, and improving the future. Children in the disaster area of Fukushima, Japan, are working together in the Soma Children's Orchestra Project; El Sistema Sweden uses family and community gatherings around food, song,

95

and games to foster understanding and respect among multiple cultures; the young violist quit his job as a vendor to audition for Neojibá – Núcleos Estaduais de Orquestras Juvenis e Infantis da Bahia – the first youth orchestra ever in Bahia. He was admitted and picked up his viola again under the baton of internationally renowned conductor Ricardo Castro.

As leaders from many different programs will demonstrate in the essays that follow, El Sistema is a powerful tool, but it cannot be effective without being molded to the community and circumstance. Its shape-shifting nature allows for the malleability that makes it a success even in diverse cultures and countries around the globe. Therefore, this section of the book is perhaps more crucial than any other; El Sistema philosophy, pedagogy, and organizational structure will be misguided and unsuccessful without meaningful consideration of the culture and setting in which it operates.

## Adaptations

To demonstrate the unique nature of El Sistema programs around the world, the first chapters delve into "case studies." I have avoided the term "model" here to describe these constructs; the very nature of El Sistema prevents a true model as each community has different resources and needs, but beyond that, none of these programs outside of Venezuela are old enough to have truly solidified in form. All continue to shift and explore in the early days of their development – and will continue to do so for years to come. Nevertheless, it may be helpful to understand the most common approaches for adapting El Sistema, so I offer below a brief summary of the most common constructs found in the United States and abroad.

*School construct, in-school:* Here, programming runs during the school day, embedded into school curriculum. The benefits to such a partnership with a school are vast – access to students, the school's built-in infra-structure and resources, and instant credibility with families. In-school programs have the potential to reach every enrolled child and to create an environment of effective collaboration between the multiple teachers and adults involved in a child's life. The in-school program may be run by a service provider who comes to the school to support or implement El Sistema education, as seen with El Sistema Colorado, a program that is further discussed in this section by its board president and NPR host, Monika Vischer. There are also examples of a school beginning and supporting an El Sistema program with its own resources, normally through the efforts of an interested music teacher (such as Lorrie Heagy, who began Juneau Alaska Music Matters at Glacier Valley Elementary School). El Sistema has also influenced nontraditional school structures such as the Conservatory Lab Charter School in Boston, where an extended day model has students learning academic subjects during the first half of the day, orchestra and music in the second half.

Factors to be considered when looking at a school for El Sistema work are administrative stability, faculty buy-in, school culture, and opportunities for continued learning for students once they matriculate to middle or high school.

*Afterschool at school:* Afterschool programs at a school site also benefit from the infrastructure and resources of the school, with pupils largely coming from the school's student body (though some afterschool at school programs extend the invitation to children in the larger community), access to free classroom space, and front office support. As with in-school programs, afterschool programs may be a part of the school's own programming or be provided in partnership with a service provider. The Miami Music Project is such an example, operating after school in multiple school sites across Miami-Dade County. The Soma Children's Orchestra, which will be further explained in this book by its founder and director Yutaka Kikugawa, has built on the existing culture of afterschool music "clubs" to build its El Sistema program in Japan.

*Professional orchestra construct:* El Sistema has become an enticing option for many symphony orchestras as they assess their ability to reach new audiences and stay relevant in the twenty-first century. Education programming has been shifting from outreach concerts where students watch to participatory music education where students play/sing. Today, the majority of El Sistema programs that fall into the professional orchestra scheme are actually a combination of several partnerships. For example, the Edmonton Symphony Orchestra embarked on partnerships with three other organizations to begin its El Sistema program – the Edmonton Catholic School District, the Rotary Clubs of Edmonton Riverview and Sherwood Park, and the Inner City Children's Program (ICCP). Partnerships are usually a necessity since symphony orchestras, as arts organizations, require additional infrastructure and expertise if they are to carry out the intensive, sustained education and community work demanded by the El Sistema philosophy. However, artistic expertise, knowhow, and opportunities are built in to this approach. Leni Boorstin and Gretchen Nielsen of the Los Angeles Philharmonic further explain the benefits and challenges of this construct in their essay on forming the first Youth Orchestra Los Angeles partnership with the Harmony Project and EXPO Center, a City of Los Angeles Department of Recreation and Parks facility.

*Youth orchestra construct:* Like their professional counterparts, traditional youth orchestras are well equipped to run rehearsals and concerts and can offer students exceptional artistic opportunities. Youth orchestras may require a restructuring, however, to delve into the more intensive educational work of El Sistema programs, since they usually rely on an audition process for children who already have considerable skill. Further, youth orchestras may require a partner in order to support work done in under-resourced neighborhoods. The San Diego Youth Symphony and Conservatory, recognizing its need for increased diversity but lack of capacity to take on El Sistema alone, created its Community Opus project in conjunction with the Chula Vista Elementary School District. Dalouge Smith, president and CEO, explains how this approach has worked to extend El Sistema education across an entire district in San Diego.

*Community center construct:* A community center or youth facility has the ability to draw a wide range of interested children. At Heart of Los Angeles (HOLA), children are drawn from seventy-five different schools. Largely, these programs operate afterschool and may operate the El Sistema program themselves or work in partnership with a service provider or partner organization. A community center typically has expertise about and is trusted in its service area. It also offers access to additional social service resources such as mental health care, food banks, housing, and crisis management. El Sistema Sweden operates within a culture center that draws children from many different schools and communities daily to music programming. As Malin Aghed from El Sistema Sweden explains, the Swedish program offers the potential to bring together a large group of people who otherwise might not interact.

*Community partnerships:* Many programs do not work in one community center or structure, but rather at the center of many organizations, programs, and services. Sistema Scotland's first project, Big Noise in

Randolph, works on a community campus where multiple schools and organizations work together to support children around the orchestra. KidZNotes in Durham, North Carolina, operates in five different elementary schools weekly, with all students and teachers brought together on Saturdays at the Holton Career and Resource Center for orchestra rehearsals. In both examples, multiple organizations, schools, and nonprofits work together to create a series of connected resources and services for students and families.

Each of these approaches is valid, and each comes with innate strengths and weaknesses that have to be measured and explored. The best construct is determined by multiple factors unique to each community. For example, a part of the reason HOLA works as a community center is its location in a high-density area of the neighborhood: within only a few blocks of HOLA are several dozen schools. Almost all students live very close by and walk to class. In a rural community where homes and schools may be more spread out and transportation options limited, this approach may limit access, making a school construct far more effective. Due diligence should be done to assess a community's resources, needs, and desires before determining the best approach.

## Asking Questions

The HOLA community is often referred to as the new Ellis Island. Culturally vibrant and ethnically diverse, it is the most densely populated area in the city, absorbing waves of immigrants from Central and South America, Mexico, Korea, and the Philippines. Though the community has incredible strengths, it also struggles with the challenges facing many immigrant communities in the United States. Several families have at least one parent, child, or relative who is undocumented. Unemployment is high and underemployment is exasperated by the low-wage and "under the table" jobs generally available. Many adults are undereducated, with nearly 60 percent having less than a high school education and only roughly 10 percent having gone to college. The poverty rate is among the highest in the city of Los Angeles, with many large families living in the cramped quarters of a studio apartment. In the music program, we have hundreds of students from six different countries. Each student and family has a story, and each of these stories has taught me the importance of asking questions rather than making assumptions.

In the early days of our El Sistema program, there was an energetic young teacher whose classroom dynamic created puzzlement. Most of her students loved her – they happily solicited attention from her and eagerly wanted to be her helper in class. However, the students in her class who had recently emigrated from Korea were a different story. While these students undoubtedly liked her, they were also slightly afraid of her, describing her demeanor as "moody" because of how quickly she would go from being fun loving to being serious and down to business. Parents had an equally split reaction to her, with many of our Korean-American parents voicing concern that she seemed angry at their children. My own observations of this teacher confirmed that she was excellent – her style echoed many I had seen in Venezuela, with fast-paced learning, high expectations, and a genuine love and concern for all of her students. Further, other colleagues who observed her found her teaching to be in line with our core values and teaching philosophy. I did not see what these Korean students and families were describing, and neither could the teacher herself.

I solicited the help of a trusted colleague who had extensive teaching experience in Korea. After only thirty minutes of observing the teacher, she slipped out of the classroom. "It's the eye contact. That's where this is all stemming from." She went on to explain to me that in Korean culture, direct, sustained eye contact is considered extremely aggressive – especially when used in moments of confrontation or, as was the case with the teacher, discipline and classroom management. When the teacher said "sit up straight, please" in a matter of fact tone, she would hold eye contact with her student. To her way of thinking, doing so demonstrated that she was aware of the student and valued her or him. For most of the students, these mini-corrections were perceived as minor, and this approach worked as the teacher intended. However, for the Korean-American students, the direct look was felt like an angry stare, turning every small correction or disciplinary action into a significant reproach. As a result, they left class feeling ashamed for being seriously reprimanded several times. When the teacher then seemed happy and joking soon after, these kids were completely confused; hadn't she been full of anger only a moment ago? The result was their perception of "moodiness."

Once the teacher got this feedback, she immediately spoke with all of her students – explaining her intention, apologizing for not better understanding their needs and feelings, and promising to try an alternative behavior. She focused on using influence rather than power in her classroom management; not only did this improve how every student related to her, it also fixed several other challenges in her classroom. Over the course of years, this problem has never repeated itself; the teacher is one of our most exceptional instructors.

Everyone uses personal and professional experiences to fill in gaps of knowledge. This is how we make sense of the world around us. If we are not careful, however, these assumptions can lead to chronic misunder-standing when working with students and families. Taking the time to stop and ask questions rather than assuming we "know" is a way of showing respect and compassion.

The potential for misunderstanding is also great since so many of those involved in El Sistema leadership positions outside of Latin America are often outsiders in the communities they work with. This position may be highlighted by socioeconomic status, race, ethnicity, culture, or all of the above. The argument that all of these labels are socially constructed may be valid, but their influence in terms of power and inequality is very real.

Individuals from the dominant culture may unintentionally take for granted that others share their worldview and experiences. In instances of misunderstandings around cultural heritage, the learning curve is steep but recognizable, and generally such differences are respected as traditions that need to be preserved and celebrated – they are what we think of as diversity. When misunderstandings arise around class, however, they become more complex. Values come into play along with an assumption of education and resources. For example, many HOLA middle school students have cell phones – mostly no brand Androids – despite living far below the poverty line and often struggling with food insecurity. At first, this may appear to someone from the middle or upper class to be an inappropriate use of funds – and proof that these families are in fact not truly poor. However, if you speak with parents you learn that they acquired the child's phone in a variety of ways – from saving for a birthday gift, to getting the phone for free. You also understand that the phones are on prepaid, monthly plans that often run out and get turned off by the company. More importantly, you understand that parents in the community have three main reasons for wanting their children to have phones. First is safety: parents living in a sometimes violent neighborhood want to be able to communicate with their child before and after school. Second is homework: almost none of our families have computers at home and those who do are not connected to the internet, yet many children have homework that requires the use of the internet, and a phone is a much cheaper option. Finally, there is status: giving their child a phone makes them feel like good parents, ones who can provide.

Examining our assumptions can be a daunting task – it requires stepping outside of ourselves and questioning how we understand the world. Marianne Diaz holds an unusual point of view; formerly gang-involved and incarcerated, today she is a professional counselor and trainer. Marianne believes that experiences construct reality, influencing knowledge and understanding of the world and one's place in it. Therefore, when Marianne speaks to a room of service providers, she is straightforward and unapologetic about the need to recognize that privilege affords a different set of rules to live by. She pushes those who believe they are already socially conscious and self-aware to inspect how systems and structures have influenced their lives and worldview so that they might better understand differing perspectives.

Marianne has argued that gangs are the natural result of oppression – individuals seek to find the family, meaning, power and security lacking from their neighborhood and home environments. Isaiah "Ike" McKinnon, current deputy mayor of Detroit and former chief of police, and Michael J. Witkowski, University of Detroit Mercy criminal justice professor and three-time Frederich Milton Thraser award-winner for excellence in gang research, follow this same line of thinking to examine how El Sistema programs may act as effective gang prevention.

Many school and community level prevention programs (as opposed to individual student or family programs) focus on increasing awareness and knowledge of gang activity while working to develop pro-social behaviors. For instance, the Gang Resistance Education and Training (G.R.E.A.T.) program is a school-based gang-prevention curriculum where police officers share the dangers of gang activity over a thirteen-week period. Students learn to practice refusal skills and conflict resolution so that they are better prepared.

McKinnon and Witkowski both recognize the value of such a program, but are concerned that it is a onetime curriculum that lacks a solution to the root problems of gang activity. For prevention, children living in gang neighborhoods need sustained programming that offers an alternative community, not just facts and statistics about the harsh realities of gang life. El Sistema is exactly this type of long-term intervention – lasting through the child's entire development into young adulthood. However, El Sistema practice must include awareness of gang culture if its potential is not to be squandered.

These last two essays both call for the El Sistema field to sharpen its status as a social program through thorough examination of the culture in which a núcleo operates. Understanding the multifaceted reasons for poverty, violence, or discord in a neighborhood is a crucial first step to effecting change. Without this understanding, El Sistema can be like holding a closed umbrella above your head during a rainstorm and expecting to stay dry. As Dr. Abreu has said, the orchestra is a metaphor for an ideal community. For this compelling tool to be successful in building agreement, the builders, teachers, and leaders must identify the strengths and challenges of the community and work with its members toward the necessary solutions.

– C. W.

CHAPTER 5

# Adaptations of El Sistema's Philosophy to Different Communities

## I.

## The Community Opus Project: San Diego Youth Symphony and Conservatory's Engagement With Public Schools

*Dalouge Smith*

SAN DIEGO Youth Symphony and Conservatory (SDYS) has recruited the most dedicated and ambitious local student musicians into its orchestras for seventy years. Evolving from a City of San Diego Parks and Recreation program, SDYS now serves San Diego County, an area geographically larger than Rhode Island, as well as neighboring counties and northern Baja California, Mexico. However, even as SDYS's traditional orchestras, housed in Casa del Prado in Balboa Park, have grown to include hundreds of aspiring musicians, the diversity of our musicians has not kept pace with the growing diversity of our region. The SDYS Board of Directors recognized that the entire organization and its focus on youth development through orchestral training ran the risk of becoming irrelevant unless it responded to the changing demographics of the San Diego region.

Lack of diversity is not an uncommon circumstance for an American youth orchestra. The majority of young musicians in our Balboa Park Programs come from families and communities of upper-middle class affluence. They have parents who strongly believe in music's power to help their children succeed socially and academically. Their parents also value long-term participation in music and adherence to its high standards.

With the means to ensure access to private music lessons and school districts with strong music programs, these parents seek out SDYS for the musical challenges and opportunities it offers – beyond what schools or private teachers can provide. The SDYS Board is enthusiastic to serve these students, but also wants to see children without easy access to the experience of learning an instrument have similar opportunities.

To promote diversity and expand access to its programs, SDYS developed partnerships with schools to increase enrollment by students from less affluent communities. This proved a difficult goal to achieve because low-income and English language learner students attend schools with the least music instruction available. Whatever desire they may have to participate in music and enroll in SDYS, they are far behind peers who have grown up with many more musical pathways open to them. We accommodated the variances in musical ability by growing from a single orchestra into multiple orchestra levels, guaranteeing all students a placement in our programs no matter their background. Unfortunately, not all advanced at the same rate as those who started their musical studies early or took private lessons.

Upon determining that our enrollment patterns were closely connected to the greater availability of music education for affluent children, we embraced the goal of "making music education accessible and affordable for all." All of us at SDYS knew that giving ourselves such a goal meant pushing against the trend of diminished music education in the schools. El Sistema-inspired work, with its emphasis on giving all children the opportunity to benefit from learning and performing music at an early age, seemed the appropriate model for such a push. Focusing our El Sistema-inspired efforts on San Diego County's public school districts, with enrollment of 500,000 children, seemed the only logical choice. Children and families frequent schools daily. Likewise, schools have substantial resources with which to educate and engage children. The missing piece in most public schools is the prioritization of music instruction as an essential element of each child's education.

Knowing where and how to begin our interactions with the public schools was a challenge. The local education system is decentralized, and many different factors influence access to music education. San Diego County's schools are governed by forty-two different school boards. The smallest consist of single elementary schools while the largest is San

Diego Unified School District's 200 schools. Music education continues at the middle- and high-school level in districts across the county, but elementary music is very limited in its availability. Affluent communities have supplemented school budgets with private dollars to maintain elementary music teacher positions, but hundreds of low-income elementary schools have been without music teachers for fifteen years or longer. As a consequence, students are given their first chance to learn music as twelve- or thirteen-year-olds.

We understood that bringing about school system investment in music education through El Sistema-inspired work would require a unique combination of characteristics. Our first aim was to find a district school with a substantial enrollment of low-income students but without school-day music instruction. In order to differentiate potential district partners from each other, we identified three criteria we believed essential for success. These included school principals willing to assist with recruitment, provide afterschool classroom space, and communicate with parents. We also sought a community partner to provide social service expertise and a deeper understanding of the schools and families. Finally, we wanted to be working in a neighborhood where the middle and high schools already had music programs, so that children in our El Sistema-inspired program would have music available to them as they matriculated out of elementary school.

Though we had our own criteria for identifying the ideal school partners, we also understood that SDYS could not define its new relationships exclusively on its own terms. Our first step to establishing a partnership of mutual respect and shared goals was learning the priorities and expectations of school and community leaders. For example, instead of selecting which instruments to teach, we asked prospective partners to identify the instruments they felt would be most enthusiastically received by their children and families. One of the first school districts we identified as a likely candidate was the Chula Vista Elementary School District (CVESD) – California's largest kindergarten to sixth-grade district with over 29,000 students, 50 percent of whom qualify for free and reduced federal lunch programs. The school principals and social service leaders in Chula Vista recommended orchestral string instruments because string instruments are common to Mexican-American culture. Likewise, we jointly agreed that if we worked with them, we would start with third-graders because of the important transitional role third grade plays in establishing a child's ongoing success in school.

As conversations with the principals and social service providers in Chula Vista unfolded, it became clear that we had found ideal partners for SDYS's new El Sistema-inspired program. Because principals have substantial autonomy to manage their school site budgets and set priorities, we were able to immediately work with these site leaders to plan for the launch of the program.

In October of 2010, we launched the Community Opus Project as an afterschool program for seventy third-graders, with thirty-five each at two primary schools in the CVESD. Our faculty not only taught the children how to play their instruments, but before the end of each class we also instructed them how to explain to their parents what they had learned on their instruments. By sharing their hard work and growing joy as musicians with their families, the students inspired pride in their parents and a commitment to support their musical development.

The program thrived as students and parents embraced it more deeply. We began hearing stories of how students and families were changing. Ramon was teaching his brother to play music as they reenacted music class at home with the mini-keyboard their mother purchased at a garage sale. Daniel wasn't as disruptive in school or being sent to the principal as often. Maria talked about music helping her not feel so sad after a family tragedy. School and district leaders began seeing these changes too and asked SDYS to expand the Community Opus Project during the second year from two schools to six. To help make this happen, the school district invested funds in the expansion.

The rapid growth in year two, as well as a first wave of Opus musicians auditioning into SDYS's Balboa Park Programs, brought a variety of challenges. Growth is always a challenge, but tripling the size of a program on short notice is guaranteed to create strain. In the case of the Community Opus Project, the greatest short-term difficulty was finding new faculty. We needed teachers with the musical and teaching skills to work with beginner and early stage instrumentalists, but we also needed them to be sensitive to the socioeconomic and cultural realities of each student and school site. The shallow pool of local music teachers up to this task was to be expected given the limited number of positions open to music teachers in San Diego. However, even now, in our fourth year, finding teachers that fit well into the Opus Project requires constant recruitment.

Along with the challenge of securing teachers, we found ourselves initially unprepared for the exponentially greater volume of instruments and corresponding instrument care required to serve 200 more students. We'd never needed to manage or provide so many instruments for the traditional youth orchestra program because it serves musicians who bring their own. Because CVESD hadn't offered music in many years, it no longer had staff experienced in the management of musical instruments. Fortunately, the local high school district, Sweetwater Union High School District (SUHSD), had extra wind and brass instruments to loan, so we only needed to secure donations for string instruments.

On another front, the admittance of students from the Community Opus Project into the Balboa Park Programs at the beginning of Opus's second year was far more unsettling than expected. A small group of families questioned the quality of Opus Project instruction, and several faculty members were concerned that SDYS was lowering its standards in order to give Opus students access to music education. The ensuing tension built for several months. It was resolved with the departure of multiple faculty members and families who chose to leave SDYS halfway through the season. Despite this disruption, we successfully recruited new faculty for the Balboa Park Program. Fortuitously, they came with more experience and a greater commitment to SDYS's overall goal of making music available to all.

The third year of the Community Opus Project brought an even deeper collaboration between SDYS and Chula Vista district. For the first time in fifteen years, the district wanted to see music instruction return to the school day, and it needed SDYS's help to make it happen. Even as the afterschool program continued, we brought school–day music instruction to third-grade classes at six Opus schools and to a kindergarten class at a school selected for a federal Department of Education Promise Neighborhood Grant. The federal grant fully funded the kindergarten music, while CVESD funded the third-grade music.

Extending the reach of Opus into the school day demanded a new level of cooperation between SDYS and the schools. Music classes changed the nature of campus life as classroom teachers interacted with the new music teachers. Principals discovered the need to dedicate classroom space to music and to learn how to create a schedule that accommodated efficient transitions from one music class to the next. SDYS's staff worked side by side with the schools through each new step. By the end of the year a set of principals was prepared to return full-time music teachers to their campuses so all of their students could participate in music.

The connections between the Community Opus Project and the Balboa Park Programs continued to grow in year three as well. Twenty-seven Opus students travelled from Chula Vista to the park and several successfully auditioned from the entry level string ensemble to the second level. Simultaneously, advanced Balboa Park musicians began volunteering at Opus during spring and summer camps. Having these older students on site as mentors and role models ultimately inspired even more students to audition for Balboa Park at the end of year three. Now, over fifty Opus students are enrolled in the Balboa Park Programs in three levels of ensemble.

The connection between the Community Opus Project and the high school district also deepened during year three. High school campuses played host to Opus's fall, spring, and summer camps ,as well as a new community youth orchestra formed by SDYS. In addition, all Opus concerts were held on these campuses. A tradition of joint all-grade community concerts with the local middle and high school bands and orchestra started in the first year of Opus evolved into large festive events with over 400 student musicians and nearly a thousand family members in attendance.

Through all these years, SDYS had been keeping relevant foundations apprised of its progress with the Community Opus Project and Chula Vista's increasing commitment to music education. Among these organizations was VH1 Save the Music Foundation, a nonprofit group that grew out of the VH1 cable music channel and which is dedicated to raising awareness about music education and promoting instrumental instruction in public schools. At a meeting in San Diego in January of 2013, the foundation's program manager informed Chula Vista's assistant superintendent that the district could become the sole recipient of a new instrument grant – and become a long-term grantee of the foundation as well – if the district made a commitment to returning music education to every school. Only two weeks after this meeting, inspired by this incentive and the positive academic and social benefits of Opus, the district's leadership team surprised us all by announcing that it was committed to restoring music education in 100 percent of its schools within ten years. They had seen the advanced Opus students perform many times, and were acutely aware of the connection between their academic and musical success.

The balance of year three and the focus of year four have been dedicated to assisting the district with the daunting task of making this goal a reality. In the process, SDYS is undertaking unexpected tasks and roles. We've advised the district human resources staff on how to recruit highly qualified music educators to fill their newly created full-time positions. Principals have included us in their interviews and observation of music teachers. We've provided guidance on the purchase, set-up, and maintenance of musical instruments and equipment. Through this collaborative effort, four full-time music teachers were placed at four different schools to teach all kindergarten through sixth grade students.

In January of 2014, the VH1 foundation program manager returned to Chula Vista to award CVESD and Lauderbach School, one of the two original Opus schools (and the first to create a full-time music teacher position), a $30,000 string instrument grant. With this news came the even bigger announcement that for the 2014–2015 school year the foundation would award grants to four more CVESD schools and then continue awarding grants to multiple schools each year until they had all hired full-time music teachers and received musical instruments. With this announcement, six new schools asked to pilot third-grade music during the second half of the school year. SDYS is again running the third-grade music, while working with four of these schools to add full-time music teachers to their campuses next year.

As music gets underway in the school day, SDYS is preparing to evolve the afterschool Community Opus Project into a district orchestra and district band. We intend to also engage middle and high school students in the community youth orchestra. This phase two model emulates the stairway structure of El Sistema. School-day music will play a role similar to a núcleo, though it won't achieve the same level of musical intensity as the afterschool offerings. The district and community orchestras will function like city youth orchestras in Venezuela for higher achieving musicians, and our Balboa Park programs will be the regional destination for the most ambitious.

SDYS is now looking to extend this model beyond Chula Vista. Our partnership with CVESD proves that it is possible to make music education a part of every child's experience. Other school districts in southern California have requested our assistance in establishing their own El Sistema-inspired music programs. We aim to provide this needed assistance by applying the knowledge and experience of our work in Chula Vista to these new community settings. We'll simultaneously seek to share what we've discovered with others in the El Sistema movement so they too can deepen their relationships with school systems.

We've taken on many more roles and tasks than we anticipated when we launched the Community Opus Project. With our focus on "making music education accessible and affordable for all," we've learned that the most important task we can undertake is to be adaptable. We encourage others to be equally ambitious and dynamic with their El Sistema-inspired work.


# II.

# An Afterschool Music Program for Japan's "Aftershock Zone"

## *Yutaka Kikugawa*


When Friends of El Sistema Japan (FESJ) was established on March 23, 2012, I became its executive director. Having worked as a coordinator of the Japan Committee for UNICEF's Earthquake and Tsunami Relief, I believed that a long-term reconstruction effort was needed in the areas affected, and that El Sistema's educational philosophy could provide important help for children who were struck hardest by the March 2011 disaster, especially those who suffered both mentally and physically from the Fukushima nuclear accident. That same year, on May 7, FESJ reached an agreement with the city of Soma, one of the areas that had felt the greatest impact from the earthquake and tsunami and subsequent nuclear power station accident. This agreement established "The Fostering Zest for Living through Music Project" (Soma Children's Orchestra and Chorus). Its aim: to help restore the dignity and rights of Soma's citizens and to give them dreams and hopes. In addition, on July 24, the FESJ

111

reached a memorandum of understanding with Fundación Musical Simón Bolívar for exchange and training purposes.

The Soma City Board of Education operates the Soma Children's Orchestra and Chorus (SCOC) with both technical and financial support from FESJ; the program is part of the city's official reconstruction plan under the education subsection. In that document the SCOC is defined as a comprehensive life skill education initiative that instructs and engages children in classical orchestral and chorus music programs inspired by such core values of El Sistema as teamwork, peer teaching/learning, and joy.

Soma was chosen as FESJ's first project site for several reasons. First, we believed that an El Sistema-inspired program had great potential to heal not only the participating children but also help many Soma citizens in the long-term reconstruction and economic challenges that lay ahead (and for this reason we were careful to word our charter to encompass a broad range of problems). Second, the city has a firm commitment to psychosocial care, support, and education. Soma was filled with passionate people in both the public and private domains who believed in the power of music to transform the lives of Soma's children. Third, Soma has long been renowned for its rich cultural heritage of folk music and dance and has a strong tradition of afterschool music club activities. Finally, Soma had already faced an economic decline in manufacturing and an aging population before March 2011, a condition typical for much of rural Japan during the last decade.

## How the Program Works

Although the organizational framework for the SCCO has been evolving, as of fall 2013 it consisted mainly of three different components; (1) Monday-to-Friday afterschool music club activities at limited schools; (2) weekly weekend strings classes, including an orchestral ensemble session, open to students from all the city's schools; and (3) in-curricular music class support, including the presentation of professional and semi-professional musicians' performances in the classroom. In this chapter, I will focus on our weekday and weekend activities.

## 1. Afterschool Program on Weekdays

Before explaining the details of our afterschool programs, I should emphasize the unique nature of afterschool club activities within the

Japanese school setting. Although they are extracurricular sport, music, or art programs, at the junior and high school level they are really an official and mandatory part of school life (though the policy varies from school to school), and even at the elementary level they are often seen as an essential part of school life. Club members are usually expected to participate in the activities daily, or at least several times a week, and over the weekend. The music clubs often compete with other clubs in contests at the local, regional, and eventually national level. In Soma, almost all junior and high school students are enrolled in a club, and some primary schools also sponsor such intensive afterschool clubs.

Nakamura No.1 Primary School (450 students from grades one through six as of March 2014) is the oldest school in Soma, with a more than 150-year history, including a period under the control of the samurai. Its string ensemble, the only afterschool club at the school, is one of the oldest clubs of its kind at the primary school level in Japan, and won a national competition for children's orchestras back in the 1960s. This glorious record stood firmly in the past, however, when FESJ signed its cooperation agreement with the city of Soma in May 2012. The club had twenty-seven members from third to sixth grade and was suffering badly the aftershock of March 2011. Maintenance and repair of the club's instruments was very poor, and the music teachers faced a daily challenge: trying to provide instruction on string instruments when only one of them was conversant with such instruments. Given this situation, Soma's mayor and its Board of Education recognized that the then poorly supported string ensemble could be utilized as an initial platform to realize Japan's first El Sistema-inspired project.

In addition to purchasing and repairing the necessary musical instruments, FESJ helped Nakamura No.1 Primary School to hire Ms. Asako Suto, a local violin teacher, to assist the schoolteachers. For the last twenty years Ms. Suto, the only strings specialist in the Soma region, had been running a small but lively violin class in Odaka, Minami-Soma, 20 kilometers south of Soma and 30 kilometers north of the Fukushima No.1 nuclear power station. After the nuclear accident, Odaka became an uninhabitable zone and Ms. Soto was forced to return to Soma, her birthplace. Educated through the Suzuki method a long time ago, she developed on her own a violin method with a strong emphasis on rhythmical body exercise and effective muscle movement for holding the bow and keeping correct posture. Ms. Suto provides the expertise for the teachers who run Nakamura No. 1's afterschool music club that meets four times a week for two hours each day and also leads our weekly three-hour weekend strings sessions. In addition to this weekend string session, many players come to Ms. Suto on weekdays for regular practice sessions with their friends.

After FESJ's success with Nakamura No.1 Primary School, the Soma Board of Education became interested in introducing a similar if less intensive afterschool violin class in another primary school. The subject was thoroughly discussed at the regular board meeting with all the city's primary school principals, and Yawata Primary School (100 students from first through sixth grade) decided to initiate a once-a-week violin class. Originally held every Wednesday, the class of twelve students from second through sixth grade is now held on Thursdays and is jointly coordinated by Ms. Suto and Ms. Yoko Hoshi, FESJ Soma Project Coordinator and a former music teacher at both Yawata and Nakamura No. 1. Indeed, Ms. Hoshi was the leader of the Nakamura No. 1 strings club during the early 1990s, when she took them to the national competition. Though a small class and meeting only once a week, the Yawata Primary violin class boasts a high-level concentration and its members learn to play some basic string tunes after a few months' instruction.

Sakuragaoka Primary School Chorus is another long-established school club in the city, with thirty-eight students from fourth to sixth grade. The group practices every school day for an hour and half after regular classes. Ms. Yayoi Ojima, a school music teacher, provides the regular instruction while, as FESJ's senior advisor, Mr. Fujio Furuhashi, an acclaimed children's chorus expert and authority on the Kodaly method, comes to Soma from Tokyo monthly for an intensive class that includes voice training; he also offers conducting lessons to Ms. Ojima and her other colleagues at school.

## 2. Weekend Program

One of the challenges FESJ quickly encountered with its support for these weekday elementary school programs was that students above seventh grade could not continue playing a string instrument or singing in school. In the junior high schools they now attended almost all students were mandated to join one or another of each school's afterschool club

114

activities, and unfortunately the only music club program was brass band. Many of the newly graduated Nakamura No.1 sixth-graders who really wished to keep on playing strings asked us and the Board of Education to consider starting a new weekend program that any junior high student could join. Starting with the new school calendar that began in April 2013, this idea was put into practice, with Ms. Suto in charge. At the beginning, this weekend strings class was attended by six seventh-graders and one eighth-grader from two different junior high schools (Nakamura No. 1 and Kouyou) as well as one tenth-grade student; they were joined by roughly fifteen primary school students from Nakamura No. 1 and Yawata primary schools.

While Ms. Suto has been responsible for the musical pedagogy at this weekend class, the presence of more advanced-level students who would soon be taking on a full orchestra portfolio made us look for someone who could both provide more technical guidance and design a medium- and long-term training plan for Ms. Suto to manage. Fortunately Mr. Yohei Asaoka, a well-known professional cellist with a long artistic and teaching career in the United States, has generously offered his fortnightly professional support as FESJ's senior advisor since the inception of the program in April 2013.

An expert on Dalcroze method, Mr. Asaoka's emphasis on body-based movement as the core foundation for playing string instruments aligns perfectly with Ms. Suto's pedagogical approach. Further, they have worked hard to ensure that advanced students adopt the El Sistema role model of peer educators to the younger students. This became all the more relevant when some sixty new students joined the weekend orchestra at the end of July 2013 when the Board of Education decided to open the doors of the new Soma Children's Orchestra to every school-aged child in Soma. With such a large number of beginner children, we needed many more music volunteers who could assist Ms. Suto during her regular sessions and lead the advanced children acting as peer educators. Somehow we manage to run this weekend class by using the many enthusiastic university students and young business people interested in this kind of volunteer work. Many of these young volunteers do not or did not study music as their major subject, but have been playing the violin since they were small.

Until recently, the "children's chorus" simply meant the Sakuragaoka

Primary School Chorus Ensemble but, as with the formation of a weekend strings session for older students, primary school graduates who used to be Sakuragaoka chorus members now regularly come to a special training weekend class to sing with their peers. Membership was exclusive to Sakuragaoka students during a transition period, but starting in April of 2014, this weekend ensemble also opened its door to every child who wants to sing.

**Challenges and Benefits**
Given the current structure of our weekend strings class, it is difficult to secure sufficient practice time as an ensemble, though many of the students have separate group or individual sessions with Ms. Suto and elementary-age students can practice during their regular afterschool club activities. However, the curriculum at Japanese junior high schools is very crowded and it's already hard for students to secure the time to practice string instruments. This forces us to make the most of available weekend time and we endeavor to organize a quality ensemble session where every child can concentrate on performance. We know our students appreciate it. For example, eighth-grader Ayuka, who lost her home on account of the tsunami and started viola lessons three years ago after moving inland, says, "Playing viola at Soma Children's Orchestra with my friends is something that makes me feel at home."

Another challenge is reaching children who are in very difficult socio-economic situations. One case is that of an eleven-year-old fifth-grader who lost his mother in the tsunami, lives in a temporary shelter, and occasionally gets into trouble with the law. He recently made an appeal to the music instructors responsible for our in-curricular programs that he be allowed to continue learning how to read musical notation, even if he has had many troubles. In Soma a boy like this is not an isolated example, and we feel we need to strengthen our capacity for counseling and mentoring so that we can provide customized support to such vulnerable children.

The most positive news to emerge out of our intervention in Soma is that the Soma City Council, through its Board of Education, is now considering making a funding commitment that means taking on full ownership of the SCCO. Of course FESJ will still provide comprehensive support; but the more the council pays, the more this afterschool model becomes truly sustainable in a local context. Such a development has strong policy implications for future El Sistema-inspired programs within Japan. The Soma project is not simply about creating a new Venezuelan style music class, but about ensuring every child's equal opportunity to quality, ensemble-based music education. We believe we can truly "foster the zest for living" through the existing public education system – a system hardly known for its flexibility when it comes to new ventures such as ours.

It is still too early to identify the tangible impact of our intervention in terms of post-traumatic stress alleviation or the enhancement of children's communication skills through El Sistema-style peer learning and teaching, but an external evaluation research study has been undertaken by a team from Aoyama Gakuin University led by Professor Toshifumi Kariyado, a well-known expert on arts project evaluation as well as workshop design and life skill assessment. The first year's study findings, based on the observation of daily activities and questionnaires and interviews conducted with students as well as their parents, are about to be released. They tell us that both quantitative and qualitative data prove the positive impact of peer-learning on participating children's motivation and skills, let alone their family and community environment.

The Fukushima recovery period coincides with the formative years of these children. We will accompany the children in Soma as they build a sustainable system rooted in local culture that cherishes local identities and is based on the love for one's hometown.

# III.

# Understanding Vänstay, the Social Core of El Sistema Sweden

*Malin Aghed and El Sistema Sweden*

In May 2009, the Gothenburg Symphony Orchestra and Gustavo Dudamel performed a magical concert of Beethoven's Fifth Symphony for 600 adults and children in a local gymnasium in Hammarkullen, a suburb of northeast Gothenburg. The energy after this concert sparked a partnership with the Angered Municipal School of Fine Arts and the beginning of an El Sistema program in Sweden. Five years later, El Sistema Sweden has grown and spread to all ten districts of Gothenburg and to six other cities in Sweden, from Umeå in the north to Malmö in the south. This has been made possible through the local schools of fine arts, the Gothenburg Symphony Orchestra, the nonprofit organization Friends of El Sistema in Gothenburg, and the National Foundation of El Sistema in Sweden.

Hammarkullen, the geographic area where El Sistema Sweden began, has its difficulties, with almost a hundred different nationalities and languages, high unemployment, gang activity, and drug abuse. But it's also an area with many engaged and skilled people who want to contribute to both their local neighborhood and to society at large. Hammarkullen is a colorful place in a crucial stage of its development – it could either get really bad, or, with all good forces working together, it could improve and be a very good area to live in. The Gothenburg Symphony Orchestra and Maestro Dudamel arrived right on time.

Some of us from the Angered Municipal School of Fine Arts who had organized the concert took an interest in digging deeper into the El Sistema movement. Led by our principal Camilla Sarner, we decided to start an El Sistema program, within the school and jointly with the Gothenburg Symphony Orchestra, Sweden's national orchestra. To honor Maestro Abreu and Maestro Dudamel, we kept the name El Sistema. With a great deal of passion, we tried to find the families that needed El Sistema the most, visiting all the local schools and performing in their schoolyards. We played scenes from Bizet's *Carmen* with a cello, a clarinet, and a singer. We talked about Venezuela, about the power of music, about how we wanted to create a dialogue and a platform for the entire family, we talked about democracy and a sharing community, and that we believed in the inherent capacity of every single child. And we had a lot of fun.

Besides these visits, we held our first parent meeting in one of the schools on a Wednesday at 5 p.m., where we talked about the very same things. Very few people came, but having Maestro Abreu in mind, we didn't give up. We kept having parent meetings at the same time and place every week, and slowly the local community started to take notice. More and more parents began to come. We translated our information into the seven most commonly used languages in the area. It was indeed a struggle. Little did we know that three years later we would have more than 1,500 families in the program, in all ten parts of Gothenburg, taught by fifty-two very dedicated teachers. We did it together, and that word – *together* – has been our great strength since day one. It still is.

Gothenburg is a very segregated city – not only ethnically, but also according to age, class, school. A change is needed. El Sistema can be a powerful tool to engage people from different cultures and backgrounds in a unifying activity and purpose. Through this idea – which includes the concept of a regular Wednesday afternoon get-together we've named Vänstay – we have been able to start building trust and understanding between parents and teachers, trust within families, and between parents from different backgrounds. Trust takes time to build up, especially among people who have been let down by society over and over again. Writing about it in a couple of pages like these is not easy: it might sound like it's possible to just do it and then it's done. That is, of course, not the truth. It's an ongoing engagement, with no ending.

We believe that the mere consistency of our Wednesday afternoon Vänstay has been one of the most important parameters in creating this trust and contact. Every single week at the same time we open the same door; families know we are there. Every week. Sounds simple, but only time shows that we are serious. Time. Continuity. Insistence. Warmth. Contact. After a while, the parents begin to trust that the door will open again next week, the same time, with the same people. Then they start to participate and to confide in us.

**The Background of Vänstay**
We agree strongly with Italian educator Loris Malaguzzi when he says that a child is "born with 100 languages," and that in growing up these languages are all too often lost or repressed. El Sistema intends to give back some of these lost language skills: singing, playing, dancing, daring to grow freely and be creative, expressing oneself, communicating, believing in yourself as well as in your neighbor, whether she lives next door or on the other side of the world. And we want to do this through music. Our aim is to reach not only the children: to make a sustainable change we need to involve the whole family. We believe El Sistema can change small worlds as well as big ones.

To reach our goals of a safer day-to-day life, a feeling of meaning in life and to fight many children's lack of self-confidence and low self-esteem,

119

we wanted to include as many people as possible who are involved with a given child. We decided to expand our primary weekly parental meetings to also include siblings, grandparents, friends . . . everyone who wishes any and every specific child happiness, stability, safety, and a prosperous life with free choices. And so, the idea of Vänstay was born. Besides the three-to-five orchestra or choir lessons per week for every child, we planned this weekly social gathering. The initial focus was simple: to make every individual feel personally welcome. The structure is much the same now as in the beginning. We try to achieve this by having the teachers who work with the children greet each visitor by name as she or he arrives. Then, we all sing together an especially composed call-and-response song before sitting down for some food. After this brief introduction, happening every week in the same way, the actual program for the day can commence.

Planning this structure we realized we needed to have a name for it. *Vänstay* is a play on words: *Vän* means friend, *stay* means staying in the program, staying after the scheduled lessons, and staying together with friends. Vänstay also sounds like *Wednesday* pronounced with a Swedish accent, and Wednesday is the day the meetings occur. Vänstay means basically: to have fun and do musical things in an unpretentious way, as a family.

**Practically, Vänstay is:**
- a social gathering for El Sistema families, teachers and musicians held every Wednesday between 5 p.m. and 6 p.m.;
- open to every child involved in the El Sistema program as well as every parent, adult, sibling, or friend of that child;
- mutually organized by all the El Sistema teachers in every particular núcleo;
- usually located in the dining hall of the nearest public school.

**Philosophically, the aim of Vänstay is to become:**
- a reliable, unpretentious, and consistent place to meet individually or as a family;
- a safe and trusted feature of an otherwise busy or possibly insecure week;

120

- a tree in the neighborhood to sit under for exchanging ideas and experiencing different languages and cultures, whatever one's own life story, age, or address;
- a fertile ground for healthy, democratic growth;
- a tool to work with in accordance with the United Nations Convention on the Rights of the Child;
- an eye-opener for families to see what music can do;
- the social heart of El Sistema Sweden.

### The Schedule of Vänstay

First and foremost, a Vänstay always includes eating together. The basic structure remains the same every week, though programs vary. First Wednesday of the month: singing, dancing, and playing games together. Second Wednesday: having an audience and being one, with performances by the children and an open stage. Third Wednesday: guest visits, such as smaller groups from the symphonic orchestra, university students studying music, or other semi-professional orchestras and choirs that act as role models. Guests might also be the local police, the library, social workers, the local United Nations Children program, or any other organization with a similar social goal. This third Wednesday may also involve visits to other Vänstay meetings. Fourth Wednesday: potluck, for which all the parents bring food and everybody shares. A party!

### We Hope the End Result of Vänstay is:

- children discovering music as part of a bigger picture;
- demonstrating that music belongs to everyone;
- an increased closeness within families – and between families;
- a safer community and an increased individual desire to take an active, constructive role in society;
- new cross-town connections: families making friends in other parts of town;
- the idea of accessibility becoming real;
- an increased responsibility for each other and each other's children (actually making a better neighborhood, where more adults take responsibility and more children feel they can trust grown-ups).

**About Where and How We Work**

One year after El Sistema Hammarkullen was launched, we opened El Sistema in three other districts of Gothenburg. We had already developed the idea of integration and exchange – so we made sure that as El Sistema spread, so did the Vänstay concept. We realized that if we all kept the same structure and shared our repertoire, playing and singing the same songs, we would also build in the possibility of exchanges on a regular basis.

Since 2014, El Sistema Sweden has had at least one núcleo in every district of Gothenburg. Having these núcleos actively involved in a regular exchange, we bring distant neighborhoods closer together. We encourage families to meet on a regular basis, and introduce the idea of integration by enabling families to make contacts and friends in other parts of town. And since El Sistema is now active in other towns across Sweden, the possibilities for exchange have increased significantly. This way we introduce otherwise isolated families to a huge range of different cultures, languages, and social structures. At least once a month the kids, parents, and teachers travel to other areas of Gothenburg, or receive visitors from another Vänstay. Sometimes we organize exchanges for individual musical sections (strings, woodwind, choir, percussion, or brass). On such a day all students from a particular section visit one special Vänstay along with their families and teachers. In November 2013, for example, ninety-five string students and their parents from six different El Sistema núcleos all over Gothenburg went to the Västra Vänstay. Between 4 and 5 p.m. we held a string workshop with our best string teachers, and at 5 p.m. Vänstay started, with a string quartet coming from the Gothenburg Symphony Orchestra, playing for and together with the children. Another instance involved a visit from the Venezuelan Percussion Ensemble to a Vänstay meeting at which they played together with all of our percussion students.

One characteristic of El Sistema Gothenburg may need explaining: not all of the sites are in socioeconomically hardhit areas. The idea of integration is an important part of our program: we want to reach everybody. Each of our fifty-two teachers in El Sistema Gothenburg (and the forty teachers of El Sistema in the rest of the country) works with this in mind. So that while we are active in "hard" neighborhoods with a high degree of ethnic tension, we are also active in wealthy areas. As Maestro Abreu often stresses: we should harbor a broad view of poverty. In his 2009 TED speech he referred to the words of Mother Teresa when she pointed out that a lack of self-confidence, a lack of self-esteem, and a lack of identification are all factors of poverty. These aspects can be found among both the rich and the poor.

In Gothenburg we find many different languages and cultures, and are confronted with significant hurdles to integration. We struggle with pride and with conflicts that are often deep-rooted in people's personal histories and home countries – and we also deal with alienation within our own society. We are painfully aware of how naïve we often are about the situations of others. We don't know what it's like for immigrants who have been living with a war in their native country, or who do not know whether or not they will be allowed to stay in Sweden. We regularly meet such children and their families through our work, and some parents have even told us that being a part of the El Sistema family is the one thing that keeps them going and gives them hope.

We will always work hard to reach such families, but we will never lose the thought that to make lasting peace in a society we must reach and incorporate all parts of our society and areas of our city, country, and world. After going to Vänstay every week for three months in a neighborhood with a very different and diverse socioeconomic community than the one she was used to, a mother once said to one of us: "Don't think that I don't get what you're trying to do here. You want me to sit over there, with people that I don't know. You have to understand, I want that to happen too. You just have to give me some time." And indeed, as time passes, cross-cultural friendships are formed; for example, families from totally different backgrounds and different parts of the city meet to go swimming together. We have stories about parents who lived in this country for thirty years and never dared leave their neighborhood who now bring their children to concerts downtown and sing in our parental choirs. We have kids from different backgrounds making friends with each other – they know the same songs and they can play together and that is how it should be! We hope they can continue doing so into adult life, and over time lessen racism, fear, and ignorance. With access to themselves and to music as a universal language, such integration becomes easier.

If El Sistema concentrated only on the so-called "poorer" neighborhoods, such diverse sociocultural integration would not be possible. For as Maestro Abreu also says: as soon as a person knows how to play an instrument or how to express themselves, then he or she is no longer poor. Working with El Sistema is and will probably always be a massive challenge for everyone involved. Many are the times when the teachers have been so tired they almost couldn't work anymore. Some children and their families left El Sistema, leaving us sad and feeling hopeless. We struggle against a society that is becoming harder and colder, and keeping the flame alive is not easy. But we do it together, and having support from the international El Sistema family being just an email away keeps us going. We must *never* become too proud or afraid to show each other our weaknesses! Only by asking for and accepting help can we develop further. But the will to make an impact and to turn segregation into integration through music is greater than all tiredness and feelings of inadequacy.

## The Music

After all this talk about social aims, we need to say loudly: none of this could happen without the music. This paper is about Vänstay and the social impact a functional Vänstay can have on kids and families as well as society, so I've left out talking much about the music. As Eduardo Mendez, the executive director of FundaMusical Simón Bolívar in Venezuela, says when asked if the core value of El Sistema is social or musical: "Music is social. Any other questions?"

## How to Continue Measuring Vänstay Values

We continue to work on ways to demonstrate the benefits of a continuous Vänstay in every El Sistema núcleo in Sweden. These values are not easily quantifiable, but we are convinced that, in the long run, the results will speak for themselves. Vänstay is the social core of our program. This weekly gathering strengthens the students' learning and cohesion, and builds bonds among families. The importance of bringing in parents cannot be overrated. Only then can a true change happen for the child and ultimately within the child's social group.

A big risk is that El Sistema work is viewed as just another well-meaning project that eventually will end through lack of money. So from the very beginning we refused to call it a project, and instead talked about wanting to change lives and society for good. We are still confronted by people who see this vision as too bold, but it is what keeps us going. The dream is vivid: a new society gradually evolving with the fundamental value of TOGETHER.

With the strength of El Sistema Venezuela, Sistema Scotland, the newly formed network Sistema Europe, and the Gothenburg Symphony Orchestra behind us we'll keep going even when times are rough. We have experienced lonely parents who, through El Sistema and Vänstay, have managed to interact with their kids and with other families for the first time in years. We have parents who could barely speak Swedish now proudly translating a Swedish song to someone new in the parental choir. We have seen other parents learning Swedish just by coming regularly to Vänstay – freeing their kids from having to translate for them. We've seen parents get jobs through people they met within El Sistema. On one occasion parents met to attend a demonstration they organized to try to convince the immigration board not to send an El Sistema family back to their country of origin, even though their children were born in Sweden. We have a parent who got seriously ill and was offered help getting the child to the El Sistema lesson. The stories go on. We all face fear, but together we also have a lot of power.

## The Future of El Sistema in Sweden

El Sistema may seem like a naïve way of addressing the complex social issues and problems faced by our society, but it is working on a daily, grassroots level. Instead of endless hours of discussion about seemingly unsolvable topics, we simply meet every week to eat, sing, and play together. There is still much to do, but we believe what we see is happening, one friendship and one musical experience at the time: that El Sistema (including the concept of Vänstay) is one way of developing the society we want our children to inherit. We see the beauty and the creativity in music as a human right, and a way of sharing that right with others. Music. Passion. Together.

*This text was written through my personal eyes, with input from my colleagues from El Sistema Sweden. All of us contributed in different ways to getting El Sistema started in Sweden.*

# IV.

# YOLA: A Partnership Program

*Leni Boorstin and Gretchen Nielsen*

The Los Angeles Philharmonic Association is a non-profit performing arts institution with an orchestra at its center. We inhabit and enliven two iconic venues – Walt Disney Concert Hall and the Hollywood Bowl. Within a given year, the Philharmonic produces approximately 240 concerts – symphonic, chamber, world, jazz, and popular music – serving an audience of more than 1.4 million people. The LA Phil distinguishes itself for its high level of artistry and as a financially stable, well-managed, innovative arts organization in challenging times.

Education and community engagement have been a part of the LA Phil's programming for decades. Family concerts, young musician training programs, and pre-concert talks deepen meaning for and connection to our audience. The LA Phil's education and community programs began as an effort to develop audiences and maintain the vitality of our art form. For example, since 1919, family concerts have offered a uniquely suited outlet for parents and grandparents to introduce their offspring to the orchestra, building a tradition of concert-going that we expect will pay off when these children become adults.

Today, education and community engagement have developed far beyond audience acquisition and musical appreciation. The contemporary world requires the kind of "social, or moral" imperative articulated by LA Phil president and CEO Deborah Borda: to remain relevant, orchestras must create public value, acting on the belief that our art form and the ways in which we deliver it is vital to the betterment of society. With this mindset, the LA Phil turned to Dr. José Abreu's mission of music for social change to create YOLA – Youth Orchestra Los Angeles. YOLA was shaped by El Sistema, and the belief that every child in Los Angeles, regardless of economic status, should have access to music education. It has grown into a communitywide initiative that engages students, families, schools, and communities with symphonic music.

126

## Background

As the landscape of public education changed across the country starting in the late 1970s, Los Angeles took a huge hit to public education financing. Passage of Proposition 13 in 1978 took a specific toll on in-school arts education. This ballot initiative limited the use of California property taxes to fund public education, forcing all funds to come from the state. As a consequence, overall school budgets began to decrease, with pervasive cuts to "non-essentials" such as electives and special services. From that point on, California children had less and less access to the arts as part of their public education. Many middle- and upper-middle-class and Anglo families left the public education system. Simultaneously, immigration patterns changed. As a result of the last thirty-five years, we now see nearly two generations of children, now adults, who have had little to no access, let alone training, in the arts. Families with financial means may have chosen to support their children through private lessons and arts experience outside of the school day, but people with limited funds have had no such luck. The phenomenon has had an impact on teachers in California as well – with only a small percentage of teachers having been introduced to the arts in their own education. This deficit feeds into the devaluing of the arts in society.

Naturally the LA Phil noticed the fissures developing in public music education, and through the years devised residencies in schools to help introduce young children to music and build an awareness of the importance of music to a complete education. By attempting to plug some of the gaping holes, and, by supporting the work of a reduced number of existing music teachers, the LA Phil began to be perceived as a "good citizen" – with acknowledgement and dollars flowing in from funders who cared about waning in-school music education, and to public officials offering their thanks for bringing resources to underserved constituents in their district. The LA Phil had started down the long road of creating public value.

Seeking community relevance has been a tradition of the LA Phil that goes beyond its school-related initiatives. In the 1960s, LA Phil former music director Zubin Mehta led concerts in African-American churches with community choirs, reflecting a connection to the civil rights movement of the era. Neighborhood concerts began anew just before the civic disturbances of 1992, a kind of echo of Mehta's initiative. Performed in community venues, often churches, these concerts were conceived of as an invitation to try out the music of the LA Phil close to home, gratis.

The LA Phil's Neighborhood Concerts were about access and inclusion. Nevertheless, despite having developed different programs over decades to support young musicians, our organization had not yet specifically addressed who had access to orchestral music-making and training in the first place. Sistema and YOLA changed the game.

## Creating YOLA: Artistic Quality with Community Partners

The shift from the LA Phil being perceived a good community citizen to an organization that created true public value kicked into gear during the organization's courtship of Gustavo Dudamel. In 2005 and 2006, while Deborah Borda was flirting with the idea of bringing this young conducting dynamo to Los Angeles, the LA Phil Education and Community Departments were in the midst of a strategic plan centered around the need to foster young musicians. When the idea of El Sistema came into focus as a consequence of Deborah and other leaders' taking a trip to Venezuela, this strategic plan converged with their efforts, suddenly acquiring heart and depth.

YOLA was launched in 2007 as the initiative of the LA Phil and its community partners to provide free instruments, intensive music training, and academic support to students from underserved neighborhoods. Seven years later, YOLA provides students ages six to eighteen a strong musical and social foundation through participation in twelve to fifteen hours of programming each week. With sites in South LA, the Rampart District and East Los Angeles, YOLA is 650-plus students strong, with seven orchestras and more to come.

We share the vision and implementation of this program with our partner organizations Harmony Project (H-P), EXPO Center, Heart of Los Angeles (HOLA), and the LA County High School for the Arts (LACHSA). The LA Phil determined from the start that developing a youth orchestra program in "tough" communities would be accomplished through partnership. The LA Phil didn't have the "street cred," skills, or literacy in the needs and wants of economically poor communities. The LA Phil had on staff someone responsible for community affairs, and through that position, had a basic understanding of the communities in which we offered our Neighborhood Concerts and the interests of civic leaders. This opened doors. However, developing ongoing partnerships meant a different magnitude of connection and social responsibility.

To become a true El Sistema-inspired program, we needed organizations that had what we did not, and who were interested in what we had to offer in exchange. By partnering, the YOLA initiative is able to care for the whole child. Our partners are experienced in social service support. By wrapping these services around orchestra education, we successfully turn musical ensemble development into what truly can be called a community and youth development program. By spending so much time together, the kids relate to one another as a community. Parent engagement, through workshops and again, simple time together at the program sites, adds to community (demonstrated by parents taking on registration assistance, snacks, and potluck gatherings), as does the stability and depth of commitment of the teaching staff. Having program managers and other staff of the program sites in communication with families and schools about their students builds YOLA as a community, and even as what some might call a family.

Prior to launching YOLA, the LA Phil had a pre-existing relationship with Harmony Project (H-P), the focus of the rest of this brief discussion. H-P offered free group lessons to kids in Title One schools, and we had connected with them in order to extend the value of our in-school residencies by adding a new element: H-P teaching artist-led afterschool group lessons, paid for by the LA Phil.

H-P's (pre-El Sistema) programs constituted an elementary-through-high school commitment to the child and family, unlike most afterschool instrumental programs linked only to a school itself. The continuity of H-P's program design aligned well with the need for sequential and sustained service to students. Additionally Margaret Martin, H-P's founder, had a background in public health and linked music learning to community well-being. Mission alignment between H-P and the LA Phil for a Sistema-inspired program was clear.

In 2006, H-P offered classes to forty students in four different instruments at the EXPO Center in South LA, a community we were interested in serving. The neighborhoods surrounding EXPO Center, while originally African-American, now were heavily Latino as well. We were also attracted to the EXPO Center because it had just completed a $32 million renovation supported by an active "friends of" board, and their operating budget was supported through the City of Los Angeles Department of Recreation and Parks.

We approached H-P and the leadership of EXPO Center to ask if they would like to partner with us to develop a youth orchestra program in the style of El Sistema. H-P's classes at that site did not have the intensity that defines Sistema programs, nor an orchestra element on that site. But H-P did have a cadre of teaching artists experienced in giving group lessons to beginners – a skill harder to find among the performing musicians of the LA Phil. We also valued H-P's experience in recruitment of students and families through their demonstrations of instruments and mini-performances in neighboring schools, and the family orientation and contract process that they had established. We wanted a faster-growing program with an orchestra at the center and family commitment four and five days a week – a more ambitious effort than H-P and the LA Phil could make on their own. We were learning what it meant to be Sistema-influenced and, as partners, were sharing that learning and developing the pedagogy and new program design together.

To establish common vision, goals, and beginning program design, we held several facilitated planning meetings with white paper all around the room. Present were not just H-P and LA Phil staff, but also EXPO Center Executive Director Belinda Jackson, and Steve Venz from the Los Angeles Unified School District arts branch, who had been helping with mapping the surrounding schools and assessing the existing elementary and middle school music programs. It was a three-way partnership. The EXPO Center did not see itself as just space to be turned over to the program; Belinda knew that we had different work styles and organizational cultures to blend together, and assigned staff to work with us. Without her particular vision and commitment, YOLA at EXPO would not have had the stability and growth in this first site. Belinda, along with H-P Executive Director Myka Miller and the LA Phil, kept her eye on the prize through the bumps in the road, and there were plenty. Partnership is not a static achievement; it takes ongoing work.

One of those bumps: space allocation. When EXPO Center signed on, it was aware of the space required for an orchestra and the smaller spaces needed for group lessons. As the program grew from 80 and 100 students to 320, we needed space for that many more lessons and sectionals – but also three orchestras. Belinda had not counted on that, and it took some time for EXPO to understand the need for three levels of orchestra for a program of that size. Parent-related programs took space. So did the students-teaching-students aspects of the program. Belinda was and is balancing the needs of EXPO Center – a recreation and parks facility that also functions as a pre-school, senior center, music school, technology center, etc., etc.

Another "bump": we are partners of unequal size. The LA Phil with Gustavo Dudamel, a substantial PR team, and its stature as a leading cultural organization has often received more press attention for YOLA than have its partners, who rarely feel adequately noted and appreciated. We address this by having our staffs meet together to discuss the issues and to learn how better to take advantage of press attention, but it's an ongoing struggle. While we all think that a thriving partnership is itself a "story," the press is more interested in the kids and families. The biggest PR success probably came with the Southwest Airlines 2013 *Spirit* magazine cover article, "The Kids Are Alright," in which each partner felt recognized, so much so that our partners could be found walking up and down the aisles of some Southwest flights, pointing out with great pride *their* program.

From the beginning, the city required an official memorandum of understanding (MOU for short) for the LA Phil and H-P to work within the Department of Recreation and Parks facility. We found it extremely useful to put in writing our common goals, roles and responsibilities, and planned growth. Besides this MOU for the city, H-P and LA Phil also signed a formal joint venture agreement. Developing a contractual relationship was new territory for the LA Phil and our partner, since previous collaborations had been more informal. For H-P, it took time to realize that we were "in it" not just as a funder of their program, but as a full partner that would insist on designing a better and better program as the venture grew. Items outlined in the joint venture agreement included that the YOLA at EXPO's teaching artist staff and program manager were on H-P's payroll, but jointly paid for by both organizations; that the YOLA conductor was hired and funded by the LA Phil; that music instruments were paid for by the LA Phil but maintained and inventoried by H-P. The first agreement with H-P outlined the LA Phil's idea that over time, the capacity of the other partnering organizations would grow sufficiently to take over the program as we established new partnerships elsewhere. That first agreement specified that over a five-year period the LA Phil financial commitment would grow along with the number of students, and then would taper off in the last years of partnership, along with its responsibilities Within the first year of operation, however, the board of the LA Phil stepped in with a different commitment, namely that of being the managing partner in any YOLA program it established. We hired a YOLA manager to oversee all YOLA partnerships as the program expanded. Success and sustainability could not be left up to community partners: over five to seven years, the LA Phil would establish three or more YOLA sites with partners, and remain in the partnership throughout the tenure of the program itself. Failure would not be an option.

Learning together with partners needs to be intentional. At the beginning, some of the musicians hired by H-P approached their teaching artist role as one more piece of their freelance existence. They could teach a group lesson in the instrument, but didn't think much about what was involved in students coming together for a core ensemble experience, or consider the consequences of a teacher's relationship with the kids and families when teaching them some fifteen hours each week. For YOLA, they were asked to think differently: to focus on group preparation for the ensemble work that became a part of the weekly program; to work together as a team, and eventually, as a faculty to support musical and social aspects of each child. The LA Phil brought experience with planning; financial resources, solid educational philosophy and pedagogy, artistic resources, and growing experience with El Sistema itself with multiple trips to Venezuela. Among its other strengths, H-P had the infrastructure to track family and student involvement over periods of time.

After our initial launch we learned fast about even more aspects of Sistema work, and "backward designed" what we had missed when the program started. Mentorship and students teaching other students were not program elements from day one, but were then quickly added as layers of program design. Now, student leadership is a bigger part of the social development along with music skills. The work is never over; many, many hours are still spent in meetings of all sorts at all levels – among the teaching artists, the program managers from the different organizations, and the administrators/directors. All stakeholders in the partnership need ongoing attention, as our programs are not static but evolving and growing.

Each partner has taken lessons from this first YOLA partnership into other partnerships. We learned with H-P the importance of a parent liaison as part of the social work and counseling aspects of the program. When identifying Heart of Los Angeles (HOLA) as a partner for our second YOLA site, we were quick to value and celebrate such strengths as academic support and counseling, not to mention nutritional support. Thrilling for us, although also challenging, is the multiculturalism of YOLA participants at every site. Evolving neighborhood demographics make every location a laboratory of cross-cultural communication and relationships. Until the first generation of students returns as the program teachers and administrators, we will not truly reflect the communities we serve.

## YOLA's Influence on the Institutional Culture

YOLA's power has changed the LA Phil as an organization and altered our own self-definition. With this musical and social program as a catalyst, the LA Phil has been re-created on a foundation of interdependence between artistry and social responsibility. We showcase this interdependence when we regularly invite YOLA students to be musical and educational ambassadors on international tours of the orchestra, include YOLA musicians in side-by-side opportunities with the LA Phil and the Simón Bolívar Symphony Orchestra of Venezuela, and feature YOLA on major artistic programs of the LA Phil that are meant to communicate the multiple facets of our organization.

As the Los Angeles Philharmonic continues on this path of big dreams, we may need to respond to some potentially outrageous change in the future. How do we attract a younger, more ethnically and socioeconomically diverse audience for our orchestra concerts if many cannot afford our ticket prices? What will we do about audiences who don't have transportation to our concert halls? Should we consider building community performing centers or bring in the Japanese "blow-up" concert halls to underserved neighborhoods? As an increasing number of our students approach high school and college age, what are our responsibilities to develop the social and academic supports they may require? Asking these questions keeps the LA Phil relevant, vital, and vibrant within our communities, since our vision for the future is about being the change we want to see.

# V.

# The Public School Perspective

*Monika Vischer*

Maestro Abreu underscored a dramatic difference between Venezuela and the United States in Tricia Tunstall's book, *Changing Lives*: "You have such incredible resources in the United States. Excellent instruments, excellent buildings. And most important: excellent teachers!" Harnessing these resources to serve powerfully all children in need is one of our greatest challenges. At El Sistema Colorado, in Denver, we decided that the most effective way to tap into these resources was through key community partnerships, starting with three of the city's Title 1 public schools.

### A Non-profit Embedded at a Public School. Odd Bedfellows?

We started El Sistema Colorado (ESC) as a grassroots non-profit in 2011, garnering funding from local foundations and individuals across Denver (I am the board president). When it came time to choose our launch site, a public school did not seem the ideal choice. Too risky. Too many important details left in someone else's hands. Too close an association with what many consider a broken education system, especially in the arts. In Venezuela, the model was the community center, and indeed it seemed this was our greatest chance for success. We surmised that youth from various schools could attend, more deeply engaging families from surrounding neighborhoods. The thought of working with school district bureaucracy wasn't appealing either.

Our funders depended on us to be wise stewards with the grants and donations they'd entrusted to us. To this end, we wanted to maintain control over the program. So, how could a school be the better option? At a site-based school, the principal holds huge power, able to cut programs, school staff, and expenses on a whim. An entire school could be shut down at the district's discretion due to poor testing scores.

The list of risks went on: How open would a public school truly be to hosting ESC after school, let alone in-school? Would other programs compete for students' attention after school? If there was an existing music teacher, what was his/her approach and openness to working with ESC? Unlike families who choose to engage in an independent program, what support could we expect from public school staff, parents, and community? What was the capacity for flexibility at this school (e.g., use of space, teacher participation, possible integration with school curriculum, etc.)? What would the partner site provide (e.g., space, volunteers, transportation, staff, and office support)?

These critical variables made us uneasy about committing to a public school setting. But our vetting process revealed limitations with the community or "rec" centers on our shortlist. In every case, there were space constraints as we looked to build a 100- to 150-piece orchestra in the near term. Community centers wanted to work with us, but couldn't offer an adequate rehearsal room. Consistently, the hours we could operate were limited. And . . . we make a lot of noise, a hang-up for some community center leaders. The concerns continued: Securing safe transport home was less certain than at schools. Additionally, recruiting our first young musicians and maintaining regular attendance was a clear challenge. Suddenly, the community center idea became less appealing. We needed a pilot site that assured our success, and as a fledgling start-up we certainly weren't in a position to buy or build our own.

Conversely, the notion of starting ESC at a public school began looking brighter. We explored further and discovered a bevy of practical advantages that – given a thoughtful and wise choice – made a school site the far better option. Our pilot site launched in January 2012. Garden Place Elementary was the first of three Title 1 Denver public schools we now work with. Garden Place principal Rebecca Salomon has been the key. She saw ESC as core to her academic, social, emotional, and behavioral intervention strategy for students at risk for falling behind in school – the majority of the Garden Place population. Many are statistically on track to eventually drop out, or experiment early in drugs, crime, or gangs. Rebecca conveys her support of ESC both in-school and afterschool consistently to her staff, and provides us critical access to the school's many assets.

The school is located in the heart of Globeville, one of the poorest and most underserved communities in Denver. Because it's a school, Garden

Place is highly trusted in the community as a safe place for the students we wish to engage. (Over 97 percent of the student population at Garden Place qualifies for free and reduced lunch, while 97 percent are also Hispanic.) The school offers free space, a familiar place, as well as the propinquity of hundreds of students within reach. This is where the students already are; they don't have to be transported to us. Time is maximized. As soon as school ends, the herds thunder into the afterschool program, the instrument cases crack open, and the music begins. Ms. Salomon also welcomed our in-school program, which serves pre-schoolers and kindergartners Monday through Friday, during regular hours. This program planted important early roots for an ESC feeder pattern.

We started by serving 100 kindergarten students in-school and 30 third-graders after school. Two years into ESC's operations at Garden Place, we've grown to serve 200 students across all grade levels: half of the school population. Classroom teachers encourage student participation after school. They also know these children well. ESC teaching artists can draw on this knowledge to gain a better understanding of the students we serve. ESC can build on and reinforce behavioral expectations already established at the school. Young ESC musicians also play for the student body, a point of pride for them and a great incentive to recruit other students at Garden Place.

Other assets include access to valuable student data for attendance, behavioral, and academic evaluation. We have access to resources such as the school social worker and front office support. Ms. Salomon promotes ESC within the school district, which in turn gives us visibility and our students opportunities (such as Denver Public School Honors Orchestra and performances at district-wide public school events). During the summer program, Denver Public Schools provides hot lunch at the school's cafeteria each day. This is a major cost saving for us and a big incentive for families. The school either provides busing, or office support in ordering buses for multiple performances our students give in the community throughout the year.

Partnering with a school also allows us to leverage and support the existing in-school music programs and teachers. By ESC working in tandem with the school music teacher, the overall value of music education at the school grows. This momentum not only builds the ESC orchestra and choir, but student engagement at the school increases on the whole. In ESC's January 2014 survey of Garden Place teachers, 100 percent of respondents credited the program with positive changes in student behavior among participating students, while 75 percent said they saw a positive change in academic success. One teacher highlighted students' "better discipline to start and complete their work," and that they are "aware of their behavior and making efforts to do what is expected." Such testimony underscores how music has not only become a core subject area at the school, but that ESC's work supports all subject areas and learning in the classroom. In short: we are far stronger together than apart. Or in the words of Aristotle: the whole is greater than the sum of its parts.

It's not hard to see the larger implications. And we are, in fact, already expanding. In addition to Garden Place, ESC is now in nearby Swansea Elementary, as well as Bruce Randolph Middle and High School, which had been without arts for nearly ten years. The principal, Cesar Cedillo, received mill-levy arts funding approved by Denver voters in 2012. Due to our success at Garden Place, he used a significant portion of this funding in welcoming ESC to his school. He hired, full-time, our recommendation-certified music teacher – a professional musician whose full-time job straddles in school and after school, doubling as the full-time ESC lead teaching artist. Cedillo has provided further support for building an orchestra at the school, such as the repair and purchase of instruments.

ESC now serves a total of over 400 students across the three schools. This early trajectory is a strong indication that partnering with schools seems the ultimate direction for our sustainability.

## Key Principles in Working Within the School

El Sistema Colorado (ESC) follows key principles to honor the existing school culture and create meaningful partnerships with school staff. At Garden Place, the most mature and established of the sites, we embed a full-time ESC lead teaching artist. This person works daily with the school music teacher, meets weekly with the principal, and attends meetings alongside school staff. Likewise, Garden Place's music teacher meets with ESC staff, and she and the lead teaching artist experiment with different ways to work in tandem. We also develop music curriculum in close partnership with the Garden Place music teacher and involve her in ESC hiring and professional development. She works for and reports to Denver

Public Schools, but is also on ESC's payroll for afterschool and Saturday rehearsals and performances she's able to help with.

In general, we leverage the relationships and valuable knowledge of school administration and teachers who work daily with our students, staying in close communication with school teachers about students' socioemotional, behavioral, and academic status to help inform our work. We are a part of the school. We plan school and ESC events together. ESC aligns with school policies and disciplinary measures and conducts regular in-school performances.

Critically, strong relationships between ESC and school staff breed trust, which in turn breeds patience. This is pivotal and takes consistent communication. The payoff is necessary room and flexibility to make mistakes. We do make them. And learn from them. But in this context, we all learn from them together. To what end? Better bonds with the kids, more effective teaching, and deeper, more joyful student engagement.

Winning advocates among school staff is as important as engendering robust family support. When staff and families feel a sense of ownership in ESC, roots grow deeper at the school. The more ESC becomes a part of overall school success, the more it becomes a part of the community and the more likely it will weather changes at the school.

### The View From the Garden Place Music Teacher, Monica Johnson

Lorrie Heagy of Juneau, Alaska Music Matters (JAMM) program, visited Denver to lead professional development just as our program was launching in January 2012. Alaska's 2011 State Teacher of the Year, Heagy immediately pegged Monica Johnson as the glue holding together our success at Garden Place. From Kansas City, Johnson started teaching at Garden Place in 2010 and is now pursuing her master's degree in counseling. Bright and young with a winning smile, Monica's spunk and spirit are a good match for the energetic challenges she faces each day in her music classroom. She's always three steps ahead of the kids. To ESC's great benefit, Monica has taught our ESC teaching artists many invaluable tricks in classroom management. She also collaborates regularly with the in-school ESC teaching artists on music the students are learning, and corroborates the afterschool program.

Monica was not excited to hear about ESC coming to Garden Place. She was concerned about how it would affect her job security. But she knew that she couldn't offer her students access to an orchestra or choir program of any significance without the help of such a program. "Because of this, I chose to keep an open mind about El Sistema," she said. "Once I learned more about the history and philosophy of El Sistema I was wholly on board." Garden Place principal Rebecca Salomon also bumped Monica's position from half time to full time in preparation for ESC's launch. Now in her second year working with ESC, Monica has found that the program furthers her own curriculum goals and supports her development as a music teacher.

"From a music standpoint, I can honestly say that El Sistema supports what I am doing in my classroom and that my students are growing in ways that I would never have been able to accomplish as a lone music teacher at the school. I only see my students once every three days for forty minutes. I find it difficult to teach all of the skills/knowledge that I would like to cover. With the help of El Sistema, many of my students are growing as musicians and meeting goals that I would never be able to help them achieve in the limited amount of time I have with them. Also, my students who are a part of ESC are serving as positive models and mentors to those students who are not in ESC, thus helping me to reach more academic goals with those students, too."

On her relationship with the ESC teaching artists, Monica said "Usually, there is only one music teacher in an elementary school, leaving them on their own to problem solve or grow as a teacher. El Sistema has given me a huge network of wonderful music teachers to learn from. They also challenge and encourage me to grow as a musician as well as a teacher."

At Garden Place, the ESC lead teaching artist is thought of as Garden Place staff. Likewise, Monica Johnson is thought of as ESC staff, involved in program decisions and a vital link to the school. She chalks it up to the kind of support provided by principal Salomon, "Rebecca has not only given ESC the opportunity to work with every one of our early childhood and kindergarten students, but she has encouraged and supported the integration of ESC into our school community. Without this integration, ESC would be like any other afterschool program: the Garden Place teachers/staff might know of them, but wouldn't really work with them."

Monica notes, "Obviously, sharing one's room, materials (and even students!) with other music teachers offers some challenges. I have found that keeping open lines of communication with the El Sistema Colorado teaching artists and actively collaborating with each of them is the best way to solve any problems that may arise. In this way, the Garden Place music program and ESC support each other instead of compete with each other."

## The View From the Other Classroom Teachers
El Sistema Colorado (ESC) serves all kindergartners and four-year-olds every day during school through a strings program. Garden Place kindergarten teachers have seen an impact on their students and families. Kindergarten educator Stephanie Kless sees them exhibit pride about their musical skills. "They carry their violins with huge smiles, my kinders tell me about their siblings' concerts, and families of first- and second-grade students have become devotees of the program. My students are extremely excited about learning how to play a violin." Like Monica Johnson, she has great confidence in her principal and notes the principal's advocacy of arts at the school, which "only works to increase my support of her school vision." Kindergarten teacher Kristina Stevenson said, "They are so proud of the work they do . . . they always look forward to when they get to go to El Sistema and are always in a great mood when they return. I think it is helping to build their self-confidence and self-regulation skills."

Likewise, teachers are seeing unusually high family involvement. Stephanie Kless: "I had almost 100 percent turnout on paper violin night and the parents were all eager to help out. It is always such a joyous experience." Kristina Stevenson: "The families are more engaged regarding ESC than other activities in my classroom. For example, parents who have not helped their student turn in homework or responded to field trip chaperone letters *have* attended violin making night and concerts on the weekend."

ESC and schoolteachers also work effectively to serve students with disabilities. Garden Place kindergarten teacher Veronica Castillo said that in addition to regularly discussing students' behavior and academic performance, the ESC teaching artist helps students with special needs. She likes how the ESC teaching artist "understands and helps make special accommodations for" students on an IEP [Individual Education Plans – kids with delayed skills or other disabilities], especially if they don't understand English." The population at the school is overwhelmingly Hispanic, and the ESC teaching artist is always helpful, even when not a Spanish speaker.

ESC can offer more powerful stories of change. Garden Place lead teaching artist William Hinkie told one notable story of a fourth-grader in the afterschool program: "Carlos Rosas has perfect pitch. He came into the program angry and resistant. Now he wants to do anything and everything. We have to hold him back from doing too much! He has a long-term view of how this will affect his life. His most precious quote is 'One day when I am a famous musician, I will make sure I will get you a backstage pass.'"

Hollie Bennett is at once a school music teacher and ESC's lead teaching artist at Bruce Randolph Middle and High School. She speaks Spanish and as a first-year teacher, is getting her sea legs. We recommended the school set her hours from 10 a.m. to 6 p.m. to create, as Lorrie Heagy says, "common culture" between the in-school and afterschool portion of ESC. Hollie teaches music during school to all 200 sixth- and seventh-graders, then stays to lead the afterschool program each day. Early on, Hollie saw the power of music work in the lives of her students. "I have a specific student who has serious behavioral issues . . . and is failing all of his classes, even the music class he has with me during the day. He needs to constantly be the center of attention, refuses to follow directions, barely does work, moves throughout the room, distracts other students. If you hand him a violin though, he is a completely different person. The individualized attention he has received in this program has changed him and I wish we could have him for more time. The pride that he puts into his violin playing makes him seem like a completely different person. It's only been two months, but it will be interesting to see if/when this excellence begins to translate into the rest of his life."

## The View From the Principal Rebecca Salomon
Garden Place principal Rebecca Salomon was sold on El Sistema from the start. "El Sistema offers hope-filled and capacity-building opportunities for our students." She's determined to help her students succeed even though the odds are against them.

In 2008, Denver's Piton Foundation described Globeville, the area in which Garden Place is situated, as an area that has "a higher crime rate, a higher percentage of gang and drug activity, a widespread poverty rate, and an overabundance of dilapidated real estate when compared to the other surrounding communities of Denver." Rebecca said, "At Garden

Place, not only do we believe that our community resembles so much more than its statistics, we believe it is a community that can transcend those statistics, if we bring in the resources necessary that promote social justice and that provide equitable student learning opportunities. El Sistema has the ability to transform the lives of children through innovative and engaging teaching and learning opportunities, and it has the ability to change the trajectory of students' lives and create a long-term investment for the school and community. El Sistema is one resource we have found to be unprecedented in its impact on children's lives and futures."

Rebecca said that ESC has already created a secondary family and support network. "Friendships and relationships have been developed. El Sistema has created a safe and nurturing environment where student confidence has increased, individuality is encouraged, and students are not afraid to take risks – a necessity in learning. El Sistema has helped students stay engaged in school and it seems to have helped our students think about their futures and to dream."

## The View From Denver Public Schools Arts Director Mark Hudson

Upper-level Denver Public Schools administration continues to take an increasing interest in El Sistema Colorado's (ESC's) partnership with Garden Place Elementary, Swansea Elementary, and Bruce Middle and High School, even though ESC is just two years old. "Most of our support has come from our superintendent, Tom Boasberg," noted Rebecca. "He always asks about our El Sistema program and has talked about it across the district. He has been supportive of the in-school and afterschool program and has supported the expansion. He is an advocate for El Sistema."

Mark Hudson is arts director for Denver Public Schools and president of the Colorado Music Educators Association. He observed that, according to Monica Johnson at Garden Place, "the apparent impact has been twofold: one, students who are participating in ESC are well above their peers in the classroom with regard to conceptual learning and understanding of music. Two, a noticeable improvement in engagement, behavior, and "citizenship" seems to be a global change in these students. Not only are kids more effectively learning music as an art, but the twenty-first century skills of communication and collaboration are evident in the classroom. In a culture that continues to see fading orchestra programs as well as dwindling audiences for symphonic music, El Sistema may be a catalyst in bringing a whole new generation to a perspective of value and comfort with the American symphonic tradition."

He said that, based on observation and discussion with teachers at Garden Place, "the partnership between El Sistema Colorado and Garden Place is a positive one, with students as the primary beneficiaries. This is due in no small way to the very careful and respectful manner in which El Sistema Colorado has addressed building a relationship with Garden Place."

Mark noted the importance of this relationship. "Although many arts educators feel threatened or uneasy about having 'external providers' come into their building and work with students (for a number of reasons), El Sistema Colorado has purposefully and thoughtfully engaged Monica Johnson at Garden Place from the beginning. In fact, she was deeply involved in the planning, even the hiring of El Sistema teaching artists. The curricular design and implementation in school music classes has been collaborative and non-invasive, to the point that the Garden Place music teacher feels that ESC is truly a partner in the business of teaching students the art of music."

So what kind of change would it take for Denver Public Schools to consider taking ESC to scale across the district? Mark didn't have a clear answer for that question, but felt that a "15 to 20 percent reduction in absenteeism, attributable to ESC, would be sufficient to gain notice. Likewise, a reduction in student behavioral referrals."

## The Challenges Ahead
For all of our successes thus far, we remain mindful of the challenges before us. First, maintaining clear and open communication between all ESC and school staff is critical to meaningful problem solving. Second, before branching out to new sites, we need to be sure our current young musicians remain our top priority, including our relationships with school music teachers, principals, and school staff. Finally, we must continue seeking out best practices in effective school integration among our El Sistema peers and music educators as a whole in Colorado, the United States, and beyond. One of Eric Booth's great pearls of wisdom applies: "The quality of sharing among peers determines the strength of the program." In so doing, we aim to succeed in heeding Maestro Abreu's call to harness our resources in the United States, so that we can enrich the lives of the children we serve to the fullest extent imaginable.

# CHAPTER 6

# From the Stance of Empowerment

*Marianne Diaz*

A S the Director of Outreach Services at the Southern California Counseling Center, I provide community counseling training to people from agencies that serve high-risk populations and underserved communities. This role is important to me both professionally and personally. As a person of color who grew up poor in the most powerful country in the world, I am deeply aware that the *way* services are provided to a community proves as important as the services themselves.

The individuals trained and certified for community counseling at the center are very much like the teachers and leaders of the El Sistema movement in the United States: people from various backgrounds and experiences brought together to provide services to the underserved. However well intentioned, these "helpers" may stumble and fall in community work if they are not mindful in actions and with their words.

I wish to share two main points with all those engaged in El Sistema-inspired work. First: underserved communities, children, and families are already filled with the solutions and strength necessary to combat the realities of oppression; the role of the service provider is to help them access their inner solutions and strength. Second: the complexities of a community or person in crisis need to be addressed in ways that are constantly mindful of *culture, context, and the realities of inequity*.

My beliefs and practices have been informed through my experiences with systematic oppression. Gang life, incarceration, and violence were a substantial part of my past. I also write this essay from the point of view of a professional therapist who has worked with youth, communities, and clients from all walks of life. In addition to working with individual clients, I created and facilitate a variety of community-based therapy groups, including rage resolution groups, teen violence prevention groups, and youth empowerment sessions in schools. When I speak of the *client* in this essay, I am referring to anyone I see through my therapy work. You as an El Sistema teacher or leader may wish to substitute *student*, *parent*, or *community* to help situate my experience within your own context.

## Moving Away From the "Expert Stance"

As a training counselor, I seek to level out hierarchy within systems that place the expertise with an "authority" who then imposes that expert knowledge on another person's reality from a position of power. "Power" is at play when one comes to see another seeking support, training, learning, or guidance. What must the person seeking support do to earn it? How does that person feel when needing support? If mandated to get support, does he or she feel in need of this support?

It can be difficult for the person sought out to not feel like the "expert" in the situations I've mentioned. What is it we think we know when we work with individuals, students, families, or communities? Being a part of the system that trains people seeking to become marriage and family therapists (MFTs), I see that there is a need to have an expert position when it comes to theory and pathology. We value the idea of "knowing," and our system does indeed depend on "knowing" something.

But the truth is, all we can really know is how to place the expertise of people's life back within themselves. When we act as a facilitator rather than an all-knowing expert who can "fix" a person's problems, we are trusting that the person in front of us is the one best able to identify and use the solutions to her challenges because she is the one experiencing them. I come from the perspective that we are all experts on our own lives. To take that expertise away from someone is incredibly disempowering. So in my work I attempt to redistribute expertise from those who provide services back to those who receive them. The expertise does not lie with me, the therapist, the case manager, or the well-intentioned person. The expertise lies within the client.

I often talk about the need for anyone working with clients to place him- or herself in the position of the tourist instead of the expert. I have not traveled the world. Still, I have a sense that when in another country it's best to stay curious about the traditions, cultural values, and differences – and not enter the country like a bull in a glass shop pushing my own traditions, cultural values, and ideas about what is appropriate. That way I'd leave behind nothing but broken glass.

Here is an example. I have a sense of footing when I am working with a client who shares something from my own background and experiences. I am comfortable working with issues such as gangs, violence, poverty, or a sense of being oppressed. One of my clients, however – a Persian-Jewish woman – came from a culture I had no familiarity with. She was seeing me because she was unhappy in the relationship with her husband. In my first session I did what I do with most clients: I heard her truth about what was going on in her relationship. It seemed to me that power and control was determinant in this emotionally violent and oppressive relationship. When I used the "walking on egg shells" analogy, she said "yes!" And here it could have become sticky. I could easily have gone in the direction of talking about agencies that assist in separating women from situations of domestic violence. But I was careful enough to hold off and first consult with a colleague who is also a Persian-Jewish woman. The first thing she said to me was, "Do not bring up separation or divorce in any form or fashion. This is not an option for our culture unless you want to be shunned by the Persian-Jewish male community."

Wow, that was interesting. I do not have strong feelings about marriage nor do I believe someone should stay with someone and not be happy. That is my stuff. That is the culture I come from. As a person of color I am still acculturated to many of the norms of this United States culture. Intead of imposing my values or norms, it was imperative that I ask questions and stay curious in order to walk with her. Had I said to her, even very gently, "Have you ever imagined leaving the relationship?" that alone might have been the difference between her staying in therapy and leaving. Cultural miscues can be that subtle and that powerful.

I remember once being in a supervision group with an intern who had just seen a person of color in a therapy session. The intern, in describing her session, stated that her client was very angry at an incident involving her white teacher, and the therapist kept trying to convince the client that sadness underlay her anger. Now, when we start deciding for another human being in any capacity in life what they are feeling, we are not being supportive or effective in the relationship. We become rather the expert in that person's life, experience, and feelings. In my opinion this is a form of violence against a person's reality. It is disempowering. What we are subtly

146

saying is, "You are not capable of handling this yourself. This situation is beyond your ability. You don't even know your own feelings."

It is hard not to get seduced into the expert stance. It feels good to be the one with the answers. We all want to be validated in our knowledge; that's how society validates us. We are a culture with a collective "fix it" mentality, and we want to have things fixed fast. I have been in therapy now for most of the second part of my life and I can tell you this: I do not need fixing. I need validation in my experiences and in my reality. My work, the work I do with my therapist, and the work I do in the training I provide is about validation of another person's reality.

There are, however, instances of "case management" where an expert may be needed. If a youth is thinking of committing suicide, has a plan, and is letting you know it is imminent, you are in a crisis conversation. While you can still draw on the young person's expertise and be a strong listener, you also need to know about the critical resources and services available to support you and the child. When a child is endangered, you may be mandated by law to report the case, and you now become a case manager.

A case manager plays a distinctively different role than does a therapist. Case managers are more directional and are expected to provide and link resources and track those linkages. Case managers attend meetings of service providers and often make recommendations for additional support. They often have a deadline or end goal for the case manager/client relationship. Transparency is important. You as the case manager must be completely honest and specific with a client about what actions are expected of you, and doing so removes the wondering about why you are or are not pushing for particular outcomes.

Therapists, on the other hand, are not and should not be directional. They are meant to provide a safe place in which clients can move at their own pace. The client should be in the driver's seat of conversations with a community counselor. There is no deadline to the therapy conversation; talk therapy is about what is helpful, not what is expected of the client. Both case manager and therapist roles are necessary and the best outcome is when both are working on an empowerment model – believing in the client's expertise over his own life.

Besides crisis situations, circumstances involving a parent or child approaching you for guidance also often call for you to act as a case manager rather than a therapist. It may sometimes be difficult to know whether a parent or child wants a "case manager" or a "therapist" when they come to you. It is best in these situations to wait for the approaching party to *ask* for a referral to additional resources and support before immediately offering them. Often, people just want to be heard, and need you to be a strong listener. Jumping into the role of the "fixer" can make you feel better about a situation, but it may not be meeting the needs of the person in front of you.

Listening is one of the hardest skills to master and the most effective way of validating a human being. When I say listening, I mean getting out of the way of a person's process and staying connected without words. We, the service providers, need to stay open-minded and constantly curious when listening, even when we think we are recognizing a familiar pattern: we might think we already know where a conversation is going or the deeper meaning behind a person's statement before they have finished. This is not good listening. When you really listen, you hear each word the client says to you and you ask questions to make sure you understand.

When you are really good at listening you begin to notice exceptions to what is often considered by the client as *alwayses* and *nevers*. What I mean by this is that most people have a clear view of negatives – things that they feel always go wrong or never work out. Problems are often at the center of most conversations steered by experts. The "problem" and how to solve it gets a lot of attention. This means the *exceptions* – the things the client does well or areas of his life that are successful – are often left out of supportive conversations. I am not one to have a problem-saturated conversation when working with youth or community members seeking counseling. I believe in working the *exception* muscle enough that the client recognizes times when he or she has succeeded. Success can be rare, or small, and hard to recognize when one is overwhelmed by poverty, racism, classism, and marginalization. That means examining and championing these exceptions is incredibly important. This is how we empower clients to recognize their ability to meet challenges. The client must be the one to find and apply her own solutions. As well meaning as we may be, we cannot support our clients or students once they leave our offices, programs, or agencies and go back to their lives. Clients are the only ones who can truly understand what they deal with every day. How can we tell our clients what they need to do to better their situation if we have not lived in their reality?

## Context, Culture, and the Reality of Inequity

Those providing services to communities in crisis are most effective when they stay mindful of the cultural and contextual reality of the community. Culture and context play a large role in how people relate to the world. As an example: in the many hundreds of discussions I have had with individuals mandated for therapy by the court due to some real, alleged, or assumed act, I have run across thousands of definitions of *respect*. *Respect* is a huge word with a strong meaning within the gang culture I come from, and I have an understanding of what respect might mean in neighborhoods and communities with a gang cultural element as a part of the collective experience. In a gang culture, respect and fear are not distinguishable. To be "respected" means to have people under you and to have power. As a gang member, if I showed respect to someone, it took away my position of power. I had to lower myself to respect someone else. They had to lower themselves to respect me. In a gang or prison system, the power that comes from respect is necessary for survival. Because my cultural experience has given me such a strong understanding of this word, I must be extra careful when a client says to me that they feel disrespected. It is not enough that I marinate this statement in my head so that it means to me what my experience and consciousness tells me it means. What matters is what it means to that person in front of me, who may have a very different definition. I must keep a vigilant eye on my own interpretation: my experience may be different than the client's. I am in that client's country, and I need to learn the meaning of respect as it relates to his cultural context. If I am not careful, I may completely misunderstand what he is saying.

It is easy to make the mistake of thinking that everyone has a similar understanding of the world. I have trained under many great therapists and counselors. I have also been the client of many – and not always by choice. I remember one therapist in particular who seemed to think that respect meant the same to me as it meant to her. She did not realize that in my contextual reality, respect was not mutual – it was about power. Later, when a therapist actually asked the question, "What does respect mean to you?" I felt it to be an enormously respectful question. It allowed me to educate the therapist about how complex and culturally loaded a word can be. I told her that for me, respect was about maintaining integrity. If I said I was going to do something – even if it was not positive – I needed to follow through on it to maintain my integrity and keep my respect and status in the neighborhood. For me as for so many people coming from oppressed communities, respect was all I had and all I could control, and so it was incredibly important to keep it. In my street life and prison life, it was imperative that people saw me as a superior – it was how I stayed safe and in control. I also did not want to be prejudged or talked down to – people who were condescending to me would make me flare up in anger because they were being disrespectful. As a gang member, I had a scary exterior at that time, but it didn't describe who I was on the inside. Further, personal space was big for me. I lived in a dangerous world and so I wanted people to stay at arm's length at all times. In my view, those who didn't understand my need for space were "disrespectful" to me.

Upon hearing this, my therapist recognized that her own definition of respect was different and that she might make missteps with me because of it. So she asked the question, "How will I know if I am being disrespect-ful?" I told her I would let her know – in my understanding of respect, there was no conversation about it, since being disrespected was a threat. She then asked, "Would you rather that I was respectful to you because I understand where you're coming from, or respectful because I'm afraid of you?" This allowed me to explain further my position and understanding. As she came to understand my definition of respect, she was able to help me see that often the things I viewed as being disrespectful were in fact unintentional, and that many people had a different understanding of respect. When I could understand that disrespect wasn't always the intention, that some people just didn't understand my way then of being in the world, I found a different way to feel it and talk about it. We often take for granted that we know the meaning of a word. Adding in the cultural context can show us that words or ideas may have a different interpretation that are not at all what you have experienced or understood by them.

Knowing how much our experiences shape the way we see and experience the world, I am often asked if there is any way to remove bias, assumptions, and judgment from a conversation. The simple answer is no. I do not pretend that I do not have some ideas about the way a person or groups of people should be. But I do think it's important to recognize my own assumptions, bias, and judgment. This is the only way I can keep an eye on them. I sat with Kaleem, a young man in Los Angeles who came to me to vent about something that had happened to him. He had moved to

YOLA at EXPO violist in rehearsal with her string quartet. MATHEW IMAGING

Students from Union City Music Project in concert.

San Diego Youth Symphony and Conservatory's Community Opus Project students perform their Spring Music Camp Concert, June 2014. KEN JACQUES

Students engaged in peer learning through El Sistema Japan. MARIKO TAGASHIRA

young violinist from El Sistema Sweden. LEE KEARNEY

indergarten students from El Sistema Colorado, Swansea Elementary, at their Paper Violin Concert.
RIGID MCAULIFFE

YOLA at HOLA students exchanging a look of excitement on stage at opening night of the Hollywood Bowl in Los Angeles, California, 2012. FRANCINE ORR/LOS ANGELES TIMES

JAMM second graders pose for an end-of-year photo. This grade level marks the transition from an in-school model to an after-school program in JAMM. XIA GUOHUA

OLA students perform a team building and leadership exercise with Rebecca Sigel at the first YOLA summer camp in June 2014. DAN BERKOWITZ

ach year, Corona Youth Music Project presents a Bucket Drum Circle for the Make Music NY Festival at Corona Plaza, ne of the busiest corners in the neighborhood. All children are invited to participate, and CYMP students take turns ading the ensemble. EUN LEE

**Dr. José Antonio Abreu hugs a YOLA at HOLA student after the first YOLA/Simón Bolívar Symphony Orchestra of Venezuela concert in Los Angeles, California, 2012.** MATHEW IMAGING

e YOLA Heart of LA Youth Orchestra performing outside in La Fayette Park, Los Angeles in 2013. DAN BERKOWITZ

OLA at HOLA students perform on paper violins for Gustavo Dudamel in the Fall of 2010. MATHEW IMAGING

**Gustavo Dudamel Visits YOLA at HOLA, October, 2010.** MATHEW IMAGING/LA PHIL

West Hollywood from Florida in an attempt to escape racism and the real possibility he might not make it past his thirtieth birthday. He came to me angry: rageful but calm. He is an African-American, gay man. He felt West Hollywood would be an accepting and safe place for him. Yet he experienced what many young men of color experience. On his way walking to an audition he was stopped by sheriff deputies and thrown up against a car. The deputies then put him in the back seat of the patrol car. They then stated that there was a report of a crime that involved someone for whom he fit the description: an African-American male with braids. Kaleem did not have braids, but dreadlocks. Regardless, he was seen as suspicious. As we spoke, I immediately thought, "Well, dreadlocks bring attention." If I had not been aware of how I was processing Kaleem's story, I might have asked him, "Do you think if you didn't have the dreads, then maybe you wouldn't be so much of a target?" I went there in my head. If I had not been aware of my own bias, I might have asked Kaleem what he could have done to prevent the incident. Instead, I asked a question about what it means for a society that black young men with dreads are viewed as suspicious. This second question is aligned with what I believe, and I was able to access it because I now know how to look at my reactions to situations and know when my assumptions, bias, and judgment are coming into play. We often expect the victims to change themselves so they can maneuver more smoothly in a judgmental world. I know I have wished my Latino sons would not shave their heads. They are not gang members at all, they are athletes, and they get stopped repeatedly by law enforcement for how they appear. Certain assumptions exist in the larger culture and they influence us all. Being aware helps us to not call on those assumptions when we are working with a client.

## Privilege and Diversity

As a person of color, I continue to always be aware of the ways in which reputation, suspicion, bias, and assumptions have worked against me. Though often on the receiving end, I have also been a perpetrator, like all human beings. Still, something different is going on when suspicion or bias is wielded by those in the privileged position over a person of color, a person of difference, the *Other*.

What is this privileged position? If you never have thought about it, you are most likely in it. This is one of the greatest challenges of privilege –

that it can be incredibly difficult for one living in privilege to recognize their privilege. The dominant culture is created for and by people in the privileged position, so everything in the world reaffirms that person's way of life. Those on the outside of privilege are always aware of their place in the world – they see how it is different from the dominant culture's expectations and vision. Those living in privilege don't need to think of their place because it's a given. A good example: the white people who honestly believe racism no longer exists in the United States, since they have never experienced it and perhaps have never perpetrated it. Indeed, racism does not exist in their world – which does not, however, mean that racism is eradicated for people of color living in the same country. Explaining the challenges that people outside the privileged position face to someone living in privilege is like explaining to a fish about the challenges of living on land. To be clear, this is not an indictment of those in this country living in the privileged position. I do not begrudge people having a comfortable life. I also understand that privilege is fluid – I am incredibly privileged in some contexts and not at all in others. However, those working in service agencies frequently come from outside the community they serve and frequently come from a position of privilege. Being aware of how this position influences you and your relationship to others is important. Staying mindful of it will allow you to stay aware of your bias and judgments and help you not to alienate your clients.

It takes constant, mindful work not to impose your beliefs on someone else's reality, especially if you come from the privileged position. The best way to be present for your clients or students is to know yourself. What scares you? What do you consider normal? What expectations were placed on you growing up? What kind of trauma is working on you at any given moment? It is hard work. It can be very painful to realize you may be racist or at least more suspicious of some people. You may find that you are classist: thinking that all people have access to the same basics, food, clothing, shelter, transportation, and dedicated space. Simple realities like how many people live together in one room can influence how well a person can or cannot cope. Does an individual have space to think, to work on their projects, or to breathe? Have you ever thought of breathing itself as a luxury? Pushing yourself to consider what you take for granted is important for success in community work.

The last thing I would like to suggest in working in diverse communities is to try not to think of everyone as the same. We are not. White has its privilege, especially in the United States, and given the history of oppression suffered by people of color it is disrespectful not to acknowledge the different cultural experiences of white people and people of color. Why is this important? I believe that much of what marginalized communities wrestle with is the natural consequence of oppression. I am aware that all people have their challenges regardless of their appearance and their cultural history. I also know that some cultures are facing systemic forces that work upon them actually and subconsciously every day. People of color have a very different experience in this country. They and other marginalized populations such as the disabled, seniors, homeless, and LGBTQ have to face things that many people do not even consider. A difference for people of color is that we cannot choose when to be seen. We are judged and seen as brown or black people and looked on particularly suspiciously if young men. If you are not of color and you sit with someone who is, you may not understand the complexities of the maneuvering this person must do to stay out of the vigilant and suspicious eye of the dominant culture.

Along these same lines, many "helpers" try to get their clients to reach certain cultural norms that are actually part of privilege, norms which if not examined as a part of a "helper's" bias may lead to misunderstandings or broken relationships. Many in my field of work tend to use the words *resistant* and *defended* when talking about a client's willingness to embrace such norms. What I try to teach is that there is no such thing as resistant or defended in working with marginalized populations. I believe resistant is another way of saying a person doesn't want to be "normal" or "conform." The dominant culture has a clear cultural norm for white, middle-class American success: college, career, marriage, homeownership, and kids. Of course, many white, middle-class Americans do not identify with this as their narrative. In fact, those in community-based work have already deviated from this path. However, it is important to keep in mind that if the path was open to you in the first place, you began from a position of privilege. Marginalized people are not automatically invited to enter this pathway to success, and therefore their experiences and expectations inside American society are altogether different from those inside the dominant culture.

This is when you have to check out how you got your own values. Was college a given in your family? Did your parents go to college? Has access been a part of your experience? Do you have a car, home, or savings? Do you have the finances to deal with a problem if it arises? We all make assumptions based on our experiences and values, so when these are not aligned with the community we serve – as is the case for so many in community work – it is essential to stay mindful and to ask questions.

## Beyond Oppression

I've had many experiences speaking with adults about young people's attitudes toward school and whether or not they are invested in it. My own stance is that if they are on campus, they are invested. All my conversations with youth center on why they continue to come to school – even though many of them have to overcome real obstacles before they leave their home, car, or other place they slept (if they slept at all). I was working at one of the many continuation schools run by the Los Angeles Unified School District, facilitating a youth empowerment group, when the vice principal of the school called me and one of my students into her office. Then, she announced that she had to kick him out of school because he was late every day. In response, I started asking the student in front of the vice principal the same questions I would have asked him in counseling: (1) Who wakes you up for school?; (2) Do you eat before you come to school?; (3) How do you get to school?

The answers to each of these questions obviously surprised the vice principal. The young man started to describe his mornings while I continued to ask more specific questions. The student, it turned out, had no one to wake him up in the morning. Both parents worked two jobs, one morning and one night job, to make ends meet, and there were always gaps in the budget. He had to travel by bus from Florence/Firestone, an unincorporated community in South Central, through various gang neighborhoods, where he had to watch his back and sometimes get off and onto another, safer bus, so this made him late. He told us he had been stabbed twice on the bus, but that both times they got his backpack worse than they got him.

He then said that he had an eight-year-old sister whom he loved and felt responsible for. He was not going to leave for school until one of the parents got home from work. He was not going to leave his sister alone in a community he considered unsafe for little girls or anyone. He told us that he had had this conversation with his parents and they tried their best to leave their minimum-wage jobs as soon as possible but it was up to their bosses, who felt no concern for their problems. I asked him, "How did you become so responsible and why do you keep coming to school even though it is hard, dangerous, and you are late?" He answered, "It is the way I am going to get my family out of this situation. I have to finish school and get a good job so my parents can rest."

The student's explanations had given the vice principal pause, but she soon gained her footing. I asked her how she got to work every day, knowing she had a brand new car in the lot. I knew it was uncomfortable for her because she did not answer me and instead said, through her watery eyes, "Well maybe you just have to get up earlier and find a sitter for your sister." Who had become "resistant and defended" now?

I want to pause here to explain more about the vice principal. It may be easy to see her as an uncaring, out-of-touch administrator – someone very different from you or me. But the truth is, the vice principal cares deeply for her students and has passed up promotions to stay at her inner city school because she wants to see progress. She wants each and every one of her students to attend college. She is the one who hired me to begin the youth empowerment group. The vice principal was not an unfair, uncaring person. Nonetheless, she made a crucial mistake by making assumptions about the resources and support available to her student. These assumptions may have been reasonable in the neighborhood where she grew up; perhaps everyone there has a car, a parent at home, breakfast in the morning, a place to sleep, safe passage to school. Her experience did not in any way prepare her for this boy's reality. She was prepared to expel him based on her assumptions.

I sat with the vice principal for a long time explaining how different her life is and how I understood that she wanted these kids to pick themselves up by their bootstraps – but that they had to have boots to start with. After a lot of conversation about her challenges in understanding realities she has never had to face she said that she was challenged right now by having a broken leg and still coming to school. Of course, the difference between her challenge (caused by a skiing injury) and the systematic challenge of her student was logically clear to the vice principal, but emotionally at that moment she had begun to engage in what I call the "oppression Olympics."

I want to be fair to all of you working in this field when having conversations like these. If you are privileged, you will feel shame, hesitation, fear, and discomfort. These are not easy emotions. If you are able, think about what it must be like to be uncomfortable your whole life. To be the one under suspicion is exhausting, and can leave feelings of rage and appropriate paranoia toward anyone who represents any system.

It's important to hold on to the fact of systemic oppression and racism. Those who have lived in these communities know that something is weighing on them. They can see clearly that the person getting paid the very most money, with access to the greatest amounts of wealth and resources, does not work harder than they do. Poor people often work themselves to death and get very little in compensation. These challenges have a daily impact on complete communities and cultures. Parents struggle to keep food on the table and the lights on. Youth is often the recipient of frustration from these parents, and sometimes violence. These young people meet each other in school full of unresolved sadness, hurt, and rage. Teachers feel overwhelmed and undercompensated. The system often steps in with a description of and solution for the situation. Usually this involves "correcting the problem" in the individual, family, or community by imposing the values, beliefs, and norms of the dominant culture upon the community through such extensions of the system as therapist, case manager, and social programs.

And here is where you can do the most good. You can have a conversation unpacking the strengths in spite of the challenges. You can see beyond the oppression to seek and find resilience. Your ability to be a tourist in another person's life can bring forth their values and traditions.

Empowerment conversations come from the genuine belief that the community and its members possess the ability to solve their own problems if given a sense of fairness and equity. We can't change the system completely or quickly. Too many privileged people depend on the status quo. What we can do is bring forward conversations that remind our clients that they are not solely responsible for their situation. An historic, purposeful, and systemic collaboration of forces has been working upon them and their communities. If they come to us for help, we are the privileged and we hold the power. To have a more equal footing for the conversation, we need to level out the hierarchy as much as possible. Give of yourself conversationally. Give yourself the right to be in the position of *not knowing*. And be kind to yourself when you, like all of us, injure someone unintentionally and emotionally through cultural blindness. Vulnerability is a scary but amazing way to invite the less powered into a truly transparent conversation. This is where each person can feel safe in the space we create together as human beings. To all of you with boots on the ground in our most oppressed communities: I wish you peace.

# CHAPTER 7

# El Sistema as a Rival to Gangs

*Dr. Isaiah McKinnon and Dr. Michael J. Witkowski*

G ANGS are not new or recent. According to some researchers, they have existed since antiquity, and were even found in Rome. Street gangs in the United States began in major cities, such as New York and Los Angeles, as a reaction to oppression, poverty, and racial discrimination encountered by immigrants and newcomers to the nation. They then proliferated, springing up in other urban areas across the United States where young people, concentrated in poor neighborhoods, turned to gangs for protection, power, and a sense of belonging. Today, gangs have expanded even to suburban and rural communities. The level of violence has taken thousands of lives over the last two decades: more people have died from gang violence in Los Angeles alone than in the entire sectarian fighting in Northern Ireland.

Children growing up in urban poverty throughout the United States are easily pulled into a gang culture. Even those children not directly involved in gang activity feel the influence of this culture; gang authority, violence, and graffiti infiltrate their daily lives. Both authors in this essay have seen what happens when a city deprives its young people of opportunities and gang activity ensues. Isaiah "Ike" McKinnon is the city of Detroit's former chief of police and current deputy mayor and Michael Witkowski is an expert on gangs who teaches criminal justice at the University of Detroit Mercy. By providing an alternative, positive culture, access to greater opportunities, a sense of belonging, and an elevated status, an El Sistema núcleo can combat the influence of gangs and win.

Today's gangs are substantially different from earlier versions focused on turf and reputation (think *West Side Story*). Dr. Carl Taylor's taxonomy of gangs posits three models:

(1) Scavenger gangs: Often brought together by social conditions, they tend to be impulsive and more informal in character, with much of the crime they engage in opportunistic.
(2) Territorial gangs: More formalized, with a goal of defending a specific turf. Membership has rites and initiations and often specific hand signs and symbolism.
(3) Corporate gangs: Highly organized and profit-driven groups centered primarily on drug sales and distribution.

The main motivator of gangs today in fact appears to be economic. Most youngsters growing up in urban poverty will encounter any of the above types, but are most fiercely recruited by the territorial or corporate gangs. Gangs that fail to recruit new members cannot thrive, since so many members end up in jail or are killed.

Gangs are constantly looking to bring in youngsters who appear vulnerable. Gang recruiters can boast access to money, status, and a sense of belonging to a clique. They target children who lack resources. Dominant drug gangs in Detroit have used murder of potential recruits' friends or family members to ensure participation and loyalty (no "snitchin'"). When a child has a broken home, a broken school, and no prospects for improving his life, it is easy to understand how he can feel trapped. A lack of opportunity and of necessities leads to hopelessness. While on patrol in Detroit, Chief of Police McKinnon once met a fifteen-year-old boy who had $2,500 of drug money in his pocket. He told the boy "If you continue to do this, you won't live to be sixteen," to which the young man replied, "If I don't live to be sixteen, at least I had fifteen good years." A few months later, this young man was killed.

With so much violence and tragedy around gangs, why do kids sign on to become gang members? The traditional reasons given by prominent sociological researchers are a need for collective safety, a desire for respect and power, a substitute for a dysfunctional family, and the opportunity to make financial gains. Such needs are basic, and the extent to which they are not met serves as a strong indicator for how "at risk" a child may be. Other reasons for participation range from peer pressure, a desire to impress the opposite sex, and the need to maintain generational connections (for example, some families in Hispanic gangs now go back five generations).

Some gang members see belonging as a way to achieve a level of safety, with gang gatherings as safe havens. They may also see joining a gang as a path toward economic stability and success. Both assumptions are incorrect. Under today's "corporate" gang set-up, wages are marginal and the risk of death due to drug peddling very high. One in four gang members will die violently at the hands of rivals or of their own peers (often due to minor transgressions such as being short on narcotics or cash). In fact, the majority of gang members would make more money working at McDonald's, and with far less risk.

In 1980s Detroit, drug cliques used children to deal on street corners or from abandoned homes, and the city became famous for "pee wee" dealers. One group – the Chambers brothers – came to Detroit from rural Arkansas seeking the middle-class dream of work in the auto plants, but found drug dealing a more lucrative occupation. Once established in the city, they returned to their poverty-stricken roots in Arkansas to recruit young men Pied Piper style, bringing them in new luxury cars from their dirt-floor shacks to the Motor City. Once arrived, the kids were placed in strategically located abandoned homes to sell drugs out of a hole in the front door. These makeshift drug pads had no heat and no working plumbing. The kids might as well have been on Mars. As strangers in their environment, they had nowhere to turn and no way out.

Gangs are made up of disenfranchised individuals because the gangs are able to fill a void. Understanding this element illuminates why El Sistema can function as a gang prevention program. First, there are multiple potential "family units" within an El Sistema program: the orchestra or sectional may become a tightly knit, positive peer group. Students may also feel responsible to set a good example for younger students. Teachers serve as adult role models who set appropriate boundaries and expectations for young people. Finally, with any núcleo comes a larger, extended family network, with parents of other children, program faculty, and supporters all becoming a community of adults who watch and care for all the children. This "family" can substitute for a dysfunctional family in a far more productive and substantial way than a gang can, and also provide the need for a feeling of collective safety by allowing the student to participate in a strong, positive community. At the most basic level: the child is no longer out on the street and so the need for physical protection lessens.

When a music-learning environment is intentionally geared toward social change, students are immersed in an encouraging, constructive culture. The intensity of El Sistema programs means students are engaged within this culture multiple hours a day, several days a week. This is crucial to combating the gang recruitment efforts taking place in urban neighborhoods. In some respects it becomes a numbers game: students must be engaged in positive activities more than they are attracted by negative ones. The more hours they are playing their instruments, the fewer hours they are on the streets as potential targets.

The necessary "sense of belonging" is also addressed through the orchestra. Every young musician has a part to play in the symphony and is necessary for a successful practice or performance. They are missed when they are absent, as orchestra members depend on one another. An individual musician is an important piece in a larger whole.

Students who are also looking for a sense of respect and power when they join a gang can feel this respect and power through the "status" of an orchestra. Dr. Abreu's assertion that "the culture for the poor cannot be a poor culture" suggests that El Sistema orchestras are intended to elevate. Students recognize a well-cared-for building, gifted teachers, a top-notch orchestra, and the connection to the global El Sistema movement. These special qualities build up program credibility. Additionally, respect and power are given to students in the day-to-day operations of the program. Students are encouraged to own their own program by taking responsibility for the space, helping one another and younger students, and "representing" their program on special field trips and concerts, as ambassadors. This dynamic of being trusted and respected by key adults in their lives reverses the oppression typical outside the núcleo that pushes so many young men and women to join a gang in the first place.

The opportunity to make financial gain may not often be immediately addressed through an El Sistema program, but over the long term the potential exists here too. In Venezuela, young men and women are offered paid teaching opportunities to support their family and their education. Even without this kind of compensation, El Sistema offers children the opportunity to further their education, which in the long term increases their earning potential, opportunities for college attendance, and the social capital of their community.

Despite these benefits, talented youngsters involved in El Sistema music programs often must endure a system of challenges daily in their street environment. The phenomenon is described well by author Robert Garot in his 2010 book *Who You Claim*:

> To "bang on," "sweat," or "hit up" another means that one person approaches another . . . on a street, in a park, at school, at a flea market, or in some other public place, and in the local vernacular "tells" (not "asks") the other, "where you from." Anyone who lives in this locale knows that the instigator is demanding to know the respondent's gang affiliation.

A gang member making a "hit up," (demanding that the targeted youth reveal his/her gang affiliation) is "representing" for his "hood" as a gang member and assuming that the young person he is speaking with is also a gang member. If the youngster being questioned gives the "wrong answer," he is likely to suffer serious bodily harm at the hands of the questioner. If the youngster claims the wrong gang, he gets hurt. If he says "I don't bang" he is telling the questioner that no one "has his back" and becomes vulnerable. Further, if the young man being questioned disavows his gang and his pals hear of it, he is in equally serious danger.

Youths aged fifteen to twenty-five are the usual targets for a "hit up." Participants in the confrontation are usually the same gender. Kids wear the clothing and colors associated with the gang they belong to or have affiliation with. For instance, a blue New York Yankees cap in a Blood Gang-dominated area can elicit a challenge as to affiliation. The initiators of the "hit up" typically approach the intended target with a specific gait or walk indicated by "mobbing strides" – long lunging steps on the approach.

Young people in urban poverty face this type of challenge almost daily, along with other normal adolescent pressures. Children in an El Sistema núcleo may need to consider the routes they walk to and from home based on safety and security. Adolescence is a difficult life period for any child. Those having to endure efforts at being recruited into dangerous gangs suffer additional strain. Some can withstand the storm . . . others maybe not. Developmental psychologist Erik Erikson divided the personalities of developing youngsters into two groups he called "role diffusion" or "ego identity." The ego identity group has a strong sense of self-worth and a very clear idea about what they believe in terms of right and wrong. Young people in the "role diffusion" group are characterized by "confusion" about who they are and what they and life are all about. They have a low sense of focus and scattered interests, and a greater susceptibility to gang activities. "We band of brothers" type thinking takes hold. Walking tall down the street in the cool evening air gives youngsters a sense of collective efficacy and energy. Together, they are something special, something to be reckoned with. They can no longer be ignored. It's a heady power.

El Sistema programs offer kids a performance high and a sense of belonging to a community of musicians that can rival the attraction of the gang. Luckily, most of the youngsters attracted to the El Sistema-styled music programs fall into the ego identity group – a "blessed" group, who have a sustained sense of purpose and often know early on what they aspire to achieve. Students of both types enrolled in an El Sistema program gain focused discipline with daily and long-term goal setting through music learning. Further, the orchestra offers a sense of belonging where every musician is valued and respected.

An advantage of many El Sistema programs is the early start in musical training, which precedes the typical age of gang recruitment. This gives them a sense of purpose and feeling of success early on. Self-esteem can be enhanced under the tutelage of caring instructors and administrators. Role diffusion is prevented as the youngsters develop a strong sense of ego identity. Poverty imposes extreme limits on the lives of young musicians. Providing free musical instruction and instruments overcomes barriers to participation.

Observers often point out that El Sistema is not a "one size fits all" solution. It is open to tweaking and adjusting to fit the environment of the núcleos. Crescendo Detroit is one such El Sistema program. Located in a Dexter/Davison church building in the middle of the block, the new program gives children from the neighborhood healthy meals, band instruments, and dance instruction after school nine hours a week. A social worker is on faculty to teach life skills and supports students with serious behavior issues, while a reading specialist helps students with their homework and students are taken on field trips weekly during the summer time. In short, the students and neighborhood are made to feel special and given experiences that expand their worldview beyond the neighborhood.

Dexter/Davison is representative of Detroit's greatest challenges today:

an area with abandoned, and often burnt-out buildings and nagging crime issues. Budget cuts have stretched the police and fire departments, and other basic city maintenance services are challenged. Detroit remains optimistic, but it is known as one of the most violent cities in the United States, with underdeveloped economic opportunities and a lack of capital. With this kind of blight, gang activity blooms. Detroit gangs often form around smaller neighborhood cliques, and these gangs are fluid, with power shifting frequently. This can make for more violent, irrational gangs. Crescendo Detroit is reaching children who have extremely limited options in an effort to show them that beauty is all around and they have the ability to access it. The program's founder, Damien Crutcher, a native of Detroit, notes that the difference in self-esteem for the students is noticeable even in their appearance and dress. When the program began, there were children who looked like they "rolled out of bed" and came to class with uncombed hair and dirty clothes. However, as these same students started to go on field trips to museums, concerts, and events, this began to change. Students began to come to class cleaned up and started to take pride in their dance, music, and neighborhood.

Oklahoma City is another urban area that has seen an increase in gang activity over the past several years, earning in 2008 the distinction from the National Violent Death Reporting System as one of the five cities with the most gang homicides. Over the past two decades, Oklahoma City has seen a wave of new immigration from Central and South America and the struggles of culture clash, racism, and prejudice have unfortunately followed. Today, most of Oklahoma City's gangs are comprised of disenfranchised Hispanic young men. El Sistema Oklahoma was formed with St. Luke's United Methodist Church, the Wanda L. Bass School of Music at Oklahoma City (OKC) University, and the Foundation for Oklahoma City Public Schools and has grown to serve hundreds of children from the third through sixth grade. El Sistema Oklahoma has leveraged the community in an impressive way; by bringing so many partners together around the cause, children are given additional support and opportunities and the very tangible possibility for a college education through the connection with OKC University.

Youth Orchestra Los Angeles (YOLA) at Heart of Los Angeles (HOLA) faces great external frictions due to its geographic location. YOLA at HOLA musicians live and gather in what could be characterized as "the gang capital of the gang capital" of the United States. The Rampart area has already been glorified in music and movies for its gang rivalries and its intense conflicts with the LAPD. Adapting the El Sistema programming to this environment requires that the leadership be aware of the conflicts happening in the neighborhood, which is regularly tagged with graffiti by gangs laying "claim" to a particular area. To rival this, the program must stay constantly vigilant by reporting tagging, and suspicious people and behavior – while simultaneously creating an environment that is welcoming and open for the students and community. Being aware, knowing the gang culture and recognizing its patterns and changes – such as a ramping up of graffiti or increased "patrolling" from gang members in the neighborhood – can allow an El Sistema program to keep safety central without blocking out the community and working in isolation. By working *in* the community, rather than busing children to a different location, programs are choosing to confront the challenges that come with gang activity while still keeping students safe. Many El Sistema programs in the United States must perform this balancing act.

The core values of El Sistema programs are opposites of those of violent criminal gangs seeking to expand territory and economic profits. It is doubtful that those seeking to expand their criminal organizations, however sophisticated they may be (and some are run by long-time members) truly recognize the value and beauty of the music the children of El Sistema produce. Current gang demographic research indicates up to 60 percent of established gangs now consist of adults and not kids. Personal observations confirm that more disenfranchised men are staying with gang life as a source of economic sustenance instead of "desisting" or "aging out" as earlier gang studies had reported. Some return from prison wiser, but not deterred from the gang lifestyle. In fact, their time behind bars serves as a status enhancer.

However little the Original Gangsters ("OGs") appreciate the value of live music, reaching out to gangs through musical performance may be a powerful tool for keeping students safe because of the good reputation of a núcleo and its students. It is well documented that gang shot-callers give talented athletes from gang neighborhoods a "pass" to pursue their talents and potential. This kind of exemption can also be extended to the musically gifted. The key is to create a núcleo of such reputation and quality that even gang leaders see the value of the program and respect that it exists within the neighborhood. Sports teams have been able to elicit this kind of pride of ownership for many gangs, with logos and mascots frequently appropriated in gang dress. In Venezuela, the Simón Bolívar Symphony Orchestra has been able to evoke this type of pride largely on account of its high level of musicianship. In the United States, an equally impressive spectacle is necessary to warrant a "pass." The long-term goal of El Sistema may be to restore and rebuild communities to a place where gangs do not thrive, but in the short term, a núcleo successfully becoming a "hands off zone" would be a huge win for the safety of the program and its students and staff.

### Advice For teachers and Staff
The following information may assist teachers and staff of El Sistema programs in recognizing and handling gang activities in and around a núcleo. After all, even students who are benefiting from an El Sistema music program may fall into gang activity if they have family and friends who are so involved. The important thing for music program personnel is to catch this affiliation as early as possible. Though El Sistema programs should work to provide *prevention* – never allowing a child to enter a gang – *intervention* can be successful if addressed immediately. After the student is fully initiated, however, *suppression* – helping a child leave the gang – is the only option, and a far more difficult one. The deeper the child becomes involved in the operations of a gang, the harder it is to get out. Gang members with children and families may serve time in prison, often for many years, and still be unable to get a "pass" upon their release. It is not simple to walk away.

It is also important that you do not immediately assume that a change in your student is the result of gang involvement. A number of potential issues, like home discord and issues at school, may be playing a part. Taking the time to ask questions daily should keep you abreast of any alarming changes. Meanwhile, keep a watch out for several red flags that may come up in your work.

One indicator that youngsters are being recruited into gangs is a change of friends and the manner of dress and comportment. Impressionable youngsters may imitate the older gang members and "represent" for the gang through dress and speech. Kids who are in this stage of affiliation may be very frightened and want to back out, but fear looking like a coward or for their own safety. Having a known adult from the music program quickly address behavior changes like this can make all the difference.

Signs of graffiti inside the núcleo buildings are another frequent red flag. It is wise to photograph all current graffiti and be on the lookout for any that's new. Police officers can explain some of the scrawls used by gangs. Some graffiti may be simple "toss ups" made with pens or Sharpies and may be underestimated compared to the more ornate spray painted material. All "tagging" should be taken seriously. Drawings in music books and materials should be closely monitored.

Attitude changes can be another flag. Does a formerly helpful and polite youngster suddenly become surly and withdrawn?

Last, be aware of kids coming to the program with cuts, bruises, and black eyes, which may be due to their being initiated or "jumped in" by gang members. Many children sustain serious injuries in the process of being "beat into" the gang. Intervention is also difficult once a new recruit starts hanging with gang members, as at this point his or her loyalty will be continuously questioned. A solid relationship with a trustworthy adult role model may be the only avenue for intervening in the youngster's life after "hanging" begins.

When all good faith is exhausted it is best to let gang members leave the group. Otherwise, they may start recruiting from within the núcleo. Once they become involved in criminality on behalf of the gang they have become a liability to program success. They also attract rivals to your location, with potential violence to follow. Program safety is paramount. Remember that there are community organizations that specialize in gang "intervention" and "suppression." These experts have a strong understanding of the complexities of a gang. An El Sistema program works well as a "prevention" program in not allowing a potential problem to start, but experts are needed to help a student leave a gang. "Remember the main thing is to keep the main thing the main thing . . ." Musical training and the transformation of young lives is the main thing.

This does not mean turning your back on a gang member. Rather, it means pulling in people who can better support the child and situation, allowing you to spend your energy on the multiple children who may be teetering on the edge, rather than focusing it all on a child you may not be able to support on your own. Progress is slow, but positive impact on any single child will strengthen the community: one kid kept out of a gang over a lifetime equals dozens of children not recruited.

To keep your program and students safe, you must respond to any and all gang activity seriously. Note that youths categorized as "wannabes"(those modeling gang behavior, but not actually involved in an active gang) can be the most reckless and dangerous since they have "something to prove." Alas, we know of many cases in which school officials, housing project administrators, or business owners have ignored warning signs that, if heeded, might have averted tragic outcomes. Failures often come from a combination of denial, ignorance, and negligence. Witkowski served as an expert witness at a trial involving the gang-related murder of a thirteen-year-old student, Samuel, who was stabbed to death in a dark hallway at a middle school as students arrived for classes. Samuel was a member of the Cholos, a group of Hispanic boys who gathered together for protection. Their primary rival within the school was a Caucasian group known as "Southeast Crip Cartel." The day before the murder, a few teachers and coaches witnessed a confrontation between the two groups near the school that resulted in gunfire. No report was made and the police were not called. The following morning saw a continuation of the previous day's conflict, with tense students entering the school. A youth approached Samuel and stabbed him with a screwdriver bearing the words *SE Crip Cartel 4 Life* on its handle.

In the aftermath of this tragedy, a review of school security incident reports showed that official school police records were missing a great deal of data. Teachers had been attacked and injured by Southeast Crip Cartel members and their identified leaders. According to teachers, gang signing and representing occurred frequently. However, newspaper reports about the school touted low drop-out rates, high test scores, and low crime figures; some had even declared the school district a "miracle." Despite obvious indications in the neighborhood and on school property of gang activity, the school had insisted that gangs were not a problem. Teachers who spoke out against the gang problems claimed that school officials turned against them.

This story serves as a cautionary tale. Samuel's death might have been avoided if the record of school crimes and longstanding disputes between the two gangs had been appropriately addressed. Instead, the school administration felt it more important to maintain their reputation as a "low problem school."

It is critical for El Sistema staff members to remember that gang members are victims of circumstance. Often, they are kids just like those you are serving in the núcleo, only they had no early access to an activity like El Sistema. Many involved in gang activity would welcome a way out if realistic opportunities were presented. There is a belief among many police that gang members should be incarcerated rather than rehabilitated because they are at a high risk for becoming repeat offenders. In fact, many gang members have changed their lives for the better.

The most successful, large-scale gang intervention and suppression program in the country is Homeboy Industries, located in Los Angeles. With the motto "Jobs not Jails," formerly gang-involved men and women are enrolled in job-training, counseling, tattoo removal, education services, and more, all free of charge. The best-known job-training is the Homeboy Industries bakery, where men, often previously from rival gangs, work side by side baking bread that is sold in farmer's markets and grocery stores across southern California. Over 120,000 gang members have been served by the organization since it began in 1988, and Homeboy Industries has served as a model for more than forty other organizations around the country. In Los Angeles, Homeboy Industries is considered preeminent in gang reduction efforts. The program was created by Father Greg Boyle, a Jesuit priest who saw the escalating gang violence and membership around the Dolores Mission in Boyle Heights in the late 1980s and realized the need to provide jobs, education, and other support as alternatives.

Homeboy Industries demonstrates that the majority of gang members, when given opportunities and options, want to leave gang life. Within an El Sistema program, these opportunities are realized in several ways: young people travel for performances, meet visitors from around the world, or even receive a stipend to help around the núcleo, money that can be used to support their families. Helping young people realize there are other alternatives is fundamental to El Sistema's gang prevention potential.

Years ago McKinnon, while police chief in Detroit, secretly met with members of the four largest gangs of Southwest Detroit in St. Anne's Church. The gang members themselves had called the meeting after seeing McKinnon speak on the news about the need for solutions to the crisis of crime in their area. These young men all wanted to turn their lives around. They told McKinnon their main concerns were a lack of jobs, a lack of education, and the need to continue to take care of their families. At just seventeen and eighteen years old, the lack of other opportunities had driven them to gang life. However, they showed up and asked for help. When McKinnon and others in the community banded together to create opportunities, it was a revelation. The young men got their GEDs. They were given jobs at Ford, General Motors, Chrysler, and with the Detroit Red Wings. McKinnon arranged drivers and rides to work, saying to the former gang members, "We can't have people stealing cars to get to work." Given the opportunity and appropriate resources, most of these young men turned their lives around to become law-abiding, productive citizens.

The El Sistema-inspired programs are worthy alternatives for youngsters seeking to avoid gangs and the hassles of constant recruitment. Students and families in these music programs are thinking about the future in a new way. Hopeful children do not join a gang. They dream.

# PART III

# TEACHING AND LEARNING

In Venezuela, the word *musician* encompasses the idea of teacher/leader and performing artist. There is no separation of these roles, because it is impossible to be one without the other. A teacher and an artist are one and the same.

I have had long conversations with Venezuelan musicians who are mystified by the way these roles are clearly divided in the United States. How can you be an effective teacher or leader if you do not model the creation of art? How can your art have meaning if you are not a leader supporting the community? For an individual who grew up in El Sistema, the very essence of music is equally social and artistic.

The Venezuelan definition of musician is introduced at the top of this section on "Teaching and Learning" because working in an El Sistema program requires a broadening of one's self definition as a musician. To work in an El Sistema program, one must be an artist, a teacher, a mentor, and an advocate. Many of the individuals drawn to El Sistema work are eager to deviate from the traditional path in order to find more fulfillment, yet have been trained primarily as only a teacher or only a performer. This calls for a reinvigoration of the neglected pieces of their musicianship as understood by the Venezuelans. This section of the book is laid out to support such a fortification.

El Sistema's motto of *tocar y luchar*, or to play and to strive, demands an artistic pursuit of the highest kind for students and teachers. The orchestra works together toward an impossible musical goal (normally comprised of repertoire years above the student's current level) in a fun, fast-paced environment. My essay on the subject attempts to explain how high

171

expectations and hard work can be used to empower students, build community, and strengthen character.

Angela Duckworth's work around "grit" at the University of Pennsylvania gained attention in recent years when she found that a student's ability to bounce back after failure was a better indicator of high school graduation than I.Q. Similarly, the Teach for America organization has discovered that the candidates most likely to be successful as teachers are not those with the best education or experience, but the ones who had planned and completed a major project. In response, "character education" has gained traction in the pedagogical world today as a potential winning technique for supporting the most vulnerable students. In classrooms and school districts across the country, educators are looking at how to develop a student's "stick-to-itiveness" to improve academic performance. At the same time, these programs have come under scrutiny on account of their strong focus on individual accomplishment and their lack of a moral compass to guide character development.

As any music teacher can tell you, grit, or "perseverance and passion for long-term goals" as Duckworth defines it, is a reliable result of learning music, a process that demands consistent practice and always brings failures as well as triumphs. Yet El Sistema stands apart from traditional music and character education programs with *tocar y luchar*'s mission of social change. While practicing art for its own sake has been argued to strengthen one's moral resolve, practitioners of El Sistema work believe that everyone deserves a life of dignity and contribution and seeks to relieve social injustice. As actors in this larger mission, El Sistema teachers explore these values with their students regularly through discussions of activism and community building. Further, teachers using a *tocar y luchar* mindset place a clear emphasis on the achievement of the entire community over the achievement of the individual. Students learn in an ensemble setting rather than as soloists because individual success is measured by how it supports the community. This is a departure from many traditional schools of music education, where students are developed as individuals rather than as members of sections and told to practice solo repertoire over orchestra parts.

As you read the essay on *tocar y luchar*, consider the importance of the orchestra in the development of the non-cognitive. YOLA at HOLA middle school students explained it best one day in a conversation around the differences between school and orchestra. At school, they noted, everyone looks out for themselves. Grades and even friendships feel like an individual pursuit. In orchestra, however, they feel a sense of responsibility to one another and tangible sense of community. As one student put it, "This is my family – I count on everyone and everyone counts on me."

*Tocar y luchar* and El Sistema's alternative definition of musician can help us rethink the role of the orchestral musician in today's society. The Master of Arts in Teaching (MAT) program in El Sistema through the Longy School of Music of Bard College is attempting to do exactly this. On the campus of Heart of Los Angeles (HOLA), the degree program operates within the traditional confines of a credentialing curriculum while also examining El Sistema through an intensive teaching practicum at Youth Orchestra Los Angeles (YOLA) at HOLA. Karen Zorn herself is a strong example of a modern-day musician; as a classically trained pianist and the current president of the Longy School of Music of Bard College, Karen has acted as an educational entrepreneur, unveiling a new path for young musicians finding that the careers laid out by previous generations are not positions they want or have access to. Longy's MAT is the first credentialing program in the United States to emphasize El Sistema. By embedding the educational philosophy and practice of El Sistema within the traditional music education world, this program is pioneering an important sea change in the world of music education. The balance between the methodical music education training and the more radical "learn by fire" techniques of El Sistema means that students not only know the rules, but also how best to break them.

Gustavo Dudamel is one of the best examples of the broader definition of musician. His words to the YOLA faculty a few years ago reminded me that in El Sistema work, we are all simultaneously teachers and learners: "The moment that you feel you no longer have anything to learn as a teacher, it is time to quit . . .You must continue to have the energy for this mission, or you must quit immediately." Even the most skilled and veteran teachers are driven to seek out new methods and materials to better reach their students. Nikki Shorts, the YOLA at HOLA children's orchestra conductor and strings specialist and Loralie Heagy, founder of the El Sistema-inspired Juneau, Alaska Music Matters (JAMM) and nationally recognized music educator, are two such teachers. In their essays, Nikki and Lorrie respectively address the most common challenges faced by new

El Sistema teachers: building a productive, positive classroom culture and making content relevant and engaging for student learning.

There is a saying in teaching that goes: "Students don't care how much you know until they know how much you care." Establishing trust, love, and mutual respect as core components of the student/teacher relationship cultivates student motivation and cooperation. Nowhere is this better illustrated than in classrooms under the spell of Nikki Shorts. Nikki's approach means that when she stands at the podium during rehearsal, her eighty young elementary students are silent with rapt attention. An outsider looking in might find Ms. Nikki to be quite strict – she has incredibly high expectations for her students and she demands that they meet them. But she does this with love, compassion, and respect.

Loralie (Lorrie) Heagy has been called a "child whisperer" by many. Indeed, on multiple occasions I have observed her fully captivate young children without a single word. With hand signals, song, and dance, the 2011 Alaska Teacher of the Year has engaged children and teachers in El Sistema programs in Venezuela, Japan, Taiwan, and across the United States and around the world. Since being introduced to El Sistema in 2009, Lorrie has not only run her own Sistema program, but has worked as a teacher trainer around the country at workshops in Los Angeles, Boston, Portland and New York. Lorrie has been using stories and music to build connections to content for a long time. Over 40 percent of the students at Glacier Valley Elementary School are Alaskan Natives, with the majority coming from the Tlingit tribe. Lorrie draws on her students' experiences and heritage as much as possible to make a connection between the music students are learning and their lives.

The story described in her essay here about "Mr. Fox" hunting for food is one that resonates to the lives of all students in Alaska, but especially those from a Native Alaskan culture. Lorrie's respect for Tlingit culture has not gone unnoticed in Juneau. In 2014, she was adopted into the Kiks.ádi (Frog) clan of Sitka as part of the Tlingit tribe for her support of the community through her work teaching children music with JAMM.

After much focus on teachers supporting the classroom, Rebecca Reid Sigel's piece on leadership and group dynamics in El Sistema pivots toward students taking ownership of their own learning experience. As the YOLA manager for the Los Angeles Philharmonic, Rebecca comes to us with a wide range of experiences teaching leadership through wilderness expeditions, which she has worked to adapt to El Sistema programming.

Rebecca is not afraid to allow her students to grow through failure. She gives them the space and time to be frustrated, noting that temporary setbacks can lead to solutions and epiphanies when students are properly supported. Many students have yet to discover that they are capable of solving problems on their own. For example, in the past I worked with a student leadership group that envisioned fantastic and relevant projects, but was at an utter loss when it came to implementation. Reluctantly, I would step in to provide additional structure, but these student-directed projects moved forward slowly. Then, one day, while I was juggling multiple classrooms due to faculty absences, the group was left almost entirely alone. With this space and time away from an adult, the students took initiative and made concrete action plans. When I ducked back in the room to check on their progress, the healthy noise of productive conversation almost immediately faded and the students turned to me for directions that they did not need, but still expected. I realized then that they had been rudderless only because I had been in the room. When forced to work on their own, the students flourished. Rebecca helps us connect this kind of student leadership back to the orchestra.

Teaching and learning is at the heart of El Sistema. Without dedicated teachers, there is no music learning or social change. As Dr. Abreu explained, curriculum, infrastructure, and buildings are second to great teaching: "We started in garages and old houses . . . The only reality we had was a small group of very good teachers. This is the true seed of a program." When this seed is planted, teachers empower students to become teachers. This is how a community grows through music.

– C. W.

175

# CHAPTER 8

# *Tocar y Luchar*

## *Christine Witkowski*

WHENEVER I think of El Sistema's motto, *tocar y luchar* (to play and to strive), an *LA Times* photo from June 24, 2012 comes to mind: It is opening night at the Hollywood Bowl and thirty-five ten-year-old woodwind and brass students from Youth Orchestra Los Angeles (YOLA) at Heart of Los Angeles (HOLA) are standing on stage in front of 18,000 people, just before their performance of Brahms's Hungarian Dance No. 5. While the majority of students are deeply focused with instruments in hand, two boys are caught sharing an expression of pure joy; wide-eyed and smiling, their faces perfectly capture the exuberance of every student, teacher, and family member at that exact moment.

Though this image confirms the excitement students find in performing, its back story is what really matters. The photo does not show the months and hours of intensive rehearsals that took place a few miles away, in a much less prestigious part of the city. From this photograph alone, you cannot know about the student who came to class at HOLA every day, despite being exhausted from not having a bed to sleep in at night. Or the dad who pleaded with his employer to work through lunch each day so he could leave early to take his daughters to music class. Or that only a year and half before, none of the children pictured had ever played an instrument and that the original score of Hungarian Dance No. 5, though fascinating and engaging for the students, had been an almost impossible reach technically and artistically.

That evening, the students' performance was met with deafening applause from the family section of the audience. They were sensational. As students came off stage, they cheered and hugged one another, elated by their accomplishment. Many parents cried, overjoyed by a palpable sense of pride. The students were not simply "given" the opportunity to play opening night at the Hollywood Bowl; they (and their parents) had earned it. This is what it means to *tocar y luchar*.

*To play and to strive* has become synonymous with the high expectations, fast-paced music learning, and camaraderie of El Sistema. Images of youth orchestras in Venezuela practicing Shostakovich for eight hours a day come to mind: students and teachers achieving the seemingly impossible by playing and striving together toward a shared vision. The concept captures beautifully the non-cognitive benefits of music education; working hard to achieve a goal leads to increased resiliency, higher self-esteem, leadership skills, and the development of positive peer relationships. Practicing music – of course – is a powerful medium for cultivating these traits and skills, with promised daily opportunities for goal setting, repetitions, setbacks, and finally successes. What El Sistema adds to the equation is a supportive, inclusive community to strive for and with daily. When a community is unified around a shared dream, it becomes collaborative and therefore more capable of leveraging its resources and innate strength.

*Tocar y luchar* is a motto, but it is also a mindset. For those of us who did not grow up in El Sistema, some aspects of *tocar y luchar* may be difficult to embrace in practice. Personally, my traditional, Midwestern band education was remarkably sequential and methodical. Growth happened incrementally and strategically. The approach worked more or less for me, and I became a fine musician. The challenge for me was then to merge my own experiences and knowledge with a more fearless approach to music education – one I did not experience growing up. In the *tocar y luchar* mindset children are believed to be artists and, as such, trusted with and exposed to great beauty and challenges from the start.

Integrating *tocar y luchar* into the daily practices of a program means questioning longstanding beliefs around music education and student competence while establishing high expectations within a nurturing and engaging environment. There is no checklist or set of criteria by which to know if you have successfully implemented *tocar y luchar* – it will be a constant work in progress. You and your students will know, however, when you have succeeded. Through this essay, I hope to share lessons and anecdotes on how *tocar y luchar* can be used to build community, create a culture of high standards and support, and ultimately promote social change through musical excellence.

## Beginning With a *Tocar y Luchar* Culture

There is a popular saying in Venezuela that goes, "If there is no crisis, create one." A crisis creates an opportunity to work together toward a solution – it is how the Venezuelans fuel the fire within their students and teachers. And perhaps unsurprisingly, YOLA at HOLA began with just such a crisis.

On the first day of the program, 120 elementary students were supposed to show up, all eager to learn music. Instead, only seventy arrived for the orientation. More than half of the parents had signed their child up because we offered academic tutoring; for them, music was only an afterthought. Meanwhile, the families who *desired* music education wanted private lessons, not an orchestra program. To make matters worse, the convergence of multiple languages within one program – Korean, Spanish, and Tagalog – immediately began to create unconscious barriers.

It is challenging to be the pioneers of a new program. Norms for our newly forming community were not yet set and consensus felt very far off. By Tuesday of the first week, there was already a litany of complaints and miscommunication. Parents called me, upset that academic tutors focused on homework comprehension rather than completion; a rumor went around that we had begun on paper violins (a technique from the Caracas-based núcleo La Rinconada) because we did not have the funds to buy real violins; and, our new fourth-graders had self-segregated in music class and were using racial slurs and stereotypes to undercut one another. It was within this fragile, new ecosystem that we encountered our first "crisis": the news that Gustavo Dudamel, the internationally renowned conductor who had taken over as music director of the LA Philharmonic one year earlier, would be coming to the Rampart District to hear our students perform in only four weeks' time.

Preparing new, young musicians to play instruments in only four weeks for a world famous conductor was no small task. Add to this challenge the birth pangs of a newly minted El Sistema program and you have a true mission impossible. Nonetheless, with a common goal before us, our entire community was thrust into a *tocar y luchar* mindset. Preparations for the upcoming visit unified teachers, parents, and students. Gustavo Dudamel is a celebrity in his own right, but in Los Angeles, that status is amplified; he appears on multiple buses, billboards, TV commercials, and advertisements. All of our parents and students knew him as the "rock star" conductor. They were proud to host him in their neighborhood. A tangible sense of excitement and urgency took hold around his visit and the community began to work together.

When Gustavo Day finally came, the orchestra room was filled to capacity, parents, grandparents, and younger siblings standing shoulder to shoulder. The audience watched with excitement as the fourth-graders performed an arrangement of Wagner's Overture to *Tannhäuser* as a recorder ensemble, followed by a boisterous rendition of "Hot Cross Buns" on brand new woodwind and brass instruments. The first-grade students sang and played for Gustavo on their paper violins, decorated with stickers and macaroni, while parents proudly snapped photos and videos. When they finished performing, Gustavo jumped up and announced that these younger students were now ready for real instruments and handed them their first violins. He also gave a new goal to the community: "Now you have a complete orchestra and next time, I am coming back to conduct."

As first concerts go, this was a remarkable experience. It was imperfect and fledgling, but also full of promise and possibility. All of the hard work and dedication the parents had poured into supporting their children suddenly had a beautiful result. Gustavo Dudamel's compliments made every student feel special and valued – they now had a sense of pride and identity around their music program. For most in our community, this was the first orchestra concert they had ever attended. Any confusion around the direction of the program was erased. After the concert, parents and students were able to picture what the orchestra was capable of achieving. With this at the beginning, anything was possible.

A George Patton quote comes to mind when I think about these frantic beginnings: "A good plan violently executed now is better than a perfect plan executed next week." To have begun our program in this way set a powerful precedent. Of course, thoughtful planning and strategy is crucial to long-term success. There are certainly things that happened in those first four weeks that we would never repeat. But I also know that learning by fire is powerful. The trust that was built between students, teachers, and parents in those weeks would have taken months without such a push. There was no time to waste and under great pressure everyone rose to the challenge.

**High Expectations Within an Engaging and Nurturing Environment**

The ideal El Sistema learning environment embodies the principles of *tocar y luchar* – a space where students are pushed to achieve lofty musical goals through a supportive, engaging process that promotes teamwork and friendship. Consistently maintaining the integrity of all these components can prove challenging for teachers and staff. I would be lying if I said that regularly achieving *tocar y luchar* "balance" was easy. For example, there are certainly times when fun and engagement trumps skill mastery or vice versa. The goal is to be constantly "in flow," but it is difficult to achieve. When these interests fall in sync, however, students move to new levels of leadership and artistry.

An *engaging environment* is key for *tocar y luchar* to be effective. Students will work hard of their own volition when the goal is relevant; they become focused and passionate when ignited by the task. The ensemble that performed at opening night at the Hollywood Bowl was not strictly "ready" to play Brahms's Hungarian Dance No. 5. However, the students were enthralled by the Hungarian folk music influence, the minor key, the varied tempos, and the very challenge. They *wanted* to play the piece, and as a result, were willing to work long hours late into the evening to make it happen. They felt a real ownership over the piece and their performance in a way that would never have happened had the teachers simply picked an "appropriate" piece for them.

*Camaraderie and community* are natural byproducts of students playing and striving together in ensemble. The ability to both contribute and belong is central to the benefits of ensemble-based learning. The semantics are subtle, but when students shift from saying "the music class I'm in" to "my music class," morale, pride, and positive behavior noticeably increases.

When students lose that sense of identity because they no longer take pride in the work, camaraderie and friendship wavers, and consequences are significant. Team Strauss was the "middle child" of our brass teams. Not the most advanced group (Team Mahler), nor the shiny new beginners (Team Shostakovich), the team began to lose its identity over the course of six months. Intentional steps were taken to rotate players between the top group and Team Strauss to keep the team from feeling lesser. However the shifting of players, rather than having a democratizing effect, diluted an already weak team identity; new players were moved up or down and the group never fully solidified. Moreover, Team Strauss happened to have a high concentration of students with inextricably difficult home lives. The team was struggling to survive.

Opportunities to travel and perform as a team were always tied to donor events, at which we were under pressure to show off our top players. As a result, Team Strauss was consistently passed up for these opportunities. Though they were pushed for great performances, such as a side-by-side with the Simón Bolívar Symphony Orchestra, they were not fully engaged with their repertoire because it did not sufficiently excite them. The group did not feel challenged musically and correctly sensed that they were not being propelled forward. Without a crisis to rally around, the identity of the group began to wane significantly. Attendance became poor. The team existed nearly as a team in waiting – students hoping to be moved up to Team Mahler.

Once we recognized the situation, we took steps to correct the lack of identity and to refocus the team and its teachers. We spoke honestly with the students of Team Strauss to get their feedback on how to shift the culture. And, from the students, a solution was born: the group spent a summer as the pep band for HOLA's sports leagues. This was a responsibility they felt excited and proud to hold. Students spent more with one another working toward a shared goal. They played games at the gym, cheered on the HOLA teams, and got frozen yogurt together. In short, they had *fun* together again doing something that made them proud. Immediately, from just these initial steps, the culture of Team Strauss began to improve – the students were excited to be challenged and through this, they regained their connection to one another and the program.

On the flip side, when camaraderie is maintained, a program culture is strong. Recently, Luis's parents began to look for a home outside the community. They wanted to live in a safer neighborhood with stronger middle school options. They had been working hard to achieve economic mobility for years – the plan had always been to move out of the neighborhood as soon as possible. But when they came to my office with their fourth-grade son, he was deeply concerned that the move would make him ineligible for participation in the orchestra. "I've thought about it a lot, and we can't move because our orchestra is a community and I helped to build it. Team Mozart will not be the same without me. So, I've decided we have to stay here." When I explained that families who move out of the neighborhood were still welcomed and encouraged to be in the orchestra, the child and parents were relieved. His dedication to his team – who he had been working with since the first grade – was so great that he and his family were willing to pass up the opportunity to improve their choice of school and home.

Creating *high expectations within a supportive environment* is perhaps the most delicate of balancing acts. We always strive to both support and push simultaneously, but there are times where a student may need one more than the other. There are a few things to consider:

*Does the student have the resources, tools and support necessary to accomplish the goal?* The environment within which students are pushed is essential. Setting a daring goal without adequate support may create anxiety and can lead to a failure the student cannot overcome later. If someone tells me to swim the English Channel in three months, they have set an audacious goal for me. However, they have not considered that I'm currently a weak swimmer, I do not have a swim coach, and I lack the time and interest to train appropriately (not to mention general athletic ability).

Bold aims are fantastic, but they have to take into account the student's access to resources, tools and support. When I first began working at HOLA, I met a high school senior who had been learning the violin at her school. She told me that she was planning to audition for Juilliard in two months and asked if I could help her with her preparations. I was thrilled that she was dreaming big, but quickly realized she was not yet ready to audition for a college music program. With only a few years of playing under her fingers, the student had real promise and drive, but limited technique and very weak reading skills. She did not know any of the pieces or scales on the audition list. When I gently asked if she had spoken with her violin teacher about her plans to audition for Juilliard, she told me that the teacher had been enthusiastic about her applying but could not teach her privately. The student had no sense of the criteria for admission into a music school and her teachers had not provided any guidance. Her goal of applying to Juilliard did not necessarily need to change, but the time line and amount of support and resources she needed to reach her goal absolutely did. She lacked the necessary tools to work effectively toward her initial goal, and was certain to fail. This failure might have been detrimental rather than an opportunity for reflection and growth, because the goal was unattainable, no matter how hard the student worked in those two months. This student ultimately decided to go to community college for a year while she furthered her musical studies and prepared for college auditions in California. Her standards are still high and she is working hard, but she now has an appropriate plan to achieve those standards.

*To whom are you really offering support?* Providing too much support can also be a danger. The line between empowering and enabling is thin. Space for failure is as important as space for success. I once pushed a student to apply for a prestigious private lesson program that was offered through a partner organization. I walked her and her mom through a rigorous application and audition process. When the parent missed our appointment to complete the paperwork, I went to meet her at her home. When the student did not come to her mock audition, I rescheduled it. She got into the program, but more problems followed. She would miss lessons or show up unprepared. She was eventually dropped. Of course, the warning signs that the program was not a good fit were there from the start. I held her hand and pushed her too far – she would have failed to get in without me, and I did not want that for her. Ultimately, I placed my own values and desires for the student above her own. If she had wanted to be in the program, she would have taken initiative. Further, if I had not done all the work to get her accepted, she might have valued the placement more. In either case, my support was about my desire to be helpful, and not about the student's needs.

*Remember that even when balancing high standards with support and resources, failures are still inevitable.* Healthy failures allow students to learn, innovate, and grow. A student who is not yet ready to win the local concerto competition will still be served by working with a teacher to prepare for the audition. If he works up to his full potential and is appropriately supported, he will have built himself room for reflection even in the face of a setback. To use failure as a learning opportunity, a child must be able to see an alternative outcome. Children may require the support of a faculty member before they can envision such a future. Even if that student feels disappointed by not winning, a teacher can help him recognize his improved abilities and he can feel proud in his effort. The knowledge that one can grow allows a child to persist in the face of setbacks. This "growth mindset" is the biggest difference between children who continue and children who give up.

*Striving vs. surviving.* Challenges and high expectations may be manifested in a variety of ways. There are a wide array of student experiences and needs within a núcleo. Given the appropriate support and resources for their needs, the majority of students are able to operate within the expectations of the program most of the time. However, I have found that there is a small, fluid group of students who need to relate to the program in a very different way. For these students, the *tocar y luchar* opportunity may simply be to come to programming each day. This period may last for a few days, weeks, or months.

Cindy went through such a period. Her mom was diagnosed with Stage 4 liver cancer and was undergoing chemotherapy. The six members of her family lived in a one-room apartment, and the illness brought additional stress to an already emotionally charged and chaotic environment. Cindy desperately wanted to continue coming to HOLA – she liked her friends and did not want to be home after school. But she couldn't concentrate in class and stopped following directions and participating. She would hide in the bathroom stalls to avoid being in class. When I asked her why, she explained that her mind kept wandering to what would happen if her mom died – where would she live? Who would take care of her? Cindy began to come to programming and sit in the office to complete homework and talk with adults who cared about her. It is not that we let go of high expectations for Cindy. She was still expected to come each day and to contribute. But a child needs to be able to survive before she or he can thrive. When the culture of the community is established and strong, it can withstand outliers like Cindy and be ready to welcome them back into the fold when the time comes.

**Not Placing Limits on Students**

Which is more important for the success of an El Sistema program: musical excellence or social development? This common question demonstrates a misunderstanding of the work itself. Social development (the idea of happy, empowered, compassionate students who contribute positively back to the community) is the clear purpose of Sistema work. This intention informs everything that happens within the núcleo. However, social development is achieved only through striving for musical excellence.

Too often, programs that reach underserved youth operate from a deficit-based approach. Adults assume that these students do not have the same abilities or motivations as their more privileged peers and do not need or require the same quality of programming. A safe, fun place to go after school with caring adults is a start, but high standards and true artistic gains are equally important. High expectations show students you believe in them, even if they do not believe in themselves. Children know quality. They are proud when they have worked hard for an accomplishment and indifferent when they have not. Self-esteem cannot be handed out – it has to be earned. When a program's expectations are low, its message is clear to students – "This is what you are worthy of, and this is the best we believe you can do." Students who receive this message from every outlet in society can quickly begin to believe it.

At school, Ivan was not allowed to participate in music class on account of his low grades. When his mom signed him up for YOLA at HOLA, his classroom teacher told her that Ivan would not be able to handle such an intensive music program due to his poor concentration and lack of language skills. The teacher suggested instead that if Ivan must play music, he do so in a less intensive program, with lower stakes. Ivan's mom wanted him to be in the orchestra and so he stayed, despite the warning. At first, Ivan tried to do the bare minimum in class, assuming that showing up would be enough. Quickly he realized that the bar was set much higher. Teachers noticed when he was missing or hadn't practiced, and held him accountable. The only assumptions made about Ivan were that he was gifted and capable. A few times, I remember Ivan protesting, "But I can't learn this, it's too hard for me," and a teacher quickly retorting, "Of course you can do it – it's just going to take some work."

Ivan soon stood out as a naturally talented flute player. He began to come to class early – at first to hang out with his friends, but soon to practice. Ivan's clever sense of humor and ability to get along with everyone made him an effective peer leader – a power that was immediately harnessed by his teachers for good, rather than evil. He was given the responsibility of playing piccolo in addition to the flute, doubling his work load. He rose to the challenge. A year later in his school, Ivan had gone up one letter grade in every subject. His classroom teacher even came to a concert that spring and remarked that she was shocked by how focused and dedicated he was to music. The experience helped her see him, and music education, in a new light.

Ivan's teacher did not believe that he was a capable pupil because she set low standards for him – and he did not prove her wrong. To be honest, Ivan does struggle from time to time in the music program – he occasionally shifts back into his old habits of apathy and has to be brought around by the teachers. Importantly, this "two steps forward, one step back" does not discourage the team from believing in Ivan or expecting great things from him. In fact, even in moments of frustration, Ivan will be the first to admit that he appreciates being believed in and held accountable. Ivan has the innate abilities and motivation to work hard and learn – they just need to be constantly drawn out.

*Tocar y luchar* can present a dilemma because, more often than not, we want to teach the way we were taught. Most of us who are steeped in traditional music education hold very strong beliefs about learning sequences and when a student should be exposed to repertoire. In El Sistema programs we need both to challenge and draw from our traditions. Venezuelan teachers do not hand out Mahler, Shostakovich, and Tchaikovsky to young students because they do not value sequential learning, but rather because they want their students to strive to create art from the beginning. Challenging yourself to use the tools and experiences you have, without allowing them to limit your student's possibilities, is a daily task.

In April of 2010, I faced my own assumptions on the capacity of children as artists, and realized they were wrong. At this time during its first of several seminars, the National Children's Orchestra of Venezuela was preparing for a national tour with Sir Simon Rattle. The 357-piece orchestra of auditioned eight- to fifteen-year-olds from around Venezuela rehearsed Mahler's First Symphony every waking hour of the day – they even ate their meals in front of a projected performance of the piece. I watched the orchestra rehearse in Caracas, standing off to the side. The quality and sound of these young students completely floored me – with every section doubled two times over, they were a force.

The orchestra was intentionally quadrupled in size during this first seminar, the intention being to re-audition and eventually pare down the group. This practice allowed younger, less qualified students to experience an intensive seminar and to take the knowledge and energy gained back to their hometowns. I was invited to sit in on the second-round horn auditions.

During the day, I had listened to the young horn section rehearse with the orchestra and been awestruck. The section was solid, despite being incredibly young (most of the students were only ten years old). That same evening, sitting in the auditions, my awe turned to utter bafflement: fourteen of the sixteen horn players were completely incapable of executing the requested excerpts from the Mahler. Passages they had successfully played in orchestra hours before were now fumbled through, as though sight-read. More often than not, the music was unrecognizable as Mahler's First Symphony.

I turned to the horn teacher, completely bewildered. How was it possible that the students were so wonderful in orchestra but then completely disintegrated on their own? He explained that something incredible – something magical – happens to students when they are playing in a section and an orchestra. They find a way to communicate and to understand one another. Alone, their level is very low – and yet when the students come together, they play years beyond their ability.

I was still reeling after the audition when the horns came back for a sectional. I identified the student who had struggled the most during the audition and sat down next to her, thinking she would need the additional support. As the horn section began to play the exact passage she had feebly fought through in the audition, I realized that she did not need my help. She played every note correctly.

If I had not had this experience, I am not sure I would believe it had happened. If those same young students had come to me before this experience and said they wanted to play Mahler's First, I would have told them it was not possible, because they could not play it individually. Due to my traditional understanding of how music should be taught and executed, I would have unnecessarily limited their possibilities.

My goal is to one day see a student run YOLA at HOLA better than I ever could. I know that my experiences, knowledge, and education are equally valuable and limiting. It is easy to pass on shortcomings or antiquated ways of thinking about the world. Today, my students are being exposed to musical and leadership opportunities that I did not experience until I was in college. At every turn, the expectations set for the students are exceeded. Trusting our students to achieve things we could not have conceived of at their age is essential. It is how they will one day surpass us.

# CHAPTER 9

# Preparing Musicians to Make a Difference in the World

*Karen Zorn*

LONGY is a music conservatory with a social imperative. We see musicians as agents of change. The musicians we train may or may not pursue a place in the elite upper echelon of the musical firmament, but they *will* seek to find a place and a community of people where they can make an impact, where they are needed, where they can have a meaningful life in music. And our role as mentors and educators is to enable them to decide for themselves what a meaningful life in music looks like, and give them the tools to make it a reality. The musicians we train will not only help transform the way we define the role of musicians in society, but they will have the skills to engage new audiences, transforming their lives in the process.

But how do we prepare our students for a world that is almost certain to change in ways we are unable to imagine today? How do we ensure that the education they receive has a shelf life and isn't bogged down by unexamined tradition or is merely reflective of the most recent entrepreneurial trend? These questions are of course not exclusive to the field of music education. But in grappling with them, as a music conservatory with a long and venerable history, Longy faced some challenges and assumptions unique to its discipline and shared by many of its peers:

*Lack of public arts funding has made engagement with classical music an ever more elite pursuit, available only to the few with means of access.* It has become a truism in some quarters that classical music is in danger, with audiences and performing opportunities dwindling because of its increasing exclusivity.

188

There is certainly no denying the cut in public arts funding and its impact. But if we as musicians and educators want to ask our students in good conscience to dedicate their lives to this path, we need a better method of preparing them for the current musical landscape. We need to prepare them for the life they are likely to live as musicians in the real world.

*Even though teaching is a part of nearly every professional musician's life, students in the conservatory historically have been given little opportunity to develop skills or gain experience as teachers.* Since teaching has been a part of the life of a musician for as long as there have been musicians, why not prepare them for this aspect of their musical lives as well?

*Success is almost always measured by the scope of a musician's performing career, and becoming a music teacher is too frequently seen as a "Plan B" for when that performing career is not successful or no longer satisfying.* Or, to boil it down to a pernicious cliché: "Those who can't do, teach." As musicians, we know the profound impact our own teachers had on our lives, both personally and artistically. So why does this false dichotomy continue to exist in many parts of the musical establishment? To be a complete musician *is* to be a teacher – performing and teaching are two sides of the same coin.

The process of clearly identifying and acknowledging these challenges, some of which were operating as hidden assumptions, enabled us to begin imagining a different path. We realized that by viewing the classical music landscape in terms of dwindling opportunities, we were actually viewing the issue through the wrong end of the telescope. Instead of thinking that the world was increasingly rejecting something that we as classical musicians had to offer, we decided to take a fresh, hard look at the world around us and identify what the world actually does want and where musicians actually are needed. From that point of view, the possibilities for our conservatory students were actually expanding. It then became a matter of identifying those areas where we were already preparing our students for the opportunities available, and those for which a different educational approach might be necessary. Looking back, it seems now quite simple. By re-examining our assumptions and rethinking our identity as a conservatory, we merely decided to catch up to the world in which our students are actually living.

One of the first significant steps Longy took as we moved from ideas to action was the implementation in 2006 of a school-wide Teaching Artist Program. This one-year curriculum, a requirement for all conservatory students, is designed to give them the skills and understanding necessary to create engaging musical experiences for anyone: those who may already be interested in music, as well as those who may feel intimidated or uncertain. Under the guidance of faculty mentors, Longy students design and implement musical projects in a range of community venues that include schools and community centers, hospitals, prisons, and shelters. Requiring this curriculum of all conservatory students enables us to reach those students who need this type of inquiry the most, but might not choose it for themselves. Our students will need to navigate life outside the conservatory eventually, and it is better to expand their options as artists while they are students and they can benefit from the support of their mentors and peers. The Teaching Artist Program sits at the center of conservatory life at Longy, and each student graduates with a Teaching Artist Certificate that acknowledges the real-life experience of their community engagement through music. Many of our graduates say that the thing they rely on the most when they begin to build a life in music after graduation is the set of skills they developed as teaching artists while students at Longy.

## Seeking Broader Reform

This emphasis on teaching and community engagement is not merely an "add-on" to Longy's existing conservatory curriculum. Instead, these aspects are an integral part of our definition of what it means to be a musician. After the success of our Teaching Artist Program, we began to explore how Longy could make an even greater impact. We were of course acutely aware of the decline of music education programs in public schools over the past few decades, the result of which has been music education becoming more and more elite. This is not just a public school problem, or an unfortunate but non-essential characteristic of the current landscape. It is an issue that should be on the mind of every music conservatory, because this reduction in the number of individuals well versed in the fundamentals of music affects the entire musical ecosystem in the United States. It has a direct impact on the number of teachers, the number of audience members – and yes, the number of potential conservatory students – in the future.

So with an eye to music education reform, we began to explore a new kind of teaching degree – one that was consistent with our definition of the complete musician. One that combined the roles of performer and teacher in equal measure. One that continued to develop the identity of the musician as performing artist, and the identity of the teacher as researcher and creative explorer. Not a musician who studied methods, but a musician who could stand in front of a disparate group of students and see kaleidoscopic possibilities. Who could take ten flutes, two guitars, and a singer and make music. And in the process, also effect change in the lives of people and communities.

With this mission in mind, it made perfect sense that Longy found the work of El Sistema compelling, in both its commitment to social justice and its spectacular results. In our search to identify the right role for Longy in the El Sistema field, we discovered a clear need; there weren't enough teachers with the array of skills required by an El Sistema-based approach to teaching music and addressing issues of social justice. Among those who were already teaching in Sistema-inspired programs, some were struggling to re-invent the traditional teaching approaches with which they were familiar, while others were looking for peers in the field from whose experience they could benefit. And so the Master of Arts in Teaching (MAT) in Music came into focus. The MAT is an innovative teaching degree that provides Longy with the opportunity to support existing Sistema-inspired programs, helps pave the way for growth in the field, and – because it confers a K-12 teaching credential, enabling our graduates to teach in public school classrooms – has the potential to reform public music education in the United States.

The MAT, based on the model created by Bard College, uses the "teaching hospital" approach, meaning that the degree program is embedded in the everyday life of a school or núcleo. We wanted our graduate students to learn the theory in a classroom, walk across the hall to put it into practice, and then return to the classroom to reflect on the experience with their peers and instructors. And with the expansion of the MAT to include a focus on El Sistema, we needed to partner with an existing núcleo that could serve as a learning laboratory for our students. After discussions with the Los Angeles Philharmonic and Heart of Los Angeles (HOLA), we selected Youth Orchestra Los Angeles (YOLA) at HOLA as the site for our Los Angeles MAT program. YOLA is a well-established núcleo that provides community-based music instruction for several hours every day, offering our MAT students extensive opportunities to observe and participate in the life of the núcleo and community. Also, HOLA's community activities take place primarily after school, which meant the center was able to provide classroom space during the day for MAT graduate courses. Faculty was drawn from the local community. Due to the intensity and individual focus of the instruction, the average incoming class is only fifteen to twenty students, and only two administrators are required to oversee the program. With all of these pieces in place, Longy launched the MAT program with a pilot class of five graduate students in January 2013 – and we graduated our first class one year later.

### Characteristics of Longy's MAT Degree Program

*The MAT degree program is an accredited teacher training program.* While the program does emphasize the El Sistema approach, MAT graduates are equally grounded in the traditions of American public school music education and are certified to teach in K-12 public school music programs, whether Sistema-inspired or not. And because of reciprocity agreements with other states, MAT graduates have the opportunity to transfer this teaching credential from the California public school system to the majority of public school systems in the United States. A credential is not, of course, necessary to teach in the majority of community-based El Sistema programs, but we feel it is an important aspect of our program for several reasons. First, the credential expands career opportunities for our graduates. Students in the MAT program may or may not know exactly where they will land after completing the degree program, and having this credential allows them to choose from a wider range of teaching positions. And should one of our MAT graduates choose to teach in a public school, which does require the credential, their position in this setting will come with a salary and benefits – no small thing for someone who has chosen a career in music.

In addition to the opportunities the teaching credential provides our graduates, we feel it can also play an important role both in supporting the growth of El Sistema and in changing the face of public music education in this country. In the current climate of continuous funding cuts, one of the greatest challenges facing any Sistema-inspired community music program is simple sustainability. With little government support for music programs per se, one way to grow sustainable El Sistema programs is for them to become a part of public schools, including charter schools – because with public schools comes public funding. Even if a public school music program is not Sistema-inspired, MAT graduates, as performing artists and teachers trained in the Sistema philosophy and approach, will have an impact on public music education over time, both musically and in terms of strengthening the qualities of citizenship and community.

*The MAT program includes classes in identity formation, cultural competency, and understanding the various social circumstances that comprise student lives.* While these issues are obviously important in Sistema contexts, they are equally important in public school settings. True to the philosophy of El Sistema, we are not just educating our MAT students musically, we are training them to understand and respond to every aspect of the children in front of them.

*By design, the MAT degree is not methods heavy.* An MAT student who arrives as an expert flautist will do more than have a week of instruction in a strings methods course; she has the opportunity for many and varied contexts in which to learn about playing a stringed instrument, arranging for strings, and teaching string instrument basics. For example, over the year-long course of study, our students might: (1) take a lab course where the basics of the various instruments are covered; (2) take studio lessons on a secondary instrument (i.e. in this case, an instrument other than flute); (3) learn from a young string player at YOLA about the basic techniques of her or his instrument; (4) create arrangements of pieces for a variety of instruments; (5) perform colleagues' arrangements on a secondary instrument; (6) work with YOLA students individually and in groups on the various instruments; and (7) have a public school practicum where they observe a variety of approaches for teaching the different instruments. We believe that a simple rotation through a series of instrument methods is not nearly as strong as a multi-experience practical approach where playing, performing, composing, arranging, and teaching with the various instruments happens simultaneously with coursework that addresses the same ideas. Our students come away with an integrated set of practical experiences that informs their individual approaches, rather than as practitioners of a certain methodology.

*The curriculum, being rooted in reflective practice, is a never-ending iterative process, with an enduring shelf life.* MAT students apply what they have learned in their classroom to their practicum teaching, and then convene for a weekly "teaching laboratory" to reflect on their experience with their peers and teachers. After this period of reflection, they return to the classroom and practicum teaching, and then once again join their peers and teachers to reflect on the experience. Through this reflective practice, the teacher develops into a researcher.

*Because the degree is adaptive rather than methods driven, students leave with the ability to think about, analyze, and build their own pedagogical approach*, one that is responsive to the wide range of environments in which they are likely to find themselves over the course of a career. If they someday find themselves in a community that is distinctly different from where they took their MAT training, they will be able to adapt their pedagogy and themselves to the new environment, becoming capable of handling challenges such as working with limited resources or with underserved communities.

*The MAT in Music places equal emphasis on development as a teacher and as an artist.* Coursework includes four graduate-level courses in education and four graduate-level courses in music. The core education courses described below are atypical for music educators, and should give MAT students the flexibility to teach in a wide range of environments.

*Identity, Culture, and the Classroom:* This course focuses on how identity development is influenced by cultural dynamics around factors such as race, gender, sexual orientation, class, ability, ethnicity, and language. An understanding of the ways in which social identity influences experience enables MAT students to see the stories and circumstances that each child brings into the learning environment. Since El Sistema is a movement for social change, this understanding of identity and individual experience is critical for building relationships with students, parents, and the larger community.

*Historical and Social Contexts of Teaching and Learning:* This course explores the many contexts in which current music learning takes place in the United States – e.g., public, private, and charter schools; community music schools and community centers; and now the rapid growth of Sistema-inspired programs. How have the various histories intertwined, conflicted, and caused confusion – as well as created collaboration?

*Learning and Teaching in Music:* This course examines the general conditions that support learning and asks central questions about curriculum design and assessment. It prepares MAT students for the work of planning and instruction as teachers in the public schools, in Sistema sites, and in community programs.

*Language, Literacy, and the Music Learner:* This course begins with the question "What is literacy?" and connects the research in theoretical models of general literacy development to those that are particularly relevant to learning in music. Since a basic principle of El Sistema is inclusion of all ages and abilities, teachers will benefit from understanding the many types of literacy they can expect to encounter in their work, musical and otherwise.

## Sistema Principles Embedded in the Mat Degree Program

In designing the MAT in Music degree, with its emphasis on teaching in Sistema-inspired programs, we embedded as many key Sistema principles in the graduate student experience as possible. Here are some of the core concepts that informed the structure of the degree program:

*The most powerful way you learn to teach is by doing it.* MAT students are introduced to the classroom in the first week, and their teaching and learning take place *simultaneously* for the duration of their degree work. Although their teaching responsibilities increase throughout the year as they gain experience, MAT students are expected from the beginning always to be in the classroom teaching.

Mentoring, a core principle in El Sistema, plays a major role in the life of an MAT student. In addition to mentoring YOLA and public school students as part of their teaching practicum, each Longy student is assigned two mentor teachers: one at YOLA at HOLA and one at an LA County public school. Since their teaching practicums take place in both public school- and community-based Sistema settings, they become familiar with both environments. In the public school, MAT students work with a certified music teacher in a highly regulated setting, the students receive a limited number of hours of instruction per week, and the participation of students is required. At YOLA at HOLA, conversely, MAT students work with music teachers who may or may not have public school certification, in a much more flexible environment; they see the YOLA students every day, and the participation of students in the program is voluntary. This range of experience allows MAT students to recognize for themselves differences and possible crossovers.

Since the degree is not methods driven, learning takes place in an integrated, laboratory-like setting. For example, an oboist will learn the basics of playing the violin by being in the room with students taking violin lessons from a mentor teacher. A violinist will help a fellow MAT student who plays brass write an arrangement for strings. Through learning to teach "on the ground" and encountering a range of real-life teaching situations with the insights of a mentor, MAT students are better able to extrapolate from these experiences and develop teaching strategies of their own.

*Performing and teaching music are inter-related and not separate endeavors.* Longy MAT students receive private instruction from members of the LA Philharmonic, because we believe that feeding the artist also feeds the teacher. A musician's development is never "done," and a high-level performer will always continue to learn. In Sistema-inspired programs, where everyone performs frequently and regularly, students are accustomed to seeing their teachers in multiple roles and contexts: as instructors, life-long students, and performers. Sistema students are also expected to teach their peers from an early age – part of learning something new is to teach it to someone else. So it is important for teachers in Sistema-inspired programs to remain fully engaged with all aspects of their artistry and musical identity. Ideally, an MAT graduate embodies the philosophy of El Sistema by making no real distinction between teaching and performing.

The music courses that make up half of the MAT curriculum are designed to support the MAT students' musical growth, but they are also pedagogically relevant to their work as teachers. For example, the Longy students become musical arrangers. This builds their chops as musicians and gives them a necessary and vital teaching tool. One of the strengths of El Sistema is having students at a variety of levels play together in an ensemble. No matter where they end up teaching, MAT graduates will always be able to accommodate any constellation of student musicians – if faced with a beginning trumpet player and three experienced violinists, their skills in arranging will enable them to integrate the multiple levels and unusual instrumentation into a meaningful musical experience.

*Social change is effected through communities, not individuals in isolation.* Keeping in mind the importance of the ensemble in El Sistema, we placed immersive community experience and engagement at the heart of the MAT degree program. First and most basically, the program itself takes place in the same building as the núcleo. The graduate school experience is fully integrated into the life of the community. Many graduate students also live in the same multicultural neighborhood as the núcleo students, sharing the same benefits and facing the same challenges: its food, festivals, and community-based organizations, as well as its lack of grocery stores, inadequate public transportation, and crime. For those MAT students whose background and experiences are different, engaging with the daily life of the community in this way gives them a deeper understanding of the many contexts in which the students and families live their lives.

## Looking Ahead

When evaluating the MAT degree program, we at Longy intend to invoke the same reflective practice and iterative process that we require of our students. Each graduating class will give us invaluable feedback when they enter the field, letting us know how the MAT education they received prepared them for the life of a teaching artist, and where there is room for improvement. We fully expect to learn as much from our graduates as they have learned from us. The program will undoubtedly change and deepen as a result of the feedback we receive from our students in the field, and this will provide new learning opportunities for future MAT students.

# CHAPTER 10

# How to Create a Classroom Culture That Yields Positive Youth Development

*Nikki Shorts*

I AM a strings teacher and conductor at an El Sistema-inspired program called YOLA at HOLA – a partnership between the Los Angeles Philharmonic's youth orchestra and the community organization, Heart of Los Angeles. All music classes take place at HOLA's site in LA's Rampart District, a community that struggles with an array of social issues including poverty, crime, violence, gangs, drugs, and a lack of resources. Recently, I spoke to my dad about my own experiences as a kid. He has been a probation officer for about twenty years, and worked in a juvenile detention center prior to that. We sometimes get into deep discussions about some of the social implications that affect the communities we work in. My dad sees the end result of what happens in adults for whom there is no successful intervention during the adolescent years. I, on the other hand, work with kids who are supported and steered in a positive direction by me, my colleagues, parents, and other members of the community. And because they are still young, there is good potential for intervention to be successful. This leads me back to why I was reflecting on my own experiences as a child.

My childhood home is in Compton, California, on the outskirts of Los Angeles, a place known for a mixed bag of socioeconomic issues that mirror what's happening in the community where I teach. In the most recent (2012) United States Census, 81 percent of California residents twenty-five years and older were high school graduates, while 30 percent had bachelor's degrees. In comparison, only 59.2 percent of city of Compton residents the same age were high school graduates, with

6.8 percent holding college degrees. I like to keep these facts in mind when I consider that my parents are both African-American and college educated. At eighteen years old, my mom was a single parent living in project housing and on welfare. She went on to complete her bachelor's degree while raising my sister, and (much later in life) earned her MBA while working a full-time job. But during my adolescent years, my mom was a secretary, and (before his job as a probation officer) my dad worked part-time at a grocery store. During this time (in the late 1980s and early 1990s) the city of Compton struggled with drugs, gangs, and political corruption; all of which culminated during the LA Riots of 1992. This outbreak of violence broke down further an already socially and economically oppressed community and caused my parents to be even more diligent with me and my sister. They sent us to school in the neighboring city of Long Beach instead of the struggling Compton Unified School District. Long Beach provided opportunities for sports, music, art, positive role models, and many activities that helped keep us focused and out of trouble.

As a teenager, I became more aware of the difference between the environment where I lived and the environment where I went to school. During my train ride home from high school in Long Beach to my home in Compton, I noticed the progressive deterioration of my surroundings. While on the train, I was often made fun of because I "sounded white" when I spoke, which was detrimental to my legitimacy as a "hood" kid. So, while on the train I would keep to myself, and when I stepped off for the 1-mile walk home, I changed my demeanor and put up an invisible wall of toughness that seemed to protect me.

The combination of these experiences shaped my point of view as I began teaching. I didn't realize it at the time, but as a kid I witnessed firsthand what can happen to a community when its youth are oppressed, misguided, and ignored. This experience became important to the core of who I am today. When I first started teaching, the first hurdle I had to overcome was my own experience with music education. Don't get me wrong, I had a wonderful music education, and I was a good student. I rarely had behavior issues that adversely affected my education, and I had talented teachers whom I admire to this day. So, when I first began teaching, that is how I envisioned things with my own students. But with my first experience teaching in an underserved community, I got a wake-up call. I was helping a friend teach strings to middle school kids in a community like my old neighborhood. I expected students would be respectful and excited about learning a string instrument, as I had been with my teachers. Yet on my first day, students didn't listen and could not have cared less about what I had to say. It was unsettling, and the feeling continued for a few weeks. I was confused: why wasn't my approach working?

This is when I began to examine my thought process about education and what it means to be a teacher. Instead of being upset at how the students were behaving, I began to think about my experience growing up in Compton and began reflecting on my views of teaching. How do I get kids to care about learning music? What motivates a kid to come to my class when he could easily choose to be somewhere else? What will keep him coming back? What skills can I give kids that will not only help them learn music, but also aid them with everyday life? In psychologist Abraham Maslow's "hierarchy of needs," food, water, and safety are basic needs that take precedence over learning the violin. So, how I do get students and their families to care about music class when they're struggling to survive?

The answers to these questions not only allowed me to eventually forge an effective bond with my middle school strings class, but led to me to a teaching philosophy rooted in a foundation of love and a genuine desire to inspire my students to want more for themselves. My philosophy: do whatever it takes to keep them enthusiastic about coming back to class. It's better that students are with me than with someone else who might steer them in a destructive direction. More important than teaching an instrument is helping to develop good human beings who will return to their communities and give back the tools they've been given.

Trying to create a classroom environment that will yield this type of development is no small task. It takes creativity, support, and teamwork from colleagues, and a teacher who is open-minded and willing to try new techniques, and very patient. Though the tools and techniques I use in my classroom vary according to the needs of my students, the focus of this chapter will be:

- Building focus and resilience
- Fostering a balanced student/teacher relationship
- Managing large classes of underserved youth.

**Building Focus and Resilience**

Resilience is a person's capacity to continue on after failure or adversity, the ability to recoup from or adjust quickly to bad luck or sudden change. Some of the factors that make someone resilient include "a positive attitude, optimism, ability to regulate emotions, and the ability to see failure as a form of helpful feedback."* These are precisely the character traits we are trying to build when teaching students how to become resilient.

Meanwhile, getting students in a classroom to *focus* is the ability to help them pay attention to and concentrate on the subject we put before them. Focusing allows most students to absorb efficiently the information being presented to them. Most people (regardless of whether or not they teach) look for physical cues to indicate if someone is focused on what they are saying. One of the biggest indicators are a person's eyes. Is she looking at the music? Is she daydreaming? Are her eyes directed on whomever is speaking? I use these indicators to help me make decisions about how to creatively capture my students' attention and engage them in the process of learning. It's also important to note that one main difference between resilience and focus is that resilience is a character trait, while focus is an action or a tool for learning.

Why is resilience important? The short answer: it's an essential life skill. Every human being faces ups and downs, and our capacity to remain resilient during these experiences helps us press on during the constant changes we confront. But if you work with children whose lives are filled with a significant amount of life stress, resilience has an even deeper meaning. In the neighborhood where I teach, the list of stressors children face every day is long: poverty, hunger, violence, gangs, drug and alcohol abuse, physical abuse, emotional distress. Resilience is both necessary for survival, and integral to success in life; it helps children rise above adverse situations and not become a victim of their surroundings.

Not every community with an El Sistema-inspired program works with children who face such heavy emotional stress, but almost all children – regardless of where they stand socioeconomically – will face some sort of obstacle to their ability to learn. For example, a lot of

---

* "Psych Basics: Resilience" (2014). Retrieved April 14, 2014 from: http://www.psychologytoday.com/basics/resilience

community music education programs take place after school. You might be teaching students who have been in school for a large portion of the day. This fact alone means students are likely experiencing physical or mental fatigue. From problems at school to issues with family, the emotional and physical load a child bears can be of significant weight. At HOLA, my students come after school four days during the school week, and again on Saturday morning. With this type of schedule, helping my students find ways to work through obstacles and be excited about learning is important to their musical and personal growth and to the overall success of the program.

But we should also be careful not to teach kids how to use focus and resilience to ignore their feelings and become workaholics in times of stress. As their mentors, we need to show them not only what it means to persevere, but to take the time to recognize and deal with their feelings during the process. If this is done in a loving way, the classroom can provide a great model for how to be focused and resilient.

The suggestions I offer below for how to build focus and resilience are based on my experience in the classroom. Every classroom environment is different; therefore there isn't a rubric for every situation. It's taken a lot of trial and error and creativity to make some of my bigger class situations successful and fun for my students. My point: do what's best for you and your students.

*1. Find realistic solutions to issues that could be affecting students' ability to focus*
To build resilience, you need to know what type of obstacles students are facing. Once you know those specific issues and challenges, address them in ways that make the most sense for *your* classroom. Some common issues we have to address at HOLA are: mental and physical fatigue, emotional stress, and hunger. Any one of these factors can derail a child's ability to learn, and we've had to be creative in finding solutions. For example, after observing mental and physical fatigue, one of my colleagues suggested that we schedule structured games and/or play time during the lesson. The result: lesson time was cut short, but students were far more focused during class, and the time we spent teaching was far more productive. Just knowing they were going to have a mental break caused students to be more willing to concentrate. Not to mention that mental rest from structured learning is essential to overall growth. During the structured

playtime, issues arose including communication, conflict resolution, and teamwork (normal for the elementary age group). The increased arguments and disagreements gave us an opportunity to build teamwork and communication skills, and eventually we included team building activities that were fun but had a greater purpose. Play time became a lesson in building social skills. Students' ability to communicate and work together improved in ways we didn't initially anticipate, all of which improved the overall classroom environment during the regular music lesson. As time went on and these same students got older, their resilience grew and we were able to shorten their play time and eventually remove it all together. Now we address mental and physical fatigue on more of an individual basis. Sometimes students need to rest and sit out for a few minutes. But typically the need lessens as they get older.

HOLA is in what is considered to be a low-income neighborhood, and hungry students is not an uncommon issue for us. If students say they're hungry, we feed them. It's not realistic to ask children to focus if one of their basic needs isn't being met. I recommend speaking with the child's family about it so that you can find a long-term solution for the future, but it doesn't hurt to buy a box of snacks for whenever the issue arises. Your students will love and appreciate you for addressing their needs.

When it comes to emotional stress, be a nurturer. In some situations this might mean talking to a student about what's going on, but at other times a child is not ready or able to verbalize her feelings. In response, find ways to bond that don't require kids to verbally express how they're feeling. For example, giving a student a special responsibility in the classroom can be a great solution. I've asked students to sharpen pencils, clean the white board, organize music, and set up chairs and stands. Most of the time they enjoy this because I (their mentor whom they look up to) asked them to do it; and we get to spend some one-on-one time together. I'll ask them about their day, what type of activities or subjects they like, and generally just get to know them. They love to help because it makes them feel special. When the student goes home at the end of the day, the feelings of sadness or anger might return, but at least those feelings have subsided for a short time while with me. They begin to associate feeling special and feeling important with being at HOLA in my classroom. I've found that after one or two days of allowing them to help me around my classroom, most students feel more comfortable opening up emotionally. Other tools like hugs, high fives, thumbs up, a proud pat on the back, a loving smile, or a special handshake are ways to communicate love and care. Giving that simple love and attention makes them want to keep coming back. Then, when you ask something of them (including to focus) they want to do it because it's a way to honor the relationship you've built with them. One note of caution: I am not a trained counselor or social worker, so if I ever sense a student needs more emotional support than I can give her or him, I'll mention it to my program director and we will work together to try and find the support needed. It's important to know when what we have to offer as teachers is not enough. Be willing to ask for additional help and support.

### 2. Be engaging: strike a balance between learning and having fun

When a child is engaged during the lesson, learning is a fun experience. If learning is fun, their ability and willingness to stay focused increases. From the student's point of view, building resilience seems effortless when they're having a blast. But being an engaging teacher requires practice and creativity. Here are few tools that can help:

*Engaging repertoire:* Find music students can connect with. It will keep them engaged and excited about learning. Sometimes they connect with classical music standards, but they might connect even more with pop tunes or other genres. Be willing to step outside your comfort zone. Experiment and find what works best for your students.

*Excitement and passion from the teacher:* Regardless of the repertoire, if the teacher is excited about the music, students will mimic that excitement. Students usually begin to connect with the music through their teacher's emotional experience of it. And if the teacher is not excited and passionate, students may mimic this indifference.

*Ignite their imagination:* The easiest way for students to emotionally connect is by using their imagination. Tell a story about the music. Use colorful metaphors. Give them some background on the composer's inspiration. Paint a mental picture.

*Intensity and pacing of the lesson:* Be intense and push them to grow, but be nurturing and make sure to give them small mental breaks throughout the lesson. Praise and recognize them for their hard work: the words "I'm proud" go a long way and make hard work seem worthwhile. Find moments to smile and laugh as a way for them to stay connected with you and to allow them to take a mental break from the lesson material.

*Think outside the box:* If you're out of existing ideas, then create something new that will keep them excited about the learning process. Create a musical game. One of my colleagues created her own version of musical jeopardy. It combines fun competition with music notation and history. I play a game I learned from another teacher called "Hot and Cold." Hide an item somewhere in the classroom. Choose a student to find the item. Using dynamics, the rest of the students help their classmate find the hidden item. As one gets closer to the item, students gradually play more loudly. And as one moves away from the hidden item, students play more softly. Students love this game, and I even used it as an incentive. If they accomplished a particular goal, they got to play "Hot and Cold." My point: try something new or do something that's never been done before.

### 3. The tools needed to focus require practice

Learning how to focus and be resilient takes practice. Give them tools, and practice using those tools in class. An example of a tool that keeps my string students focused is "shadow bowing." During rehearsals when I need to rehearse with only one section of the orchestra, the remainder of the ensemble sitting idly is prone to lose focus without any activity to keep them engaged. To counteract possible boredom, I instruct the rest of the group to put their bow in the crease of their elbow (for cellos, across their lap) while I'm working with the other section of the orchestra. Though they're not to make any sound, they follow along, moving their fingers and gliding their bows along the crease of their elbow. This keeps them from mentally checking out.

Eventually I wanted my students to make the choice to use "shadow bowing" by themselves, which meant we had to work on identifying moments when they could choose to shadow bow without having to be told or directed. This gave them a clearer idea of times when they might easily lose focus, and how to respond to prevent that. A further advantage to "shadow bowing" is that it is not only a tool to help retain focus, but constitutes actual practice (even if silent).

One of the biggest challenges is getting my six- and seven-year-olds to read and track the music as they play. This is sometimes associated with a bigger issue, namely their ability to read and write. Some of my students have trouble tracking and following along when reading books, and the same happens when reading music. This difficulty can lead to a lack of engagement, a lack of focus, and eventual behavior problems. To help avoid this, I have students sit in pairs with one pointing to the music, helping to track the notes, while the other child plays his instrument. This not only teaches kids how to focus and track the music without getting lost, it also reinforces teamwork.

**Fostering a Balanced Student/Teacher Relationship**
The most effective tool for building any skill, including focus and resilience, is a strong bond between student and teacher. In Maslow's hierarchy of needs, the third level after physiological and safety needs is love and belonging. Love and belonging is tied to our interpersonal relationships. Students who have a strong bond with their teacher are more likely to stay focused, resilient, and dedicated because of that relationship.

I've heard the phrase: "students do not need a friend, they need a teacher." I don't think the role of a teacher is so black and white, and can in fact be found somewhere in the middle. A teacher is a *mentor* – someone respected for wisdom and experience yet with the ability to love and nurture within clear boundaries. For example, I'm a mentor to my fifteen-year-old niece. We have a tight and special bond that includes a balance between respect and love. My actions have shown her that I am stable and reliable. She feels safe sharing her feelings with me because I've given her the emotional space to express herself without feeling judged. In other words I've earned her *trust*. The primary difference between my niece and my students is that with my students I am much more careful to have clear and concrete boundaries as to what I share.

Also, my personal experience as a kid has fueled my desire to build strong relationships with my students. I remember what it felt like to be a kid whose feelings and whose voice was not being heard. Many times, I just wanted someone to listen, to hear me, to help me feel less invisible. So, it's important that I provide a safe space for my students to be heard.

*1. Follow through*
When you say you're going to do something, do it. Students need to

know they can rely on you. If you aren't able to follow through on something you promised, apologize. Explain that you're human, you make mistakes, but will do your best to remedy whatever the situation is. Along these lines, if I'm unsure about being able to provide something, I'm honest about it with my students. It took me some time to practice not making promises I can't keep. I'm a people pleaser, and sometimes say I can give more than I actually can. But I'm aware of it, and try to be honest about my limitations.

*2. Be on time, be prepared, be reliable*
At YOLA at HOLA, our students' parents work hard to provide for their children. Sometimes, this includes working multiple jobs that might cause them to be absent in some way. This is why the phrase "it takes a village to raise a child" resonates with me. As their teacher, mentor, and community member, we are a part of their village. Even a small action of support can mean a lot to a child. That being said, the number one way to show students you don't care is to show up late and unprepared. Students need to know you want to give them your absolute best. They need to know that even if their day was chaotic, they can come to you and things will be stable because you've shown them day-in and day-out that they can count on you. Without realizing it, they will begin to rely on your stability. Try not to be another adult in their lives who is unreliable. If you fail to be on time, be prepared, and give your best, show your students you're human and apologize. Tell them that tomorrow you will be better, because they deserve the best. And then do it. In this way, you are mentoring by example.

*3. Show them you care*
Everyday at the beginning of class my students form a tuning line next to the piano. As I tune their instruments, I use my sixty seconds of interaction with the students to make them smile, giggle, and feel loved. If a student was absent the day before, I smile and say, "You're important to your classmates and to me, so when you're absent, I notice. Is everything okay?" After this introduction, students will usually dish pretty quickly about why they were absent. As for my very young paper violin students (five- and six-year-olds), I give each a high five when I hand them their paper instrument. Sometimes a few of them will poke the center of my

palm with their miniature fingers instead of giving a high five, and everyone giggles. A very silly, but important bonding moment. They've come to rely on my high fives so much that when I forget they remind me and run back for it!

### 4. *Allow room for self-expression*

When I was a kid, my parents divorced. There were times when I felt alone in the experience, and sometimes I was caught between the high running emotions of my parents. I was often afraid to speak to my parents (or anyone) about how I felt. As a young musician, my viola became my voice. My instrument could express things that I wasn't able to verbalize yet. It allowed me to open up and be vulnerable in a way nothing else could. A child who doesn't have a positive outlet for self-expression may express sadness or rage in ways that are destructive. This could include physical or verbal violence. So, give your students a place where they feel heard. For some teachers this might mean to carve out time in the lesson to sit with students and give them time to speak about their thoughts and feelings. For other teachers, this might mean using the emotions behind the music as a form of expression. Either way, help your students find their voice.

Having a strong and balanced bond with students has another benefit: more successful classroom management. Usually, when the relationship is strong, students will listen and honor what you ask of them because they care about you and respect you. This is especially helpful with students who struggle with behavior issues. Behavior is a choice. So, making the right choice and accepting the consequences of a poor choice is a lot easier when students trust, respect, and care about you. Then again, kids still have to learn how to choose to do what's right. It's one thing for someone to tell them what they should do, it's another for them to actually feel internally that the choice is right. Even if you have a strong relationship with students, guiding them through how and why to make good behavior choices is important. For example, I'll ask students, "Before we begin today's rehearsal: What type of behavior have we been trying to improve? Why does an orchestra have these standards of behavior?" These types of discussions help kids understand that the teacher isn't a dictator-like authority, that there is a purpose behind the rules and expectations.

**Managing Large Classes of Underserved Youth**

People often ask me about my classroom management techniques, particularly in medium to large group settings with kids who have challenging behavior issues. Though teaching and classroom management is something that feels natural to me, trial and error has been my most valuable learning tool in this area.

The biggest tool in classroom management is the teacher's relationship with her students. If you've earned their trust and respect and they are excited about learning, they will honor the behavior you ask of them. I'm now at a point where I feel comfortable working with a medium to large group of students without additional support from other adults. But in the beginnings of my teaching career, it felt overwhelming and sometimes even chaotic. In order for this overwhelming feeling to lessen, I had to be patient and try multiple approaches.

Recently, I acquired a new ensemble with about sixty-five students between the ages of seven and fifteen who are all at different levels of playing ability. They all play different instruments (recorders, winds and brass, percussion, and strings). There is no repertoire (let alone a rubric for behavior, focus, and resilience) for this type of classroom setting. This has proven a true test of my abilities to manage a classroom full of squirrely, beginning-level musicians.

*1. Manage the classroom by helping kids learn how to manage themselves*
There is only one of you, and a lot of them. In large ensembles the idea of the teacher having to manage every aspect of the classroom is not realistic. In fact, trying to do so can cause classroom behavior to derail. Instead, establishing clear routines and expectations for students to carry out on their own positively affects their behavior and lessens the teacher's stress level. So, at the beginning of the quarter/semester, make sure to create and practice routines. Here are a few I find integral to this process:

*Transitions to and from class.* What are the behavioral expectations while students are entering and exiting the classroom? Do they know where to sit? How and where do students unpack their instruments? How are their instruments being tuned? Do students know what music and equipment they need? The easiest way to make this smooth is to use tools that require very little explanation. For example, name tags or some other easy-to-remember seating system are the easiest way for students to find their seats without having to ask. Writing an agenda or list of items needed for rehearsal is a simple way to avoid confusion in preparing for rehearsal. I use a "checklist" of items and behavioral expectations that students read when entering the room. If students ask, "What music do I need?" I respond, "Please read the board. It has a list of everything you need to know before rehearsal starts." Eventually, they become so used to this routine that questions and confusion lessen.

*Responsibility.* Kids want to be trusted with responsibility. So, give it to them. They take pride in that responsibility, it keeps them connected to their environment, and they tend to take better care of the classroom. With my forty-piece string ensemble (ages eight to thirteen) I used a "Classroom Duties" pocket chart with specific duties for clean-up. The duties included: stacking chairs and stands, organizing name tags and seating charts, collecting pencils, organizing music folders, picking up lost items, collecting and counting pencils, etc. The duties rotated on a weekly basis. About six to eight months later, my students no longer needed the chart. But if any issues arise, I resurrect the chart and we revisit the expectations for classroom clean-up.

Having these types of routines in place not only allows class to begin and end smoothly. As an added bonus, whenever I have a substitute teacher, the students need very little direction with routines, and will often direct the substitute themselves!

## 2. Be conscious of how you use your voice

A few years ago, I was introduced to the concept of non-verbal classroom management through the ENVoY program ("Educational Non-Verbal Yardsticks") from Michael Grinder & Associates. During an observation, ENVoY trainer Lynn Williams noticed that I use my voice a lot. She didn't say it was wrong, but she noticed how much I use it and how my voice carries even when managing large ensembles. I was open and intrigued by her feedback, so I started to pay more attention and came to the same realization. So I asked my students "Do you think my voice is loud? Does it bother you?" Their response was an exuberant "Yes!" It's possible they were even annoyed by it (one student said, "Sometimes your voice hurts my ears"). After being humbled by this group of eight- to ten-year-olds, I chuckled and asked them to help me work on how I use my voice. We made a pact: I would try my best to keep down the volume when I spoke, and they would help by giving me their attention right away and not talking or making noise while I was giving directions. They agreed, and when they became aware that they weren't able to hear my lower, softer speaking voice, they made a real effort to uphold their end of the bargain. They even started to manage themselves, saying to each other, "I can't hear Ms. Nikki. Can you please stop talking?" Because I listened to their gripes about my loudness and responded with a reasonable solution, my students became more invested in helping me solve the problem. With large groups of students, we generally tend to use a louder voice. But when you speak with a softer voice, they will listen more intently.

### 3. Have clear and manageable "quiet" signals

In a group setting, the amount of sound from instruments and voices is often too much for one voice to speak over. As is clear from the preceding, I have a loud voice – but have still failed many times to get my students' attention. Sometimes, the loudness of my voice will cause the overall noise to increase. Once I became more conscious of this, I felt it was important to have signals that don't involve my voice at all. Having a signal that's easy for kids to recognize is crucial. When my students were young and new to a large ensemble setting, I used a gourd shaker for my quiet signal. The sound was distinct enough to be audible even with a lot of other sound in the room. Shaking it meant students were to be quiet and sit in rest position. When I first used the shaker, we had to practice a few times before my kids remembered what it meant. Within a few months, all I had to do was put the shaker in my hand (without making any sound) and they knew to get quiet. After about six months of this routine we graduated to a more simple gesture. Stepping on to the conductor podium or simply raising my hand is now their signal to quiet down. Helpful hint: If you are having trouble implementing your quiet signals, try including some incentives (points, pencils, stickers, high fives, thumbs up, etc.) when students respond quickly to your signals.

### 4. Rules and expectations that make sense

It's always important to have rules, but they don't carry any weight if students don't know what they mean and why we enforce them. Make sure to discuss the importance of each rule and its role in the learning process. Why do we sit quietly in rest position while someone is speaking? Why is it important that everyone moves to rest and play position together as one unit? What does respect mean? Why are there consequences for making a behavioral choice that is detrimental to the class? Having answers to these questions will help students better understand why they are being disciplined and prevent power struggles between the teacher and the student. Disciplining students is a less dramatic experience if they understand your reasons for doing so.

### 5. *Positive reinforcement always prevails*

Some students use negative behavior to get attention. Constantly responding to their attempts just adds fuel to the fire. My advice: calmly address their behavior only a few times during the lesson, then ignore it. Instead, keep the focus on the students who are making good behavior choices. Give them a lot of recognition and praise. The rest of the class will recognize the type of behavior that is most beneficial to their learning and to their relationship with their teacher. Eventually, the student who is used to acting out will see that his tactics are not working. And once a student has decided to make a change for the better, recognize him for it and let him know you are proud of him. Even if it's for something small. Once I had a student for whom going ten minutes without being disruptive was an achievement. When it happened, I would say to him, "You seem to be having a much better day. I'm proud of you. Keep up the good work." Eventually, ten minutes turned into twenty, and before long he could go an entire class without acting out. Since we often check in with parents about negative behavior, and fail to share the positive, I made an effort to share with the student's family the improvement in behavior. When my troublesome student saw his mother smile after I told her, he beamed with pride.

It's also important to make an effort to include positive reinforcement *before* a student starts acting out. Find something small that can create a positive interaction with the student. It might seem a little silly, but before class begins, I might say things like "I like your shirt," "cool shoes," or ask "How was school?" or "How was your day?" This type of proactive positive interaction can prevent attention-seeking negative behavior and strengthen the bond between teacher and student.

If you sense a power struggle behind a student's acting out, respond with logic, not power. For example, you might say, "The rules are A, but you chose to do B. So, C is the consequence for the choice you made." Keep your voice low, don't show anger or frustration, and keep a soft but firm tone. If a student resists the consequence, ignore her and deal with it later. Do not get into a power struggle. Instead, continue to positively reinforce the students who are doing the right thing. I have a strong personality, and I have experienced the infamous power struggle (and it sometimes still happens). But by keeping my cool and focusing on students who are making good choices, I'm able to nip it in the bud.

### 6. Take breaks

When learning, our brains need moments of rest. This helps us recuperate. from With younger children, playing a game or moving to music is a great way to breathe out. With any age group, a bathroom or water break is another simple way. Sometimes I ask students to sit in "lazy position" (slouch in their chairs) for a moment and take a few deep breaths to help them relax. Or I give them time to interact with each other, like practicing with their neighbor. Sometimes even giving students a few minutes to practice individually is a good way to break up the monotony of the regular lesson. Mix up your activities. If students have been rehearsing for a while, try listening to a recording of the music for a few minutes instead. Regardless of how or what you do, giving students little breaks will help their behavior.

### 7. Incentives and games

Incentives and games are useful when behavior fatigue rears its head part way through the semester. At YOLA at HOLA, the biggest behavioral challenges appear during the month of in-school state testing, when students are stressed and mentally fatigued. Any musical game or fun activity keeps the kids excited about learning. Lynn Williams (my ENVoY trainer) calls it "dessert." She writes the agenda on the board, and the playful item at the bottom of the list of tasks is "dessert."

### 8. Allow students to contribute their ideas

Students who have a say in what's happening in class are more connected to their learning. This is especially helpful with rules and expectations. If you're dealing with difficult students, have a discussion in which they get to create the rules. You add teacher input and they add student input. Also, try giving them a say in what they're learning – you write the list of material you need to cover, but let them choose the order in which to learn it. When I needed to create behavior incentives for my new sixty-five-piece beginning full orchestra, I asked students to help me brainstorm ideas for behavioral incentives. They gave their ideas as to what kind of behavior they need to exemplify in order to win a particular prize. As a result, my students were excited to improve their behavior.

### 9. Recognition, recognition, recognition!

When the group improves their behavior, give them recognition. On a basic level, positive reinforcement helps the overall group morale, but you can also help them notice how much more they learn when everyone has made a good behavior choice. This way good behavior is connected with better learning.

### 10. Be creative – think outside the box

Sometimes all the tools we have in our bag of classroom management tricks just aren't enough. If a solution doesn't exist, create one. For example, the difference in ages in my new ensemble of sixty-five students leads to a lot of different behavioral issues happening all at once in the same room. For the youngest students, settling down after transition and tuning time was proving to be a big challenge. The time it took to transition to class and tune was eating into our rehearsal time.

In response, I invented a way of reinforcing the behavior I expect from the younger kids. After tuning time, the younger students were instructed to sit in a special area of the room (called the "tacet" or quiet corner), away from everyone else, and near a white board on which their names were written. While they were sitting in the tacet corner, I began rehearsing with the older students. A volunteer or other staff member watched the behavior of the younger students and once a student was sitting quietly and was focused on the rehearsal that had already begun, the volunteer would draw a smiley face next to his or her name. They would start with two dots for eyes and as a student continued to show readiness for rehearsal, the volunteer would draw a mouth and then eventually a circle to complete the full smiley face. The completed smiley face was the student's signal to walk quietly to join rehearsal. If at any later point the young kids became disruptive, I asked them to return to the volunteer and earn a new smiley face.

This routine allowed the older students to focus at the beginning of rehearsal without the distraction of the younger students, and set a tone of behavior that was much more conducive to learning. For the younger students, it reinforced the need for them to tailor their behavior to the expectations I'd set before them. And, being kids, they were glad to sit out for a few minutes and take a break to compose themselves. No one told me about this classroom management tool. I just saw a problem and created a solution. If this new solution hadn't worked, I would have tried something else.

★  ★  ★

Whenever I am searching for information to help grow my teaching skills, I like to keep in mind this quote: "Take what you like, and leave the rest." I certainly don't have all the answers, so even if you dislike every idea I've presented, let that indifference be a catalyst for you: an indicator that you can give something better than I can. Haim G. Ginott, author of *Between Parent and Child* (1965), once said:

> I've come to a frightening conclusion that I am the decisive element in the classroom. It's my personal approach that creates the climate. It's my daily mood that makes the weather. As a teacher, I possess a tremendous power to make a child's life miserable or joyous. I can be a tool of torture or an instrument of inspiration. I can humiliate or heal. In all situations, it is my response that decides whether a crisis will be escalated or de-escalated and a child humanized or dehumanized.*

I agree with Ginott's notion that the level of power we have to affect a child's life can be frightening. Yet, I've come to learn that this fear is an indicator of something bigger within me. It has caused me to do a humbling amount of self-reflection on what I say, what I do, and why I do it.

When I think about my experience growing up in my old neighborhood, I remember what it looks like when there is a community that

---

* Ginott, Haim G., *Between Parent and Child*. Retrieved April 14, 2014 from:
  http://www.goodreads.com/author/show/212291.Haim_G_Ginott

ignores the needs of its youth. Across the street from our afterschool program at YOLA at HOLA, there's a park that is always active and full of people. The experiences to be had there can lead to an array of life choices. Some good, and some not so good. Instead of choosing to participate in the not so good, my students decide to spend their time with me learning music. I think about how difficult it might have been to make that choice. I want students to continue to return to my classroom with an excitement for learning and a desire to continue building the relationships that help them feel good about their choice to do something positive with their time. Therefore, I will do whatever needs to be done. If this means feed them, then so be it. If it means my lesson is cut short because they need a break, then that's what I'll give them. If they need someone to confide in, I will be that person. A teacher's role is not arbitrary. It is vital to the growth and success of every community. It takes a village to raise a child, and we are the part of the village that educates, loves, and inspires our future leaders to become more.

# CHAPTER 11

# The Importance of Story in Teaching

## *Loralie Heagy*

WHILE visiting El Sistema initiatives in Venezuela as a Sistema Fellow, I witnessed Gustavo Dudamel use storytelling to help connect members of the National Children's Symphony of Venezuela to a challenging passage they were rehearsing in Mahler's Symphony No. 1. He explained that the first few phrases were like the protestations of a young girl turning down the advances of a young man, but in the final passage she could no longer resist and the couple falls madly in love. Dudamel's expressions of the starry-eyed lovers made this orchestra of adolescents burst out laughing. But when asked to play the passage again, they did so to perfection with Dudamel's story running through their minds and fingers.

Now travel to Juneau, Alaska several months later. I had just founded an El Sistema-inspired program called Juneau, Alaska Music Matters (JAMM) at a Title I school where all sixty kindergartners receive 90 minutes of violin instruction during the week. In kindergarten, JAMM is an in-school program that serves as an intervention for school readiness skills including focus, self-confidence, family connection to school, and the understanding that it takes hard work and teamwork to accomplish something great. Over 40 percent of our students are eligible for free and reduced lunch. It's late afternoon, and as the school's music teacher, I am trying to focus a classroom of twenty-five kindergartners on their "bumpy thumb" to help them with their bow hold. Focusing so many little ones on such a subtle detail is no easy feat, so how do you make a bow-hold exercise engaging so that they'll practice it on their own at home? The answer: Turn it into a story, just like Dudamel did. For a classroom of kindergartners, a story about teenage angst won't hold their interest, but one about animals will. And to me, a bow hold looked like a fox!

From that one connection came a whole host of creative activities that motivated young children to practice their bow hold accurately and often – beyond the music classroom, into the school halls, and at home. Story helps personalize, make relevant, and create an emotional connection to what can otherwise be abstract and uninteresting practice. Instead of making it a rote exercise with no connection, we activated their imaginations: a fox with a song to accompany him. Why a fox? A fox can have a life of its own, while a bow hold remains rather stagnant. A fox can interact anytime, anywhere, while a bow hold is more specific to the music class.

For example, instead of quietly waving to a student in the hallway, I encourage my kindergartners to use the "secret hello" by showing Mr. Fox (a.k.a. bow hold) to me. Their bow hold becomes a secret handshake, which makes this violin skill relevant to young children. In doing so, I have the chance to reinforce proper bow hold technique throughout the day. Every time I see a kindergartner walking in the hall, eating lunch, or run into them at the grocery store, I am encouraging them to practice their violin skills outside of the classroom. When sharing this teaching practice at a teaching artists workshop in Juneau, one of the participants excitedly shouted out, "So that's what Darren has been doing all of this time." Turns out that one of my kindergartners attended her daycare and was talking and singing with Mr. Fox. His bow hold had become a friend of sorts. Mission accomplished! When teachers successfully extend learning beyond the classroom, they have made learning relevant for students and worth repeating several times over. Add a song, and repetition becomes interesting and memorable. This was my kindergartners' first experience with bow hold position – one filled with joy, song, story, and personal connection.

## Why Story?

There is a Scottish riddle: *What lasts forever and is visible but invisible? Is as small as a dot in space and vaster than an ocean? A story.* Kendall Haven (2007) stated: "Evolutionary biologists confirm that 100,000 years of reliance on stories have evolutionarily hardwired a predisposition into human brains to think in story terms. We are programmed to prefer stories and to think in story structures" (p. 14). As 2011 Alaska Teacher of the Year with seventeen years experience in the classroom, I can attest to the power of story to reach every learner. It has been my teaching tool of choice to reduce stress for optimal learning, gain students' attention and keep it, reach all learning styles, and improve memory and recall. For these reasons, I have dedicated most of this chapter to its use.

## Reducing Stress and Priming the Brain for Learning

There is another reason why stories are such an effective teaching tool: they embody the same five factors that get the brain's attention and keep it (Jensen, 1998). These five factors are pattern, novelty, emotion, movement, and relevance. The brain searches for meaning and familiarity through pattern recognition. All stories have a pattern: a beginning, middle, and end. Patterning helps reduce stress when taking in new information and allows the brain to connect new information to an existing framework. This balance of familiarity and novelty serves as the perfect mix for learning. In the classroom, this balancing act means teaching new content with a familiar process, or familiar content with a new process. The remaining factors of emotion, movement, and relevance are equally important. Emotionally charged events etch longer lasting memories with greater accuracy. And as Dudamel demonstrated in his humorous love story, content must be relevant in order to hook an audience. Add motion and students pay even more attention.

## Application to Lesson Planning in the Classroom

Let's return to the kindergarten classroom in Juneau . . .

*The students enter the room while I sing the American folk song, "The Fox Went Out on a Chilly Night." I gesture for them to sit down while I finish singing this song tale.*

- **Teaching point:** Reduce stress during a transition and prime them for new learning.

*After they've heard the song in its entirety, I explain that I'm going to tell them a story. Immediately, I notice their bodies relax, with all eyes focused on me.*

- **Teaching point:** Stories provide pattern, novelty, emotion, relevance, and movement structure for getting the brain's attention and keeping it.

- **Teaching point:** According to Medina (2010), "If information is presented orally, people remember about 10 percent, tested 72 hours after exposure. That figure goes up to 65 percent if you add a picture" (p. 234). Stories are moving pictures in our minds.

*I hold my hand behind my back and whisper that I have a special friend whom I'd like to introduce.*

- **Teaching point:** Balance familiarity with novelty to pique their interest.

*Show them Mr. Fox (my bow hold) and explain that he needs our help bringing home enough kill to feed his family, "eight, nine, ten." Students from our Title I school can relate to parents trying to put food on the table and children want to help! When I asked them if they could help Mr. Fox bring food home to his kits by keeping his jaw open, they were eager to oblige (establish purpose and the big picture).*

- **Teaching point:** Unless you give students the big picture within two minutes time you face the risk of losing a child's focus and will have difficulty regaining it (Medina, 2010). This is one reason why teachers should not take roll the first few minutes of class and should always be prepared. By the time teachers complete attendance or organize their materials, they lose that window of opportunity for hooking a child's attention and priming the class for success. According to Medina (2010), "Your ability to create a compelling introduction may be the most important single factor in the later success of your mission" (p. 116).

*I show the kindergartners how to make a fox with their hand, specifically focusing on the position of the thumb, which now becomes the fox's jaw, jutting out so that he can adequately feed his family. His mouth also makes an "O," which the students heard in the refrain of the song sung earlier as they entered the classroom. (They were primed ahead of time by being sung the song as they entered the class-room, which made new content familiar.)*

- **Teaching point:** The story I developed to help teach bow hold was no masterpiece, but it's short, focused, and draws attention to the important teaching element – maintaining a "bumpy thumb." Make sure your story focuses on your teaching point and that it's relevant to students.

- **Teaching point:** Establish purpose for the student. Recently our school district has been reiterating the importance for teachers to communicate to students the purpose behind every learning activity. But this request overlooks one important question: whose purpose? What makes an activity purposeful for teachers isn't necessarily meaningful to students. I care about students forming a correct habit in holding a bow, but they may not. That's why the purpose I share with students focuses on what they care about – animals, families, and food. Dudamel understood this principle!

*I sing "The Fox Went Out on a Chilly Night" and ask the children to sing the refrain with me. Each time we sing "town-o" the students open the fox's mouth, making sure his jaw makes the "O" shape. To refocus their attention on their bumpy thumb, I ask if the fox's mouth is still wide open (thumb joint is correctly bent). If so, children say, "Take a bow, Mr. Fox" and then rub their bumpy thumb (as though scratching the fox's chin). If the thumb joint is not extended, children point to Mr. Fox and say, "Behave, Mr. Fox," correcting their thumb position. This draws attention to the important element that these young musicians may overlook or find challenging.*

- **Teaching point:** By connecting bow hold practice to a song, the exercise is more interesting and more likely to be repeated at home and remembered throughout the day.
- **Teaching point:** According to Medina (2010), "Memory is enhanced by creating associations between concepts. If we can derive the meaning of the words to one another, we can much more easily recall the details. Meaning before details" (p. 84). Start with the big picture and then hang details on key ideas.
- **Teaching point:** Make the abstract concrete.

Earlier I mentioned that by transforming a bow hold into a fox, teachers bring key concepts and skills to life. The story of Mr. Fox continues . . .

Once students have mastered shaping their right hand into a bow hold, we introduce the pencil to help students take that next step toward holding a bow. The pencil now becomes a bone to help enliven the activity of lifting their thumb off and on the pencil while maintaining a bumpy thumb. This image fittingly relates to the last verse of the folksong, "The Fox Went Out on a Chilly Night," in which the fox family "never had such a supper in their life, and the little ones chewed on the bones-o." But how do you motivate your students to practice this activity at home? Have them introduce Mr. Fox to family and friends by showing them all of the tricks that Mr. Fox can do (sing, roll over, and gnaw on a bone). My students' enthusiasm for and engagement in practicing these rather mundane skills throughout the day remind me that the five factors that capture and keep the brain's attention really do work: pattern, novelty, emotion, movement, and relevance (Jensen, 1998).

**Story Packs a Powerful Punch**

Stories naturally integrate the five attention-getting factors, but also pack a powerful punch because they draw upon all three learning styles: visual, auditory, and kinesthetic (VAK). According to Keefe (1979), learning styles are the "composite of characteristic cognitive, affective, and physiological factors that serve as relatively stable indicators of how a learner perceives, interacts with, and responds to the learning environment" (p. 44). Learning styles are how individuals prefer to learn. Many online resources detail instructional methods tailored to help each specific style of learner, but I prefer to focus on methods that cater to all three: storytelling is one of them.

Stories allow learners to *hear* the emotion, *feel* the emotion, and *see* the emotion. Emotionally charged lessons have a longer lasting effect on memory and are recalled with greater accuracy than neutral memories (Medina, 2010). Visual learners prefer metaphors, pictures, and stories that allow them to see the teacher's enthusiasm through gestures, while auditory learners favor listening to an expressive voice that has emotional intensity. Kinesthetic learners enjoy audience participation and feeling the teacher's enthusiasm. By using story to introduce a lesson, I accomplish several educational outcomes in one activity: reduce stress, make the lesson accessible to all three types of learners, capture and maintain their attention, and create a multi-sensory experience that makes for more accurate and detailed recall.

Although the brain has specialized areas for processing each of the five senses, these areas are strongest and most effective when integrated with another sense: their sum is greater than their parts. According to Medina (2010):

> Groups in the multisensory environment always do better than the groups in the unisensory environments. They have more accurate recall. Their recall has better resolution and lasts longer, evident even 20 years later. Problem solving improves. In one study, the group given multisensory presentations generated more than 50 percent more creative solutions on a problem-solving test than students who saw unisensory presentations (p. 208).

Of all the senses, vision has the greatest impact because of the brain's penchant for color, orientation, size, and objects that move. Storytelling is such an effective tool because it incorporates so many of these brain-compatible strategies. While students hear a story, they are constructing a moving picture in their mind.

If you hear yourself saying, "But I'm not a storyteller," all you need to do is give it a try! Even with omissions, awkward pauses, and mistakes, you'll quickly discover how forgiving students are and how hungry they are for this type of learning. I share this experience because I was that person – fearful of standing in front of a classroom of students without a book or note cards to serve as a crutch. I still remember that day when I made the leap into storytelling. I was an elementary classroom teacher at the time and wanted my students to have an emotional connection to plate tectonics. I decided to share the story of Alfred Wegener, who first proposed the theory of continental drift.

During my telling, nerves caused starts and stops and overlooked details, yet when I looked out at my students, they were hooked! They exhibited what I now call the "storytelling spell" – eyes transfixed on the speaker, bodies relaxed, mouths slightly open, and a silence in the room full of anticipation. I chose Alfred Wegener for a reason: I thought his story would not only connect students to the scientific context, but also to their lives. Here's why: Wegener shared his theory at a Science Conference in 1915 and was ridiculed by his academic peers. My students were shocked to hear that adults would mock a man without considering his ideas. What shocked them even more was to learn that Wegener died never knowing that his hypothesis would be confirmed forty years later. In 1930, he died tragically while on an expedition in Greenland. When I explained that I'd like to create a performance in honor of Alfred Wegener, the kids were already emotionally hooked. Many of these fourth- and fifth-graders could relate to the social injustices that Wegener endured – an adult version of bullying and teasing – and understood the importance of listening to each other's ideas. Students who are now in college can recall that performance and remember the man, Alfred Wegener, who endured ridicule to advance our understanding of how the Earth works.

After that experience, I never looked back. Storytelling has become a mainstay in my classroom. When students hear the words, "I'd like to tell you a story," they immediately relax, focus, and anticipate making enduring connections to their learning. Here are a few examples of how I've used story to introduce new concepts and/or content to help motivate and engage students in the music classroom:

- Describe how Beethoven exhibited true grit, perseverance, and optimism when writing "Ode to Joy" and grappling with the devastating reality of being deaf.
- Describe how Joe Juneau (the founder of our Alaskan town) must have felt when he entered the local dance hall in 1880 after prospecting for months in the unforgiving outdoors and was greeted by the festive music of Offenbach's "Galop Infernal" (can-can).
- When trying to focus young musicians' attention on the accurate positioning of their fourth finger, encourage them to "give pinkie a chance by setting it up for success with an elbow up and forward." All students can relate to being ignored and when finally getting a chance to play, they want to be successful.
- Introduce rhythmic notation as a "Rhythm Family." A quarter note serves as older brother Ta, who sets the rules (or beat) for everyone else in the family, including his little twin sisters: Ti-ti. You can identify both family members by the way they look. Older brother Ta stands straight. The twins also stand tall because they try to imitate their older brother, but you can tell them apart because the twins have their arms around each other. They are also twice as fast as their older brother with that nagging non-stop energy and nipping at his heels, always wanting to play. Now and then, the twins will let go of each other. When that happens you can find them in the music searching and reaching out for one another (the flag) in the house (measure).

## Stories Create Episodes

Let us return to that moment in Caracas when Dudamel rehearsed Mahler's Symphony No. 1 with the National Children's Symphony of Venezuela. How is it that I still remember that specific moment of the rehearsal conducted over five years ago? We know that story reduces stress, which is a necessary component for the brain's ability to process new learning. We also know that storytelling naturally integrates the five factors responsible for gaining and sustaining the brain's attention, and also addresses simultaneously the three learning styles. Yet there is one more important reason why Dudamel's story sticks so vividly in my mind: he created an episode, and episodes easily lend themselves to forming a powerful type of memory called *episodic memory*. According to Jensen (1998), "Episodic memory has unlimited capacity, forms quickly, is easily updated, requires no practice, is effortless, and is used naturally by everyone" (p. 106). Why? Because all learning is contextual. When learning is directly linked to a specific location, emotion, and strong sensorial associations, it becomes more distinct, accurate, and memorable. This is another reason why I intentionally try to segment the lesson by changing location (or at least orientation), sensorial input, and mood for each activity. Just imagine the last time you listened to a forty-five-minute lecture, during which all of the information originated from a single podium with one speaker. Can you distinguish key talking points or did they all blur together? Change of location not only helps segment learning into meaningful episodes, but change of speaker does as well. This is one reason why peer teaching and co-teaching are such powerful teaching practices: each new speaker creates a new episode of learning. By telling a story of two young lovers, Dudamel created an episode rich with intense emotion and multi-sensory associations. He also initiated something that every teacher needs to do in order to be successful in the classroom: build meaningful relationships with your students. Storytelling is one way to help make that connection.

## References

Haven, Kendall. *Story Proof: The Science Behind the Startling Power of Story.* Westport, CT: Greenwood Publishing Group, 2007.

Jensen, Eric. *Teaching with the Brain in Mind.* Alexandria, VA: Association for Supervision and Curriculum Development, 1998.

Keefe, J. W. "Learning Style: An Overview." NASSP's Student Learning Styles: Diagnosing and Proscribing Programs (pp. 1–17). Reston, VA: National Association of Secondary School Principals, 1979.

Medina, John. *Brain Rules: Twelve Principles for Surviving and Thriving at Work, Home, and School.* Seattle: Pear Press, 2010.

CHAPTER 12

# An Expedition–Based Approach to Leadership and Group Dynamics

*Rebecca Reid Sigel*

AT the National Outdoor Leadership School (NOLS) students are immersed with a group on multi-week backcountry expeditions, wherein leadership skills are learned and applied in the high-stakes context of wilderness. When a NOLS student group goes into the wilderness for weeks or months, they take on a curriculum developed around nurturing leadership and group dynamics through the application of real back-country situations. When a student's only resources are the pack on her back and the finite group of people around her, she learns to be adaptive in interacting with the unexpected. Each turn in the weather or change in physical ability requires that the group make new decisions. These decisions – alongside the safe failures and successes that often ensue – are put in the hands of students, in an effort to develop the skills of leadership.

At eighteen, while a student participant in a semester-long NOLS course, I kept a journal in which I documented each and every day in painstaking detail: the trails, the conversations, the decisions, the frustrations, the fun, and the food. At the same time, the journal tracks my path from student learner to student leader, a transition I identify as beginning on October 9, 2006, in the Gila Wilderness of New Mexico:

> Today was an eventful day. It took us a while to get out of camp. My group (Alex, John, Kate, Van) was supposed to leave at 9:00 but ended up leaving around 10:00, after waiting a long time for Alex to pack. (It's getting annoying, dragging him along.) Once we got to the long ridge walk, we could see some ominous clouds. The instructors had warned us that thunderstorms were likely to roll in

227

later in the day; if we hadn't gotten such a late start and hiked so slowly, we would have gotten off the ridge with plenty of time.

It started to hail so we all pulled out our raincoats but kept going. Then the lightning got within a mile, so we scattered and got in lightning position. After a half hour of sitting, crouched and tense in freezing hail with lightning right on top of us, we were all frozen. The lightning moved away before the hail did, so we were able to get out of lightning position and set up a tent to warm up in. I had enough sense to make some hot tea for all of us and tell everyone to get out of their drenched clothes. Alex, John, and Van refused to change their clothes, but they did it in this weird, lazy way that made me remember what they'd taught us about hypothermia: that one of the beginning signs of hypothermia is that you won't be willing to put in a little bit of physical effort and temporary coldness, even if it means getting warmer in the long-term. They were definitely in that stage – they wouldn't take off their drenched clothes, because they were so concerned about how cold they'd be between taking the wet ones off and putting the dry ones on. I finally got them to change (I literally had to yell at them), and after a while I realized how fuzzy my brain had been during that time – I had definitely been a little hypothermic too. Weird to now know what that feels like.

The above entry comes from a few weeks into that course, and marks a transformation in my eighteen-year-old voice: in previous entries, I am a self-important, arrogant jerk – a student who teachers praised for her skills and charm, but who was quick to get frustrated when her peers didn't live up to her own personal standards of success. The mentality documented in the early journal entries is, essentially, "I am on this course to backpack through great places and learn great technical skills, and I would do that in spite of the ragtag, often lazy group that I've been saddled with." The day of the hailstorm forcibly changed that attitude. The storm forced me to come to terms with the truth that the adage by which I, self-importantly and arrogantly, swore – Emerson's solitary "Trust thyself" from *Self Reliance* – was not a good strategy for survival (or interpersonal relationships, for that matter).

After the hail subsided and we started walking again, I thought, "What if it had been me? What if I had been further impacted by hypothermia and I had been the one protesting changing into dry clothes? Would the rest of my group have taken the initiative to keep me safe and warm, identifying that they had to confront my protests or else I'd get even more hypothermic?" Dragging them along, I realized, wasn't in their best interest or mine. My safety relied on their knowledge and capacity, and vice versa. If they didn't have my knowledge or capacity, they might be unable to make good decisions in my absence, or keep me safe in the event something happened to me. I had to work with them in order to lead them, not act in spite of them, because I never knew when things might shift without warning.

Successful expedition leadership is about creating a group dynamic that can take on shifts in leadership, because any unexpected event might leave the group without its established leader. If the crew is not endowed with the same skills and emotional resilience as the expedition leader, the leadership is not successful.

Many outdoor leadership curriculums are based on this philosophy of participant leadership within groups. El Sistema programs offer an opportunity to adapt these leadership curricula to group music learning environments: an orchestra is an expedition team in which each member's contribution and success is vital to the success of the whole. As with an expedition team, an orchestra provides an opportunity for a community to be built, as if independent of the dominant culture, with its own agenda, philosophies, and culture of belief, in a community whose success depends on participant leadership. Imagine a youth orchestra that is focused and productive when the conductor is on the podium, but which falls into disarray as soon as the conductor leaves the room. A culture of participant leadership creates a group that is able to maintain stability even when the expedition leader, or conductor, leaves without tangible expectation of return.

I have lived in both of these worlds, first as a young musician, then as a student with NOLS, then as a backpacking trip leader, then as a researcher looking at El Sistema learning environments, and now with the LA Philharmonic as the YOLA coordinator. Here I have been able to take the lessons learned in both music and the outdoors and integrate them into our learning environments through direct and indirect leadership teaching – including a course for rising juniors and seniors in summer 2013 and the inaugural YOLA overnight camp in June 2014, formal programs that supplement the integrated approach to leadership development that we practice year-round at YOLA sites.

With this chapter, I hope to illuminate how tools derived from outdoor leadership curricula can be translated into their applications in El Sistema learning environments. Realizing that "leadership" is a lofty, often abstract buzzword, I want to make the roles and qualities of leadership tangible, so that staff and students can operate with a clear understanding of how and when leaders become leaders. In order to establish a common understanding of what I mean by "leader," this chapter begins with a delineation of different leadership roles, including an argument for the interconnectedness of leadership training, group dynamics, and ensemble quality. From there, the chapter moves into an explication of the tangible skills that can be fostered through leadership development programming, with some proposed models for facilitation and implementation in El Sistema programs.

**What is a Leader?**
"Leader" in the public vernacular – and often in student perception – is a status associated with those who have a title or power. The idea that leaders must have status makes an aspiration to becoming a leader a daunting prospect for those who feel that they are starting from a place of powerlessness, as many young people do. This difficulty in envisioning is compounded if an individual's identity is not validated as worthy of status by the broader culture due to race, economic status, gender, nationality, sexuality, or any other number of "others." The dominant culture convinces "others" of all ages that Leaders are X, "but I am Y. Therefore I will never be a leader." Breaking the identity of "leader" down to its skill elements can make aspiration a tangible thing for young people who may otherwise feel alienated by the system of status. Not all of the young people you work with will grow up to be their generation's Nelson Mandela, but neither will all of your students grow up to be professional musicians. The social and musical duty of an El Sistema-inspired program is to give students the grounding on which they can build the rest of their lives.

The first means of translating leadership to your students involves the realization that there are many ways of being a leader, and only one of those roles is directly related to any kind of status. These leadership roles are:

*Designated Leadership:* This is the person that people of all ages think of first when they are asked to think of a Leader. A Designated Leader is the one recognized by others as having power over a group, often with an accompanying title. Designated Leaders are either selected by others (democratically elected officials), selected by necessity (a first responder in a medical emergency), or self-appointed (dictators).

*Example:* All students in the program participate in seating auditions at the beginning of every semester. The violinist who performs the best in these seating auditions is deemed "Concertmaster" (*Designated Leader*) and is responsible for organizing and guiding the rest of the orchestra.

*Active Followership:* An Active Follower keeps her brain "on" even when someone else has taken on the role of Designated Leader. The Active Follower actively looks for areas in which the Designated Leader might benefit from support, taking initiative to fill in the gaps, and setting an engaged example for the rest of the group in the process.

*Example:* While the teacher (*Designated Leader*) tunes student violins at the beginning of class, a student (*Active Follower*) offers to put the music folders on all of the stands, recognizing that the teacher cannot do it all at once.

*Peer Leadership:* Whereas an Active Follower supports the Designated Leader, the Peer Leader looks to provide the same support to the group of followers, working to keep them on task and keep them successful.

*Example:* At a rehearsal, a student (*Peer Leader*) for whom music comes easily realizes that the student next to him doesn't know the fingering for a note in their orchestra music. The peer leader demonstrates the correct fingering to the student, in an effort to improve his classmate's abilities and, thus, heighten the quality of the group.

*Self-Leadership:* At times, an individual's best contribution to a group is to look upon themselves with self-awareness and recognize that personal development is their best contribution to their peers.

*Example:* A student (*Self-Leader*) realizes that the rest of the ensemble is progressing more quickly than he is, but acknowledges that he isn't practicing as much as everyone else. Recognizing the difficulty he has in prioritizing practicing, he decides to make an active change: he makes a practice log for himself, sets alarms to remind him to practice, and asks his teacher for some advice on structuring practice sessions.*

In adulthood, we take on each of these roles in its own time, fluctuating between all four as we determine who we are in each interaction and context. In childhood and adolescence, we're not quite as natural. Many people start with *Self-Leadership* and work their way up to *Designated Leadership*, in a linear fashion. For many students, each successive role is more difficult than the one that preceded it. A journey through young adulthood is defined by learning the ins and outs of each role, understanding where to serve as an authority (*Designated Leader*), where to serve as a supporter (*Active Follower* or *Peer Leader*), and where our best contribution to the group is to focus on self-improvement (*Self-Leadership*). Identity is a composite of these four roles. As young adults make that journey to understanding each role, group dynamics are shaped accordingly.

Sometimes, individuals' journeys are counterintuitive, because struggles are rooted in different needs. Also, the progression through the leadership roles is not always as linear as students and facilitators imagine it to be. In my years of leading hiking trips with teenagers, I dealt with many slow-hiking participants. While speed is not always a necessity on trail, an excessively slow hiker can sometimes be a risk to the group, which has to put in a longer day on trail to account for the slower pace. Depending on the motivations of the slow hiker, one of two strategies will nearly always make that hiker walk significantly more quickly:

(1) Have the student hike directly behind the counselor, so that the student can place her feet where the counselor places them, taking the doubt out of her step.
(2) Have the student go to the front of the group, setting the pace on trail with no one in front of her.

I had one such hiker on a particularly difficult hike up Mount Lafayette in New Hampshire – a mountain known for afternoon thunderstorms. Because lightning strikes the highest point, an exposed ridgeline is the last place you want to be during a thunderstorm. We would have to maintain a pace that got us past the exposed summit before the thunderstorms rolled

* http://www.nols.edu/about/leadership/leadership_roles.shtml

in, or we would be unable to summit the mountain at all. When the day started, the slow hiker positioned herself in the back of the group and struggled with every step. She spent the morning watching the rest of the group walk much faster than she did up the trail, stopping to wait for her periodically, with a trademark teenage frustration in their posture. No one was having a good time. After lunch, the slow hiker agreed to take the lead on trail. With her at the helm, the group took off at a comfortable, sustainable pace, far quicker than her earlier slow pace. After an hour or so of keeping a productive, even pace, the group was in a great mood and everyone – even the hiker who had struggled in the morning – was laughing and joking and telling stories as they walked. No one was focused on the "task" of hiking anymore; everyone was now taking in the pleasure of each other's company on a difficult walk through the woods.

At the end of the day, I asked the slow hiker to tell me what had made the change for her. She responded, "In the morning, when I was in the middle, I felt like I couldn't keep up and they were annoyed to have me there, so I kept thinking over and over about how bad I was at this. In the afternoon, when I was up front, I started off pretending they weren't even there behind me – I was only accountable to myself. Once I realized I could keep up the pace and do it comfortably and we all started talking to each other and having fun, I felt like I could actually contribute something to the group."

Leadership opportunities are often presented to the most successful students. Consider as well the students who struggle most in your music classrooms. Imagine what the feeling of "leading the pack" can do for a student who feels stuck and suffocated at the middle or bottom. An ensemble becomes stronger when individualized leadership needs are addressed.

The choir teacher of a music program had a "discipline issue" student – the kind of student whose mood completely dictated the mood of the class. This student would decide a lesson was stupid and try to rally the rest of the students to the same conclusion. Sometimes he would sway them, but more often he would just frustrate them. After weeks of this, the choir teacher decided to treat the student's behavior as a *leadership* issue rather than a *discipline* issue. The teacher began giving the student formalized avenues to express his ideas, and even had him help with the implementation of a few of the better ideas. The student began to take on the positive qualities of a Peer Leader even as he worked as an Active Follower. (Note: he had tried to be a Peer Leader from the outset, he just hadn't had the avenues available to be a *productive* one.) His investment in the content renewed, the student began actively recruiting other students to join the choir, which had previously been experiencing flagging attendance. As a result, the overall tenor and quality of the ensemble improved.

Students' needs as learners and leaders are constantly shifting as each individual continues to determine her own place in the pack. Bruce W. Tuckman's stages of group dynamics provide some formal means of conceiving of how and when these redefinitions of leadership roles occur in groups. Tuckman breaks the evolution of groups down into four stages – Form, Storm, Norm, and Perform. Sometimes these four stages happen in quick succession, as in a finite teambuilding exercise that occurs in an hour period. In longer term groups, such as musical ensembles, these four stages cycle, in perpetuity, throughout the lifecycle of the group. These cycles can take days, months, or years, depending on the triggers in the environment and the evolution of the group.

*Form:* Everything is fresh and new as the group gets excited about the unified experience they are taking on together. Issues are treated on a surface level, as individuals get a sense of one another and their place within the whole. Group members fall into the roles that seem to make the most sense on that initial surface level, not yet wanting to challenge the structure.

*Storm:* An outwardly emotional stage, this occurs when the needs of individuals and the actions of the group do not match up. Individuals become unhappy with the group structure built during the Form stage, and react in an effort to redefine that structure. If the goal of a group has been clearly articulated from the beginning (through a document of group values and goals, for example), the Storm stage can be productively navigated, with the language of productivity replacing the language of blame that often characterizes this stage in groups of young people. If the goal is ambiguous, or the group never bought into the goal, a Storm is harder to navigate. Having students themselves articulate and document goals, group beliefs, and ground rules during the Form stage can make these contentious moments significantly more productive.

*Norm:* The group is unified in a goal, committed to remaining on task and doing the right thing. In an effort not to rock the boat (not wanting to relive the storm they've just come out of), individuals prevent conflict and avoid presenting anything controversial, limiting the overall productivity of the group and quality of its product in an effort to maintain harmony.

*Perform:* Having learned, in the Norm stage, how others in the group function and what they can contribute, the group is now able to work cohesively and maximize every individual's efforts. Some individuals begin to branch out again, in an effort to establish their autonomous worth. Reaching new levels of success, the group reenters the Form stage, this one (if the Storm has been navigated properly) stronger than the previous Form.[*]

Each stage is integral to the growth and strengthening of the group; though many facilitators might wish to shy away from conflict, a group cannot get to a higher level of performance without first undertaking a Storm.

It is in the Storm stage that the group redefines its leadership roles. In each cycle of the four stages, the group determines who fits into which leadership role, based on where that individual is and what the group needs at that individual moment. When a student or students are ready to transition into a different leadership role in the group, but the group structure doesn't allow for that shift (i.e. a student wants to be taken seriously by his peers in a "peer leadership" capacity, but the group has pigeonholed him as a discipline issue who can only focus on "self-leadership," based on their previous experience with him) it is time for another Storm, to allow the group to realize new leadership roles for each student and grow more creative and productive as a result.

While leadership is often considered in largely individualistic terms, it is thoroughly intertwined with the health and dynamic of a group. Facilitating students' growth into their evolving leadership roles can help keep a group healthy and performing at the highest level, musically and otherwise.

* Tuckman, Bruce W. "Developmental Sequence in Small Groups." *Psychological Bulletin* 63/6 (1965): 384–399.

**Skills of a Leader: What do We Teach When We Teach Leadership?**
The skills taught in El Sistema classrooms are tangible and transparent: the student learns a physical skill on an instrument that is then directly applied to a piece of music he is playing. The skills of leadership, though somewhat illusive, can be made similarly tangible. There is no reason to be obtuse with students: just as you are open with them about the purposes of the musical skills they are learning, so too can you be open when giving them the language of leadership, the language of what they can achieve. Leadership empowerment can be translated to students of all ages so that they can start valuing their minds and behavioral strengths from early on; relegating young students to "cute status" without regard for their minds is like expecting less of an adult because she or he is pretty – it's condescending and begins a cycle of lowered expectations.

In an effort to make these skills tangible and transparent, NOLS has identified seven skills of a leader. While these particular categorizations were developed to be taught through a NOLS curriculum, they are cross-disciplinary and can be equally applied in music classrooms. Some are taught naturally through the model of an orchestra. Some may require more active facilitation. Either way, bring students in on this, so that they can operate with an active understanding of their own leadership path.

These seven skills of a leader are: *expedition behavior* (redubbed *orchestra behavior* in the context of this chapter); *communication*; *judgment and decision-making*; *tolerance for adversity and uncertainty*; *self-awareness*; *vision and action*; *and competence.** Below, I provide a brief definition of each, followed by commentary.

*Expedition or orchestra behavior*: cooperation, conflict resolution, motivation, and "getting along." Those with group backcountry experience know that unresolved, festering conflict and interpersonal instability are front-country (non-wilderness) luxuries. Nonetheless, many middle/high schoolers (and adults) are drawn to them: in the front-country, young people quickly divide over trivial issues, often dissolving affiliations, avoiding each other in the hallways, and ignoring each other in class on that basis. Individuals who succumb to this behavior can still successfully

---

* The definitions that accompany the skills listed below have been adapted from http://www.nols.edu/about/leadership/leadership_skills.shtml and use moderate rewordings to better reflect the context of the orchestra.

pursue their own particular interests (to ace a test, or get into a good college, for example) without having to reconcile the interpersonal conflict. On a backcountry expedition, avoiding reconciliation is an impossibility: rare is the backcountry expedition where an individual can break away on his own and pursue the same goal of survival or discovery with a differing ideology.

Dr. Abreu articulated the inherent exercise of *expedition behavior* practiced each day in El Sistema when he noted, "The orchestra is the only community that comes together for the sole purpose of agreeing with itself." In the orchestra, the stakes may be different than in the backcountry, but the need to practice good *orchestra behavior* is the same: the first clarinet player cannot pick a fight with the second clarinet player and then storm off, because the fundamental structure of their community commands that they work together in pursuit of their individualized interests. *Orchestra behavior* is inherent in the act of playing as a group. Individuals must learn to resolve conflict – musical and otherwise – amidst collaboration.

*Orchestra behavior* can often be misinterpreted as a call of "don't rock the boat," especially by teenagers who are uncomfortable expressing their opinions or discussing their own interests openly. Looking back to the stages of group dynamics, the "don't rock the boat" mentality leaves an individual locked in the Norm stage, never able to reach Perform or trigger the kind of vital Storm that might bring the group to a higher level of functioning. *Orchestra behavior* is not about withholding identity or "not rocking the boat" – the very opposite: *orchestra behavior* means learning how to communicate and collaborate productively through different worldviews, and learning not to walk away and leave disagreements to fester.

*Communication:* giving good feedback, stating needs and wants, understanding multiple perspectives during conflicts, listening. In this arena the focus is as much on the quality and timing of communication as on content. Young people who are still learning how to see the world through others' eyes may struggle with effective communication: during a frustrating rehearsal, the concertmaster has a great idea for how to get her section back on track, but waits to share the idea until the group is too frustrated to be receptive to trying her solution; a clarinet player demonstrates a concept to his neighbor in a way that feels condescending or chiding to his peer; an advanced cello player articulates an idea to younger students, but uses concepts that students don't understand, without defining them.

*Judgment and decision-making:* using experience and knowledge of the group to make situationally appropriate decisions. "Good judgment" is not a universal. The right decision on paper is not always the right decision for a specific group. *Judgment and decision-making* is as much about analyzing the particulars of a specific circumstance as it is about taking into account the particulars of the individuals involved and their skill sets.

I once found myself atop a mesa in New Mexico near the end of a long day of hiking. With a few hours to go until darkness and heavy packs on our backs, my group was about 750 feet of elevation above the valley in which we were supposed to camp that night (and fill our near-depleted water supply). As we looked down, we could see that the trail we had planned to take – a steep and sketchy trail even in ideal conditions – had been degraded through erosion, if by no means impassible.

On paper, it might have been an easy decision: we were running low on water and we had just enough time to make the descent before sundown. In reality, this particular group had found that it did its best hiking during the first few hours of the day, and often became clumsy near the end of every day. To make such a strenuous descent at the end of a long day might in fact take more time than the sun had to give us, forcing us to do some dangerous night-hiking while already struggling physically. Such a result would be destructive to morale, both physically and mentally. So the decision was made: we camped on the mesa that night, rationing water appropriately, and made the descent early the next morning when we were all fresher.

Music teachers struggle each and every day to understand how a group can be most successful: How can I challenge my students enough to keep them achieving ever higher, without devastating them with a musical challenge that proves too much of a reach? These questions and answers are completely dependent on the needs and personalities of the group members.

Student leaders take advantage of similar opportunities for *judgment and decision-making*. A group has been preparing a concert for months. Its aim: to perform three pieces for an audience of friends, family, and staff. One piece has been easy since they sight-read it months ago. The second piece has proved a significant challenge, but the group is excited to have mastered it to a performable level. On the night before the concert, the group is rehearsing the third piece, which from the beginning has been a huge reach for the group's abilities. While they were excited to take the piece on, and have shown great improvement in its performance, they're not sure they've mastered it to the point of presenting it to an audience. They are faced with this question: Will they feel more successful if (1) they perform the piece in its current state tomorrow, and follow through with their plan, or (2) they cut the piece from tomorrow's concert but continue to work on it and perform it at the next scheduled concert? In this situation, only this particular group can develop the right solution for the group.

*Tolerance for adversity and uncertainty:* adapting to unexpected changes, and turning challenging situations into opportunities. Leaders are always prepared for Murphy's Law to take effect – that is what *judgment and decision-making* is about. *Tolerance for adversity and uncertainty* identifies how individuals (and the groups they affect) deal with the consequences of those decisions, and the attitude they take when things don't go their way.

In the previous example of a group having to decide whether or not to perform a piece, their *tolerance for adversity and uncertainty* would emerge as they dealt with the disappointment of not meeting the goal they had established. Say the group elects to go with option (2), continuing to work on the piece for a later performance. Someone tolerant for adversity would be all the more motivated in advance of the eventual concert, rather than dwelling on the failure of not performing the piece as planned.

*Self-awareness:* knowing yourself and your strengths and weaknesses, while also being aware of the influence you have on others. Shifting between leadership roles requires an understanding of self and your own influence on others, including knowing where your expertise lies and where it doesn't. Self-aware leaders recognize the strengths and weaknesses in themselves and their peers, working to ensure that all group members are given the opportunity to exercise their strengths and expertise. Facilitating student leadership can often be an exercise in *self-awareness* for adult administrators: in some contexts, students have more knowledge for decision-making than adults do.

*Vision and action:* seeing the possibilities of a situation and finding creative ways to move the group forward. Inspiration is the first step toward innovation, but a strong leader is one who takes an idea (theirs or a peer's) and makes a plan of action to accomplish it. *Vision and action* is the impetus to say, "I see what this group can achieve, and I will motivate us to achieve it."

In the small-scale and concrete, a trombone player may realize that the brass section is not in tune with itself, as he wants it to be (*vision*). Rather than become frustrated that the brass section doesn't sound as good as it could, the player asks the conductor for a moment and has the section tune (*action*).

A deeper form of *vision and action* came to YOLA at EXPO in the spring of 2014, when the Neojiba Youth Orchestra from Bahia, Brazil came for a site visit. The Brazilians performed Márquez's Danzón No. 2, complete with choreography and an infectious energy. The students, who had long been passive in their desire to be a more vibrant group of performers, were not just entertained – they were inspired to action. Afterward, the YOLA at EXPO students collected themselves and said: "The excitement we feel when we watched the Brazilian Orchestra play is the excitement that we want our audiences to feel [*vision*]. To make that real, we should play Danzón No. 2 and choreograph it [*action*]."

Vision without action is inconsequential. Action without vision is uninspired. Successful innovation requires that both work in concert.

*Competence:* knowledge, skills, technical ability, and organization. I list *competence* last since it is the leadership skill most often validated in K-12 classrooms and it is the skill most students consider first when they imagine the skills of a leader (though it is by no means the most important). In fact, each of the leadership skills discussed here is a balance of hard skills (specific technical skills that can be measured) and soft skills (the intangible, immeasurable skills that are more linked to emotional aptitude). *Competence* is the skill most weighted in the "hard skills" direction. Students who excel at grasping hard skills are often given an elevated leadership function in that classroom, regardless of whether they are strong in soft skills. While *competence* may gain an imbalanced focus compared to other leadership skills, its importance can't be ignored: while some leaders have found success leading a group in a concept in which they have no hard skillset, it becomes much more difficult for a leader to gain credibility when the group does not respect her hard skillset.

*Competence* is more core to some leadership roles than it is to others.

In the orchestra, the concertmaster has to have the personality traits of a leader (soft skills), but also the ability to play the parts better than everyone else (hard skills) so that the section can keep bows together and the concertmaster can help when the group struggles.

That said, electing a concertmaster solely based on *competence* negates the importance of *communication* (how carefully can the concertmaster articulate musical nuance to the string section?), *orchestra behavior* (how well can the concertmaster navigate and motivate the different personalities in their section to keep them performing at a high level?), *tolerance for adversity and uncertainty* (how does the concertmaster react when the section does not play at its best?), and the other areas of soft skills of a leader. Prioritizing *competence* over all other leadership traits means that leadership opportunities become the prize and learning lab for students who grasp hard skills fastest, leaving students who excel in the soft skills without a venue in which to develop themselves further.

Many of the musical examples I've used to illustrate the seven leadership skills fall concretely within the context of a music classroom learning environment, but it's important to recognize that the community that supports that learning environment of an El Sistema program is equally rife for student leadership opportunities. Creative thought and vision should extend beyond students' identity as a musical ensemble. Young people are capable of reading the needs of a community more broadly and creating a vision to make it stronger, and take action toward that vision. Indeed, student leaders are likely to find creative solutions that staff wouldn't have thought of on their own.

**How is Leadership Taught?**

All educators have moments where they are "teachers" and moments where they are "facilitators." When it comes to bringing leadership skills into learning environments with students, the difference between the identities of "teacher" and "facilitator" become key. A teacher is directional – there to give students new knowledge and facts; a facilitator is positioned to enable the independent thought and introspection of a group, in whatever direction that thought may travel, letting the group explore their own learning and taking care not to give them "the answers." The facilitator only steps in to guide the conversation when necessary.

Facilitating students' learning of the previously described leadership skills can happen in many ways – a crash course, an immersive learning strategy, or any other number of practical applications within music classrooms. Leadership skills can be learned in much the same way as music. Imagine a group of advanced students sight-reading a piece of music for the first time: they may transmit all of the right notes on a page (or nearly all), but fine-tuning the complexities will take more time. On the second time through, the clarinetist may realize how his high note complements the tuba part at the same spot. While rehearsing with their section, the cellists may connect with the emotional arc of the music in a way that hadn't been apparent upon first understanding. While practicing at home, the violinist may perfect etudes that make the notes themselves play more smoothly within the group. Students can read through the list of skills of a leader, or hear the breakdown of different leadership styles, and understand the basics of each definition – just as they can play most of the notes on the page upon first sight-read. But in order to perfect these skills, they will need ongoing avenues to rehearse, practice, and understand how they fit together.

The different routes toward facilitating leadership in classrooms require different levels of intensity, programming, and staff resources. While there are infinite models for integrating student leadership in music classrooms, I envision student leadership programming as falling into three tiers of intensity, each of which trains a different level of programmatic and long-term leadership and requires a different level of staff and other resources.

1. *Leadership through the establishment of a community leadership culture.* This most basic and resource-independent tier integrates the language and structure of student leadership into the daily culture of music program-ming through the emphasis on peer teaching and the establishment of a program culture that also expects its learners to be leaders in everyday situations. By following the El Sistema adage, "If you know three notes, teach someone who knows two," utilizing pair teaching and in-classroom modeling, and adding explicit language from staff ("I see you as a leader in this class, and that means X, Y, and Z," or "You showed great leadership when you taught your peer,") teachers and facilitators can ensure that the language and actions of leaders are on students' minds every day. It's one thing for students to take part in a community leadership culture, and

another for them to understand, with agency, that they are an integral part of a community that is defined by student leadership.

Additionally, classroom models can be structured to facilitate the shifting leadership needs of students as they try on different roles. A constant rotation of student roles and responsibilities allows students to have their needs met as they relate to the group in different ways. Choosing repertoire to highlight different instruments, changing seating often, and creating time for peer teaching and teambuilding activities can create spaces for students to reinvent themselves as they try on many different hats.

2. *Direct Leadership training programming.* A leadership training course allows the facilitator to articulate the tangible skills (and implementations) of leadership to students. Trusting students with the language of leadership through a single "crash-course," followed by periodic follow-ups and assignments, can enable students to decide how they want to act as agents of the information given to them.

The scope and scale of a course is infinitely variable and dependent on the needs of your students and resources of an institution. In the summer of 2013, YOLA piloted a summer leadership course with rising high school juniors and seniors, who participated in six three-hour classes over a three-week period. Upon realizing that many of our students were uncomfortable with public speaking and had little confidence in their own perspective, we tailored the course to the needs of the group: though students gained an overview of leadership, most of our activities, assignments, and conversations focused on *communication* and *self-awareness*.

In June 2014, YOLA hosted its first overnight camp with 100 of its oldest and most advanced students. In a week that focused on musical excellence alongside leadership development, students and staff emphasized the notion that camp – an amalgam of music and the outdoors – should be considered a place to take risks, and a judgment-free zone. The previous summer's curriculum – devoted to *communication* and *self-awareness* – was supplemented with an increased focus on community building and mentorship. In an activity designed to hone in on students' teaching skills, while also giving them the opportunity to remember what it feels like to be a brand-new instrument learner, the group undertook what has since been dubbed "The Great YOLA Camp Instrument Switch." The session began with a teaching tutorial designed to give all students an idea of the specificity needed to convey a concept to a new learner. Then, each string player was paired with a wind or brass player and told they had an hour to prepare each other to play a simplified "Ode to Joy" in the orchestra. Once given this assignment, the students, ranging in age from twelve to eighteen, did not deviate even mildly from the task at hand. Teachers, who were circulating as facilitators, kept remarking on how little they actually had to do – with the tools in their own hands, and the incentive of seeing their student succeed in the orchestra, the students governed the activity themselves. When the orchestra came back together to play their newly learned instruments, each student literally saw the orchestra from a new seat and new perspective, and they did so with an enthusiasm sprung from dual successes: pride in their own achievement on a new instrument and pride in their student's new knowledge.

For programs without the time or personnel resources to devote to an intensive course, a more integrated, long-term curriculum might be utilized:

(1) Have the whole group focus on one leadership skill each week, the same way they might focus on a particular etude. The group will experience what it feels like when everyone is practicing *orchestra behavior* for the week. They will see what creative ideas are put into effect during Vision and Action Week. A curriculum might structure a Tolerance for Adversity and Uncertainty Week to coincide with a large-scale community event, so that students can see how a focus on resiliency changes how the group tackles the inevitable challenges that accompany a concert or event.

(2) Debrief the group at the end of each theme week, allowing them to articulate to each other what the group experienced when it focused on each individual skill; then take mindful action accordingly.

(3) Have students complete journals over the course of these weeks, so that they have documentation of which skills are easy for them as individuals, and which ones are harder.

(4) Once students have completed their leadership etudes, have them try more immersive skill building. Have each student select *one* skill they know to be their weakest, and have them spend a full semester focusing on that particular skill.

This route can be applied with students of any age (though you would, of course, alter the language for younger students); is an explicit, tangible, direct approach to student leadership development; and involves students in their own learning, alongside their facilitator.

3. *Student boards and decision-makers.* Creating structured opportunities for designated student leadership can prove time-intensive, since such structure requires a means through which students' ideas can actually be implemented. Opening up the door to designated student leadership means allowing students to solve real problems that carry real weight.

In-school student governing boards get a bad rap as popularity contests that lead to powerless positions, but that impotence is a symptom of the inflexibility of long-fixed school systems. Since so many El Sistema-inspired programs are still in the growing stages, they are in a better position to benefit from student perspectives generated by such boards.

The truth is that students often have more worthwhile and relevant ideas than staff members ever could. When there were recurrent issues of student tardiness at YOLA at HOLA, the student board was able to look at the student-centric issue from a personal level and put themselves in the shoes of their late-coming peers. The students came up with the idea of attendance awards that were attainable and realistic, yet still relevant and meaningful to students from a wide range of ages. The awards consisted of a personalized, screen-printed hoodie from HOLA that labeled them "Perfect Attendance Star," additional tickets for the end-of-year carnival, honors at graduation, and a breakfast with the executive director.

In another case, a staff member had an idea for a student project involving Facebook. When she took the idea to the student leadership board, they immediately responded, "no one our age uses Facebook anymore," and suggested a redesign using other, more relevant forms of social media. Facilitating student leadership is an exercise in self-awareness that makes adult leadership stronger through acknowledgment of its own shortcomings (and, lamentably, fading relevance).

**Facilitating Growth and Leadership**

An adult facilitator may have more experience by virtue of having been alive longer, but his or her experience is not, by default, more valuable (take the preceding examples of student solutions). Sometimes a teacher might facilitate, and sometimes a facilitator might teach (in leadership program, you might "teach" the particulars of the leadership roles to students before "facilitating" their application).

The role of the facilitator in all of this can be a difficult one to balance. As a facilitator who cares about the group, watching students Storm can be hard, especially since student struggles can often seem so easy to solve from an adult's perspective. As a facilitator, you can guide a Storm, but you cannot fix a Storm, tempting as it may be, because students are not chess pieces who can be situated at will. Individuals need to break things down, make active decisions about what role they want to fill, and collectively put the puzzle back together to see how it all fits.

When it comes to bringing these skills into learning environments with students, the facilitator need not overthink the debrief conversation of an activity or event. Once students get accustomed to the standard trajectory of these conversations, they will do the thinking. The standard, open-ended questions of a debrief can be broken down into the following ordered categories:

- *What?* (The event/activity summarizing question.) What happened? What did you notice? Use your memory.
- *So what?* (The discussion of the lessons of the activity itself.) What did it feel like to do that activity? What did we learn? What went well? What could have gone better? Did anything change? Would anything have made this a more positive experience?
- *Now what?* (Discussing how those lessons have broader implications.) What would we do differently next time? How can we apply what we've learned outside of this activity? Where does the group go from here?

Facilitating teambuilding activities and the debrief that follows is prescriptive and simple. It becomes complicated only by a facilitator's desire to "be in charge" or to dictate a direction for their students. The important thing to remember, from the adult perspective, is that the group may not always have the debrief conversation that the facilitator wants it to have, but the group will have the debrief conversation that it is ready for. The facilitator cannot ensure that her takeaways will also be those of the students. Not everything can be solved in a single activity or conversation.

An open-ended debrief model facilitates student-led communication and an articulation of belief, which can be a unfamiliar occurrence in a K–12 student's life. Middle and high school classrooms are often backward looking (dates, names, and summaries) and rarely get beyond the first debrief question category: "What?" The forward-looking questions of "So what?" and "Now what?" are not confronted.

In the summer of 2014, in a leadership course with rising YOLA juniors and seniors, students were asked to discuss a broad yet pointed question about social justice and music education. The students were asked to have a group conversation without faculty facilitation. The following exchange occurred:

> Facilitator: *Poses question.*
> Students: *Silence.* [There is one feeling when a group is silent in thought, and another when a group is silent in paralysis. This was the latter.]
> Facilitator: *Repeats question.*
> Students: *Silence.*
> Facilitator: There are no wrong answers.
> Students: *Silence.*
> Facilitator: Why is it so hard for us to get a conversation going in this class, do you think?
> Student: Because no one's asked us what we thought about things before. There's always a "right answer" if we're asked questions in school.

Your students may be able to express themselves beautifully through their instruments, but, without proper facilitation, they may never have the experience of expressing themselves through language, the primary means by which the dominant culture determines value and relative worth. Getting students used to an open-ended debrief model will help them answer open-ended questions on progressively more complex levels, getting past the "What?" and giving students an avenue through which to express all kinds of answers and ideas.

Empowering leadership is about facilitating belief over time, rather than teaching your own. That way, when your students sit down for a college interview and are asked, "What will you contribute to our campus?" or "Tell me about a challenge you overcame?", or sit down for a job interview and are asked bluntly, "Why should I hire you?" they'll be able to advocate for themselves based on a personal articulation of belief and understanding, without paralytically searching for the "right answer."

**Creating an Infrastructure for Success and Struggle**

I want to close by bouncing back to the journal entry I opened my chapter with, because it didn't actually end with hot tea and dry clothes in a tent. The entry ends:

> We had been in the tent for about a half hour when the instructors walked by. They saw our dry clothes, tent, and tea, and congratulated us on doing everything right. We stayed in the tent a bit longer to make sure we were okay, then got our stuff together to keep moving and stay warm. Them saying "nice job" was great, because I knew we'd navigated a tough situation properly, but it was also good to know that, if we hadn't navigated it right, they would have been a half hour behind us on trail, ready to keep us safe in case anything really bad happened. Even when it feels like we're doing these big things on our own, and when the stakes feel really high, it's good to know that the instructors are there to swoop in if things get bad.

Administrators in El Sistema-inspired programs might be tempted to protect their students from all harm and adversity, glorifying the orchestral community as the safe space independent of the inequity of the surrounding world. But it is that very safety that makes the program the best place to facilitate those practical lessons in navigating struggles. Without conversations around failure, disappointment, and improvement, students aren't able to become active agents of their own development during the time when they have a programmatic safety net to help them bounce back in case of failure.

El Sistema-inspired programs provide an opportunity for young people to take on real risks, experimenting with challenges in the learning lab of a supportive community that can help them bounce back in case of failure, in preparation for the times in the future where that safety net will be removed. These programs are a place to learn life skills in real, applied ways that students of all ages can take on as agents of their own development and learning, so long as facilitators trust their students to want to be the best versions of themselves. There's no need to hide this from students – imagine a community learning culture in which students are just as excited to master a new leadership skill as they are to master a new musical concept. It is that balance of the tangible and intangible, the hard skills and the soft skills, the socioemotional and the individualized that leads to the kinds of long-term success that we all wish for our students.

# PART IV

# GROUNDWORK

On a warm Los Angeles evening in 2012, young YOLA at HOLA string players with members of the Simón Bolívar Symphony Orchestra of Venezuela turned the outdoor basketball court of La Fayette Park into a concert hall. Crime and violence are not uncommon occurrences in the park, which is home to one of the most notorious gangs in Los Angeles – only a week earlier, the police arrested multiple gang members in the middle of the afternoon for dealing drugs. But on this particular evening, none of that violence or fear was allowed inside the park – the orchestra had taken over. As the sun slowly set on rows of violins, violas, and cellos, the audience grew rapidly; park-goers and community members began to join the ranks of proud parents and faculty members to listen to the neighborhood youth orchestra, sitting alongside some of the greatest musicians in the world. "What is this?" I heard a young man ask aloud. Before I could respond, one of the parents answered him with a smile: "This is El Sistema. This is our orchestra."

Making that orchestra happen in La Fayette Park was the result not just of philosophy and pedagogy, but of substantial ground work – building a sustainable program and hiring the team to implement it. This final section of the book covers the practical aspects of program creation, from start-up through expansion into a visionary organization. Each contributor has been a trusted thought-partner in my formation of YOLA at HOLA as well as a deliberate and fearless "architect" when approaching the unknown. They have all known how to heed Dr. Abreu's famous advice to "start small, think big" – wisdom that confirms quality and intentionality as key. These deceptively simple concepts are common themes touched upon by each author in this section. Taking an idea from inspiration to action requires a thoughtful approach rooted in the philosophy of El Sistema.

As forms of social entrepreneurship, El Sistema programs should also look outside the field for successful models of innovation. What can we learn from the world's most creative designers and entrepreneurs? Common to each is the willingness to experiment, take risks, and at times fail. However, these risks are calculated so that they will not cripple the organization over the long term. Successes and failures are determined through feedback and open discussion. Planning, implementation, and thorough assessment lead to stronger, more resilient programs.

The beginnings of the Baltimore Symphony Orchestra's (BSO's) El Sistema program, OrchKids, in 2007, is a story of such risk-taking, assessment, and experimentation. As Dan Trahey, the founder and artistic director, recounts OrchKids' beginning, he notes that and his team were prepared. They had a mission, a curriculum, and clear program expectations for students and parents. Dan and his team wanted to make a difference where it mattered most – in West Baltimore, and they chose Harriet Tubman Elementary School because it was the most in need in the entire city of Baltimore. The challenges were substantial. They held a mandatory parent meeting where no one showed up. Students had to be picked up by a parent after programming, and some would not arrive until 8 p.m., two hours after classes had ended. The OrchKids faculty knew something had to change, so they looked for feedback from the community. As a result, the team started to amend their original plan. They heard that students and parents did not care about producing great instrumentalists, but well-rounded musicians, and the program shifted from its focus on instrumental learning to also include a variety of music classes such as bucket drumming and singing. OrchKids was becoming a program of the BSO with West Baltimore rather than just a program of the BSO alone. The school felt a change – Dan and his team even spent a day painting the sign in front of the school so that their students might feel proud to come to class every day. Then, despite all this effort and hard-won success, things at the school fell apart. The Baltimore City Public Schools initiated a review process called "Expanding Great Options" which aimed to close programs and buildings deemed the "lowest performing" and "least suitable" in order to reallocate resource to strengthen those that remained. Harriet Tubman Elementary was one of the schools that was closed.

This setback might have deterred others, but for Dan Trahey and OrchKids, it served as a learning experience. They took their beginning first-graders with them to a new school and began a new program, which proved to be the beneficiary of their previous learning and knowledge. Today, OrchKids is one of the largest and most expansive El Sistema-inspired programs in the country. Dan Trahey and the program have supported and trained multiple teachers and leaders. In 2013, OrchKids was awarded a National Arts and Humanities Youth Program Award from Michelle Obama and the White House.

Great start-ups require strong leadership – after all, the very nature of a start-up is extreme uncertainty. Therefore, the founding teachers of a program are critical for longer term success. These teachers are mapping uncharted territory with students in a new program with a new curriculum and set of expectations. My own "teacher hiring guide," the first chapter in this final section, is among the more prescriptive essays found in this book as it shares my process for vetting, hiring, and supporting El Sistema teachers. I chose to share this information in such a detailed, practical way because I believe it works, as evidenced by the team at YOLA at HOLA, and questions on teaching hiring are perhaps the most common I hear from around the country. Often, individuals lament the lack of great teachers for El Sistema work outside of Venezuela. However, as I address in this essay, it is the program leadership's responsibility to maintain a culture of learning and support where teachers can develop into superb educators. Risk-taking, failure, and feedback are as essential for developing great El Sistema teachers as they are developing the program itself.

Once a start-up has ironed out its initial design kinks and found its footing, it is well-advised to take heed of Dr. Abreu's second piece of advice, "grow without fear." Tony Brown has put these words into practice at Heart of Los Angeles (HOLA) since becoming its executive director. In Los Angeles, Tony is known as an innovative non-profit leader; he is always looking ahead to identify new strategies and ideas for how to best meet the needs of the HOLA students and community and keep the organization current. Tony balances openness with a keen awareness of the organization's intention, or mission, and he uses this as his guide in each growth decision that is made.

251

Growth necessitates carefully considered planning. However, even the best laid plans require flexibility and revisions. Josbel Puche, a master teacher at La Rinconada in Venezuela visited HOLA a few years ago. As we discussed HOLA's growth and development, she smiled and shook her head at the five-year plan I had so neatly mapped out; La Rinconada, one of the most praised núcleos in all of Venezuela, with a long history, had recently decided to completely scratch their programming to start over to make improvements. "Being yet not being" still applies.

Bear this in mind when reading Dan Berkowitz's paradigm of a "system of orchestras." Dan's balanced experience building initiatives in both the for- and non-profit worlds lends itself well to creating such a structure. His example is not meant to serve as a stencil to be traced; instead, bend and reshape it to your own purposes. The essay also serves an important notice to program designers: consider early in the process future issues and opportunities that may develop only later, after the growth of a program.

Much of the influence for the sample system of orchestras was derived from núcleos across Venezuela, which Dan visited with Alvaro Rodas and me during the Sistema Fellows' first residency in the country. In our travels, one of the núcleos recognized Dan's affiliation with YOLA and Gustavo Dudamel and honored him with a performance of "Ode to Joy" – the same piece that had welcomed Gustavo to Los Angeles just five months earlier. The feeling of connection in the room was palpable.

This exemplifies the ever-expanding network of El Sistema – a movement of human connection on a deep level. Alvaro Rodas surveys the "connectors" of the movement in the final essay of the book, and in the process illustrates what a social movement using music looks like. Alvaro has been involved in El Sistema work for years – first in Guatemala, and more recently as the founder and director of Núcleo Corona in Queens, NYC. Having lived through Guatemala's struggle for a formalized national system of El Sistema, Alvaro suggests that the United States take care not to lose its organic nature too early in the game. A formal network at this point may result in more battling egos and identities than in well-taught and well-supported students. Connection in El Sistema happens around people; the more we can foster this open source network, the better.

I first met Ron Davis Álvarez in Guarico, Venezuela, where he was a young núcleo director and conductor. Several years later, Ron and I met again when he visited HOLA with his El Sistema students from the Children's Home at the Uummannaq Polar Institute in Greenland (these same children were also the cast for the film *Inuk*, the Greenlandic entry for Best Foreign Language Oscar at the 85th Academy Awards). Many YOLA at HOLA students never leave their neighborhood, so the visit and performance of students from Greenland was particularly exciting to them. But the connection doesn't stop there. A YOLA at HOLA teacher went to Venezuela to work at a seminario in June of 2014. While she was visiting, I received a message from Ron with a photo of him and the teacher together, smiling. I shared it with the students, who had been missing her during her absence, and they immediately lit up as they recognized Ron. The world for them is shrinking, and opportunity growing, thanks to their connection with the movement.

The value of being connected and learning from one another far outweighs the value of being proprietary. If you are beginning to design a program, be sure to consider its humble origins. Share your failures and successes to serve the greater Sistema family. We are all striving together to build a global Sistema.

— C. W.

# CHAPTER 13

# Identifying and Empowering Your El Sistema–Inspired Faculty

*Christine Witkowski*

WHEN YOLA at HOLA teaching artist Emily Kubitskey first met Aaron, she immediately saw his potential. Deemed "disrespectful and rude" by his teachers, Aaron was dangerously close to failing the seventh grade. His friends were moving down a path of school expulsion, violence, and drug use. It would have been easy to dismiss Aaron as a "bad kid" based on this information. Instead, Emily handed Aaron a clarinet and worked with him daily before and after programming, building his musical skills while also earning his trust. She leveraged him as a peer leader for younger students and pushed him to grow as a musician.

With this mentorship, Aaron flourished. The unhappy adolescent developed into a thoughtful young leader and artist. Two years later, Aaron was admitted into a competitive arts high school in Los Angeles as a clarinet major. He wrote his admissions essay about what it meant to have a transformative teacher: "Ms. Emily is my clarinet teacher, my friend, my mom, my one person that I know I can count on. I use to feel that I was never myself outside of music; I would behave, think, and act different with people. When I came to YOLA at HOLA I felt great – like I could be myself and enjoy life. Ms. Emily has not only helped me become a better musician, but also an improved leader . . . I now view the world as an enormous opportunity to make a change."

Where Aaron's school teachers had seen a lost cause, Emily saw promise. Her guidance, dedication, and skill helped to positively change Aaron's attitude and life trajectory. Aaron now aspires to go to college to study music and psychology. In the future, he wants to come back to YOLA at HOLA as a teacher.

As we learn from Aaron's story, effective teachers matter. The quality of teaching has more impact on student performance than any other aspect of schooling. Great teachers are crucial for students who suffer from non-school factors – such as low self-esteem or an unstable home life – that may adversely affect their performance in class. Quality teaching can help to level the playing field for underserved students. Therefore, identifying and empowering your El Sistema-inspired faculty is a high priority.

The purpose of this essay is to provide some practical inspiration for those looking to build and cultivate an El Sistema-inspired faculty. This inspiration and knowledge comes from my time in the inaugural class of Abreu Fellows at the New England Conservatory of Music and from my experience as the founding director of YOLA at HOLA, an El Sistema-inspired program in partnership with the Los Angeles Philharmonic and Heart of Los Angeles (HOLA). At HOLA, I worked to empower an incredible team of eighteen different faculty members. Finding the right individuals is a crucial first step, but the burden of high-quality teaching cannot fall on the individual teacher alone. Building a teaching faculty culture that encourages collaboration, risk, creativity, ownership, and support is critical for allowing talented teachers to contribute up to their full potential.

**Who is an El Sistema Teacher?**
During my 2010 visit to Valle de la Pascua, Venezuela, Núcleo director Miguel Sanchez explained to me what it means to be a teacher in El Sistema. He made it clear that teaching music alone was not enough. "This is a social program. It is not that music comes second – rather, music is the vehicle. Every teacher must be a father, a friend, a priest, a musician, a mentor. We have to be everything."

The foundation of an El Sistema teacher is a *strong dedication to the mission* of Dr. Abreu. One must be passionate about creating social change through musical excellence, believe that access to music education should be open to all, and find value in building community through ensemble-based learning. The intention of social change informs every pedagogical decision an El Sistema teacher makes, from ensemble placements to curriculum development. Without a strong belief in the overarching philosophy, a teacher cannot be effective or satisfied in delivering the mission of El Sistema.

In the music world, there are many wonderful teachers who see their role as creating the highest quality artistic experience for the student. Their programs audition for placement and have limited spaces. Many resources are channeled toward a small number of talented, driven students who are thus nurtured into strong, refined young musicians. No question, these programs have merit and value; they may even be reaching underserved youth. However, these programs and teachers funnel resources and prioritize goals quite differently than does a program steeped in the philosophy of El Sistema. Though artistic expression and quality are central objectives for El Sistema teachers, they do not trump the goals of open access or community building as they would in a traditional, selective music program. Talent and ability are not measures by which students are excluded from the orchestra. Orchestral instruction and growth is prioritized over solo repertoire. Time is taken away from music learning to emphasize pro-social behaviors and community engagement. There are skilled, dedicated teachers who would be frustrated working under these constraints. Teachers who believe in the mission of El Sistema, on the other hand, thrive in this environment. They see their role as mentor, music teacher, and community leader.

When Dylan first started as a YOLA at HOLA student, Blake Cooper, a teaching artist and tuba player, immediately pegged him for the low brass section. In the fourth grade, Dylan was nearly six feet tall and easily 150 pounds, so he certainly fit the tuba, but this was not Blake's primary consideration. Blake had learned that Dylan's dad was incarcerated and had noticed that he seemed eager for attention. Blake wanted Dylan in his section so that he could keep an eye on him. Dylan latched on to Blake and was eager to share in his hobbies – he would spend hours on the library computer, looking up different mouthpieces in order to quiz Blake on the pros and cons of various rim and shank styles. As we grew to know Dylan better, it was clear that he was struggling at home. His mom was often unwell, and Dylan was frequently responsible for taking care of the family. He would disappear for weeks at a time. But he always came back and always showed excitement about playing the tuba – the same instrument as Mr. Blake. Dylan's poor attendance did not make for fast musical progress, but because he was on tuba, Blake was able to coach him individually and to keep him caught up. Blake also held him accountable for communicating his schedule to us and for practicing at home. If Blake had not viewed his role as a mentor as well as a music teacher, he would have given up on Dylan and kicked him out of the class long ago. Had Dylan not been with us in those early years, he would have been hanging out in the park after school and easily become a prime target for gang recruitment.

In addition to having a core philosophical understanding, *an El Sistema teacher must be (or become) highly skilled in the art of teaching*. Someone who fully believes in the mission but lacks the hard teaching skills necessary to be effective in the classroom will not be successful in fulfilling it. Her students will not make progress socially or musically because she is unable to manage the classroom, deliver content, or develop sequential curriculum.

There are exceptional, credentialed teachers who spent years learning and training in a formal teacher education program. There are also excellent, intuitive teachers who have no formal training at all. Credentialed teachers will likely come to the table with more concrete and articulated tools for instructional strategies, student assessment, and curriculum development. These critical tools for success can be learned and refined over the course of a teaching career. This is often referred to as the "science" of teaching – pedagogies, techniques, and methods that can be measured.

The "artistry" of teaching, however – intuition, creativity, drive, and compassion – is far more elusive. It is how a teacher fully engages and empowers a group of students. Though this artistry manifests itself differently from teacher to teacher, it yields similar results: a transformative classroom experience. This art of teaching is incredibly difficult, if not impossible, to teach. Rather, it is sparked by an innate intuition and passion for teaching and students. This spark separates good teachers from great teachers.

*Musicianship – or subject expertise – is critical* for the El Sistema teacher. Teaching strategies and passion are rendered useless by insufficient expertise from which to draw content. Imagine a successful and engaging science teacher being asked to teach beginning violin. His knowledge base would limit how far he could take the students. I once met a young violin student who had been taught exclusively by an amateur violinist. The student told me she was going to quit because it was too hard and she was not getting any better. I quickly realized that she had never been taught a proper bow hold and that this was the cause for her consistent frustration: playing the instrument as she had been taught was far more difficult than necessary.

Though these two areas – teaching skill and subject expertise – are central to success in the classroom, they are not fixed – someone who is willing can learn and grow in both these areas. *Adaptability and resourcefulness* are thus also important qualities of an El Sistema teacher, especially in remote areas where the pool of expertise may be limited. Being adaptable allows a seasoned K–5 music teacher with no string experience to begin a violin class. Being resourceful and pulling in expertise from outside is what allows this violin class to be successful. The best teachers see themselves as lifelong learners and are willing to grow and adapt for their students.

Several years ago, the YOLA at HOLA youth orchestra was preparing an arrangement of Sibelius's *Finlandia* for a performance. The average age of the string section at that time was eight and the range of developmental needs proved vast; some students excelled at the violin while others were growing frustrated. It became clear that the kinesthetic learners – the students who needed to move in order to learn – would not benefit from additional violin rehearsals. They needed something different. Seeing this struggle, the music creativity teacher was quick to come up with a brilliant solution – she arranged the orchestral percussion parts from *Finlandia* for Orff instruments. These instruments involve significant physicality while requiring fewer fine motor skills. Students were allowed to choose whether they wanted to play violin in the concert or participate as a percussionist. This offered a wonderful solution for students in need of a different pathway for success in the orchestra. Rehearsals immediately improved, and the end result was a successful concert where every child felt proud of his contribution.

Finally, *collaboration* is key for the El Sistema teacher. Working with a team of other El Sistema teachers, a faculty member is able to share and gain ideas and resources to meet the needs of the students. As the orchestra is the main stage for any El Sistema program, teachers cannot work in a silo to prepare their section, but rather must work in tandem with the rest of the faculty. This is also essential, as the goal of El Sistema is to create a collaborative, caring community through the life of the orchestra. This must be modeled from the top down by the teachers.

## How to Identify and Hire Your Teaching Faculty

The effectiveness of an El Sistema teacher cannot be judged by his or her credentials or experience, but rather by performance. This can make the hiring process somewhat daunting. Resumes, cover letters, and interviews are not enough.

Two steps have proven valuable when added to the conventional hiring process: an El *Sistema resource review* and a *group teaching audition*. The first can be used to judge mission alignment, initiative, and adaptability, while the second creates a venue for assessing teaching skill, musicianship, and collaborative potential.

*El Sistema resource review*

The interview is the best time to gauge a qualified candidate's affinity for El Sistema. Applicants with the strongest resumes and cover letters are sent an email that requests a phone interview and includes several attached readings and videos on El Sistema. The applicants are not explicitly asked to review the resources – the email states that these materials are provided to help the applicant know more about the position.

This resource review strategy is effective for identifying candidates who are invested in the mission, self-motivated, and willing to learn. After asking more standard interview questions around a candidate's experiences and goals, one open-ended question about the resources can be quite telling ("Was there anything in the resources I sent that resonated with you as a teacher or learner?"). From there, follow-up questions can create a dialog that reveals the candidate's vantage point on El Sistema. Knowing the answer to this question frequently helps me categorize candidates into three groups: teachers who have "the gig mentality," those who are inflexible skeptics, and those with "program alignment."

The "gig mentality" group is comprised of candidates who do not review the materials. They either admit to this openly or fumble badly through the resource question. This is a red flag. A candidate who does not show initiative during the interview process will not show initiative on the job – in fact, that quality is likely to diminish once the position is secured because the teacher is either spread too thin outside the position to fully engage or was not truly excited about the mission in the first place. This kind of teacher will keep students and other faculty at arm's length.

The inflexible skeptics are those who reviewed the materials, but found the philosophy to be contrary to their own line of thinking. They push back against the idea of putting kids in an orchestra before years of training, or are indignant when asked if they would be comfortable stepping outside their expertise to assist a colleague or class. This group fundamentally disagrees with the concept of open access and makes suggestions for how the quality of a program could be improved through auditions and stronger criteria for entry.

I enjoy my conversations with these candidates, and believe that a healthy dose of skepticism can keep us from becoming complacent. In fact, several teachers who ultimately are passed on to the next round in the hiring process also ask difficult questions that challenge the tenets of El Sistema. The main difference between candidates who fall squarely into the "skeptical" category and those who fall into the "alignment" category lies in how fixed their mindset appears during the conversation. As discussed above, it is important that a teacher see his role quite broadly in an El Sistema context, especially in the start-up phase of a program, when the culture of a faculty can be particularly fragile. Inflexible candidates are unlikely to broaden their self-identification, and a faculty with a united sense of purpose is vital for a program's success. Of course, it is possible that a closed skeptic's mindset can be changed through experience within an El Sistema program. Indeed, when beginning at a site or school where a skeptical music teacher is already employed, program directors are prudent to attempt to work through that faculty member's skepticism. However, when hiring a new teacher from the outside, it is best to hire a candidate who does not need convincing.

Candidates who engage fully and openly with the resources sent are in the "program alignment" category. These candidates are ignited by what they have read and learned about El Sistema. They respond to the open-ended question with thoughtful, deep reflections. I remember a candidate saying to me, "Everything resonated with me. I felt like for the first time I was being given a vocabulary to express my own philosophy." She went on to talk about her personal experiences as a music teacher and the challenges she had with the way the music education system was constructed. "I don't want to perpetuate a broken system that limits access, but I still want to teach music. It has been an ongoing struggle for me and when I started to learn about El Sistema, it felt like the path I should be on." This candidate demonstrated initiative and a strong personal connection to the mission of El Sistema. She is the type of candidate you want to see in front of the classroom.

*Group teaching auditions*

The next step is to identify the teachers in the "alignment" category who will be inspiring, effective teachers and collaborative faculty members. The best way to do this is through a group teaching audition.

Group teaching auditions are short lessons presented by the candidate to a group of students with the hiring committee and the candidate's peers (other auditioning teachers) observing. The hiring committee is made up of the director and selected faculty who will work alongside the candidate. During these auditions, the hiring committee is looking at candidates' teaching skills and style, as well as their collaborative potential.

*Assessment of teaching skills and style:* Each candidate is asked to prepare a fifteen-minute lesson to a group of students on a subject relevant to the job position. Here is what to look for in these lessons:

- Relevant, appropriately challenging, and engaging teaching
- Lessons that are well paced, organized, and scaffolded (the lessons present a concept in a way that is relevant for the students, demonstrate and model that concept, actively engage the students in practicing the concept, and finally reflect on the learning)
- Subject expertise
- Successful classroom management skills and a teacher personality/style that fit the program's philosophy.

The planning and pacing of these fifteen minutes tell a great deal about the skill and experience level of the teacher. A very green teacher may try to cram far too much into this short period and fail to build a logical sequence with a beginning, middle, and end. These are the candidates who do not finish their lessons in time due to a lack of organization and focus.

When the YOLA at HOLA choir teacher auditioned, she started her short lesson with a story of her hometown in Australia that described its mountains, rolling hills, and daffodils. Immediately, the students were excited to learn about a new teacher from a new country with a new accent. This story served as an engaging introduction to Ms. Emma Joleen, while priming students for their lessons. She taught them a song that "boys and girls in Australia learn" called "I Love the Mountains." The students instantly recognized that the lyrics corresponded to the story Ms. Emma had told about her hometown and felt connected to it. Through this lesson, Emma established her expertise as a choral teacher by pitching the song appropriately for the age group, helping the students consistently sing in their head voice through fun and effective techniques, and modeling superb singing. She also demonstrated skill as a teacher through the way she constructed her lesson, the multiple learning styles she engaged through white board use, body movement and call-and-response and her ability to effectively manage small behavior issues without interrupting the flow of her lesson.

The candidate's personality and compatibility with the students also becomes clear during these auditions. A candidate once auditioned with a group of middle school boys using a lesson on "ostinato" that involved singing and dancing. Initially, my heart sank – this group of kids was at the height of the middle school "too cool" phase and I was not sure the teacher could pull them successfully through his exercise. However, his personality, confidence, and enthusiasm was so infectious that the boys willingly interacted with him.

Assessing these teaching skills is important if you want to find the right fit for your position. Some candidates will be impressive on paper and speak passionately about the mission of El Sistema, but may be completely unable to deliver once in front of a classroom. There are also teachers who will show incredible potential during the audition with clear room to grow. Your capacity and expertise to guide and nurture these green teachers – as well as the kind of position you have available – may determine whether or not they are the right fit for your faculty.

*Assessing collaborative potential*
At the end of all audition lessons, candidates are brought into the office to participate in a facilitated feedback session with their peers and the hiring committee. Candidates are asked to listen and respond to feedback on their own lesson and offer feedback to others.

Typically the facilitator will ask purposefully open-ended questions to the group such as:

- Was there anything you would change about your lesson if you could do it again?
- . What teaching strategies did you appreciate in other people's lessons?
- Do you have any ideas or suggestions for other people in the group?
- Is there anything you saw this afternoon that you want to use or try in the future?

The most recent teaching audition I facilitated was for a cello teaching position. There were four cello TA candidates and two staff members. I began by asking if any candidates would change something about their lesson if they could do it over. Immediately, one of the candidates breathed a sigh of relief and smiled, "Of course! I wish I had done a better job of engaging the kids who need to move. I didn't ever really get that handful of boys on track through my whole lesson, and I wish I had brought something for them to hold and manipulate during the white board work."

This candidate enjoyed the opportunity to validate her intentions and preparations, and to show she had ideas for how to solve the challenges that came up. Then, when I asked the group if they had suggestions for others, I was surprised by the way this same candidate, so open with her self-criticism, was also quick to give very direct and abrasive advice to a room full of strangers – many of whom had executed far more successful lessons. I believe she felt under pressure to establish herself as a leader with a strong knowledge base, and did not intend to overstep. However, I knew immediately that her type of communication style would not mesh well with my team.

Ultimately, the strongest candidate was one capable of appreciating feedback while offering valuable, considerate ideas. Careful with his language and presumptions, he qualified his comments about the others as "wonderings" and ideas rather than facts. He was engaged and excited by the process of analyzing lessons because he saw it as a learning opportunity.

Through such facilitated feedback, the hiring committee has the opportunity to see how candidates interact with others. A candidate's communication style, consideration toward others, and ability to contribute and propel the conversation all become apparent during the discussion, as does his facility for interacting with existing faculty. To be clear: faculty compatibility does not mean conformity. Diversity of experience will strengthen your team's collaborative potential. If many on your team come from the same background, you are likely to see a certain sameness to the challenges they face and the benefits and solutions they bring to their work. A faculty member with an alternative view can be a positive addition. The purpose of the facilitated feedback session, in other words, is not to ascertain that candidates think the same way as you, but that they are capable of listening, reflecting, and openly collaborating with others.

In addition to offering a look into a candidate's collaborative potential, the feedback session is emblematic of the character of El Sistema as a community of learners. It offers the candidates an opportunity to reflect, learn, and grow after the audition. It is important that all teachers who come through the door – whether or not they are ultimately hired – feel they have been valued and respected for sharing their experience and expertise.

The group auditions also allow the candidates to connect and meet one another, which in turn encourages an informal network of musicians and teachers interested in El Sistema. A candidate who has made it to this final round but is not hired may well be a potential substitute teacher or the right candidate for a future position. Realizing that these candidates may meet again as colleagues makes it important to set an expectation of mutual respect and collaboration.

The process described above should yield a qualified, dedicated team that meets the needs of your program. Finding the right individuals to fill the spaces on a team is crucial. But even the highest caliber teachers will become mediocre if put in a stifling environment. Creating a culture where a supportive, collaborative, inquiry-based faculty can thrive is the essential next step to the faculty building process.

### The Value of a Collaborative, Inquiry Based Faculty

In the winter of 2012, behavior among the YOLA at HOLA lower elementary students was starting to concern the faculty. The air con-ditioner in our building that had failed to work all summer, despite the 90-degree heat, was now blasting us with full force. It was January, the sun set each day by 5 p.m., and each classroom was colder inside than it was outside. Students were lethargic and irritable, and to make matters worse, each class had reached the "Storming" phase of group dynamics and was constantly pushing the boundaries. Students, no longer cooperating and caring for one another as they had in the fall, were being sent to my office hourly. Something had to change quickly.

Sitting around the table together, the faculty started to toss out ideas for how to turn the culture around. Little time was wasted on the constraints we could not control – the limited daylight hours and the broken air conditioner. Instead, the question quickly became "How can we keep our kids engaged, happy, and working together?" One teacher began by asking the group to come up with an incentive that teachers could share from room to room – a tangible goal that the kids could rally around to give them focus and promote teamwork. A flurry of ideas were considered: a field day for classrooms that upheld the core values; teachers dancing for students whenever they demonstrated positive communication; private lessons for students who helped to teach others. The group listened and considered one another's ideas carefully while continuing to refer back to the initial question and goal.

Finally, the faculty decided to create the "Chain of Champions." The name of an individual or class would be written on a strip of construction paper when that person or group did something positive for the community. The acts could be very small things, like demonstrating a fantastic rest position in rehearsal, or larger ones, such as staying after class to help a friend practice a tricky passage. That strip of paper would then become a link on a chain that was hung on the walls of each classroom. Both teachers and students were eligible for recognizing something "champion-worthy." The goal: to create chains long enough so they could wrap all around the classrooms and into the hallway, eventually connecting every room in the building. When that indeed finally happened several weeks later, the students earned a party to celebrate their efforts.

While the air conditioner continued to blast for the remainder of winter (and turned off promptly before summer), the attitude of the students and teachers shifted. The broad guidelines for which one could earn a link meant every student and team – including those who truly struggled to maintain the core values – had their name on the chain at least once. This acted as a daily reminder that they were capable of doing terrific things and that other people noticed and appreciated when they did. Further, the kids were no longer focused on "tattling" on one another – instead, they hoped to "catch" someone in an act of kindness. They showed gratitude for these acts by immediately sharing the good deed with the teacher. This shift began to set in as a new habit. Before long, the bar for what most students considered "champion-worthy" was raised, because their base line of interaction had so improved. By the time they earned their celebration, an entirely new student culture had emerged.

The roundtable meeting that formulated the "Chain of Champions" idea is one small example of how a collaborative, inquiry-based faculty works together. The process frequently begins with a question such as "How can we . . .?" From here the team delves into further questioning and suggestions around how to best achieve the shared goal. A conscious effort is placed on rephrasing worries and concerns as ideas or questions so that problems are presented with potential solutions and the faculty communication stays positive. This kind of joint brainstorming allows teachers to create shared practices that maintain consistency from class to class for parents and students while reinforcing the larger program culture. A collaborative faculty meets frequently to plan, discuss new ideas, questions, strategies, successes, and challenges. Often, the exchange of ideas is so fluid that no individual can take credit for a specific concept or suggestion. Instead, over time these become shared best practices used by each teacher in the program.

### Empowering Teachers to Take Risks

A renowned horn player once explained that if the conductor dictates exactly what he wants from an orchestra, the musicians give the conductor exactly that – and not an ounce more. But, if a conductor lays out a vision and allows the musician to contribute to it artistically, they will go above and beyond and give their full effort. This is what makes for the most profound and moving concerts.

An El Sistema faculty needs both creative freedom and a clear vision. Enabling constraints and appropriate supports are essential – they are what make a job manageable and clear. But to dictate exactly what is to be taught with no room for imagination, risk-taking, or inquiry stifles growth and creativity. When teachers are respected and trusted as the experts on the ground capable of developing curriculum and objectives, they create strong classrooms where students thrive and teacher satisfaction is high.

Last summer, one of my teachers, Ben Ede, came to the realization that his musical improvisation course needed reconsideration. "Spotlight

Syndrome" – the sense that everyone was scrutinizing their every move – was plaguing our sixth- and seventh-graders. Though comfortable playing in front of one another off written sheet music, they completely froze when asked to improvise on their instruments. The teacher knew he could get the students to understand and practice musical improvisation through the course, but he worried that anxiety would prevent some from fully embracing it.

So instead, the teacher restructured the quarter-long course around increasing student confidence and overcoming performance anxiety. Instruments were put aside for the course in order to focus on actor's improvisation games, personal reflection through poetry writing, and texts on overcoming stage fright, such as Don Green's *Fight Your Fear and Win*. The students loved this course and grew tremendously through it. Where only a few weeks before they had cowered in front of their peers, they now read their poetry aloud and encouraged freedom of expression within themselves and one another.

This course was a deviation from the curriculum plan and a complete experiment. The improvisation class, in its original conception, would have been fine – most if not all students would have gained knowledge and practiced new skills. However, the new course was far more relevant and appropriate for our students. The learning that took place transcended the music classroom; students bonded with one another and reported feeling more confident in social situations and class presentations. Later on, these students learned the skills of musical improvisation much faster than their peers who had not participated in the performance anxiety course. The time spent developing confidence and performance techniques paid back in dividends as far as the original content was concerned. A stronger program can be built when teacher ideas and experiments are valued. Empowered teachers lead to empowered students.

However, risk-taking also means taking time for effecting change and evaluating it. The leadership needs to trust the teachers to maintain the integrity of the program, even through periods of experimentation in the classroom. New strategies and classes do not come to fruition overnight. If a teacher is not given the space to suffer small setbacks in order to accomplish a larger gain, he may not ever accomplish it.

If you do encourage this type of risk-taking, you will most certainly have failures. Not every experiment is a good one. A three-week marker is good for judging how a classroom experiment is going: if no progress has been made after that, you may consider reevaluating your strategy. In any event, experimentation needs to happen within the program's overall vision, core values, and goals to ensure that any failures are not detrimental in the long term to the program or students.

Constraints and supports are necessary for ideas to flourish. Open-ended demands for creativity normally result in paralysis. Years ago I participated in a drumming workshop where older students were encouraged to walk up to the drum and play any rhythm they wanted. The room was still. Almost all students retreated into themselves, heads down, avoiding eye contact with the teacher. No one was willing to begin. However, once the teacher added in a perceptible constraint – a call and response where students could choose to repeat his rhythm exactly or create their own four-beat pattern – the weight lifted from the room, and students engaged with the process. The same care and structure is necessary for adults.

Several enabling constraints were in place before my initial YOLA at HOLA team was hired and stepped into the building: the philosophy and core values of El Sistema and HOLA, the class sizes, the population of students, the instruments available, and the number of hours and times a week classes could meet. Within this framework, the faculty worked together to set clear musical and social objectives for students and pathways for meeting those objectives. We spent hours together poring over the tenets of El Sistema and what our objectives in the Rampart District might look like in one, three, five, and ten years. My role as the director of the program was to help create those constraints and then step back and allow my faculty to contribute fully to the vision. Through this process, the teachers became invested in the program and its goals. The teachers have the necessary freedom and support to create content and to use techniques that work well for them. This assumes trust in the teacher and a belief that they will be most effective when teaching curriculum that excites them through strategies that work for them.

Program leaders who give so much autonomy to teachers must be consistently present to offer help and guidance when needed. This is how teachers and classes stay aligned with the program goals. A faculty-driven program requires constant communication, weekly meetings and frequent assessment and reworking. Dictating clear objectives from the top down is a much simpler way to move forward. But giving teachers room to experiment and invest in the curriculum and outcomes is ultimately far more rewarding for both teachers and students.

El Sistema programs have the opportunity to create a new culture in education – one in which teachers are trusted, valued, and respected as the true experts on the ground. Given that one goal of El Sistema is to change the patterns of oppression by empowering students, it is important that we do not reconstruct a top-down leadership that muffles the voices of teachers (and by proxy students as well). Every child has the opportunity to become her best present and future self. A transformative teacher believes in the innate potential of each of his students. As first responders, teachers are true agents of change. Finding the right team can be a challenge, but once those individuals are in place, they have the ability to enlighten, mentor, and inspire students and one another.

# CHAPTER 14

# Using Mission to Lead Heart of Los Angeles

*Tony Brown*

HEART of Los Angeles (HOLA) is a non-profit organization that provides underserved and at-risk youth with exceptional academic, arts, and athletics programs in neighborhoods often overrun by poverty, crime, and a feeling of hopelessness. The challenges of our community are numerous. The need is huge and growing, as the density of our neighborhood increases and the quality of schools diminishes. To meet that need, we stay focused on our mission. Our mission is comprised of our purpose, goals, core values, and vision. Together, these four components serve as the foundation that guides the organization not just in our daily operations, but also keeps us focused during times of exponential growth. When we drift into areas outside of our expertise and capacity we are throwing pebbles of services into an ocean of need and the impact is minimal.

## Background

In 1989, Mitchel Moore, a young professional living in the Rampart District of Los Angeles, founded HOLA in response to what he was witnessing in the neighborhood. He became deeply concerned as he watched kids getting shot on the streets and being successfully recruited by violent gang members. These kids didn't have a safe place to just hang out and they lacked any sort of positive role models. These youth were headed down a road marked by poverty and criminal behavior. He began simply by inviting a handful of young kids to play basketball in an old dilapidated gym located in the back of a local church. As word spread, more students came looking for any kind of positive outlet, a listening ear, and a safe haven from the world around them. Mitch recruited his friends to help out with art, music, and dance classes, as well as helping these kids with their homework.

I was on staff in the early years, returning in 2003 as the director of development. I have been the executive director since 2007. When I returned, I focused my efforts on building out HOLA's education programs, expanding HOLA's capacity, and securing a $1 million grant to help renovate the La Fayette Park Recreation Center in partnership with the Department of Recreation and Parks. With this partnership, HOLA was able to expand the number of youth served by 60 percent and today, more than two decades later, HOLA serves 2,400 youth each year through structured and rigorous programs.

The vast majority of the adults living in the community surrounding HOLA are immigrants. Most do not speak English and have less than a high school level of education. They want to support their children's education, but most do not have the experience or knowledge to navigate the Los Angeles Unified School District bureaucracy. The graduation rates at the local high schools are extremely low and very few kids make it to four-year institutions. Of the kids that do go on to college, less than half graduate within five years. To counter these staggering conditions, HOLA provides nine different rigorous and engaging programs that aim to invest in the welfare of each student.

The academic needs of the students are met through HOLA's Smart Start Elementary, Bridges Middle School, and Preparing Achievers for Tomorrow (PAT) High School Education Programs and are led by highly trained, credentialed teachers who invest daily in the academic well-being of each student, helping them to prepare for college and change their life trajectory. HOLA provides a full complement of arts and athletics programs, including a youth orchestra and choir program, private and group music lessons, visual art classes, premiere soccer and basketball leagues, science, technology, engineering, and math (STEM) classes, leadership training and more. All of HOLA's programs are free, an essential feature for the area's impoverished families.

HOLA invests in youth to build stronger communities. It gives some of the city's most vulnerable youth a chance to succeed in life. As HOLA's executive director, I coordinate and guide a large team of individuals around a clear, unifying mission. Our goals and purpose are then realized through actions modeling our core values. This focused, intentional work is how we make an impact in the community and what drives us to make our vision a reality.

## Mission

Several components combined together create an organization's mission. These components are its purpose, primary goals, core values, and vision. The mission statement is a tool that helps to articulate its purpose and measure the impact of its work. HOLA's mission statement – to provide underserved youth with exceptional programs in academics, arts, and athletics within a nurturing environment, empowering them to develop their potential, pursue their education, and strengthen their communities – has been tweaked and updated over the years, but it has always had the kids at its core. That statement is how we measure and assess what we are doing and where we are headed. We use it to filter what specific activities, teachers, opportunities, or partnerships we pursue. Is the person, partnership, or activity a good fit; is she or it contextually relevant for our at-risk and vulnerable youth? Measuring activities against our mission statement keeps us true to our purpose for being – to level the playing field and give kids a chance to succeed in life.

When I returned to HOLA in 2003, it wasn't long before I realized that while we continued to provide the kids a safe place, many didn't have the basic reading and writing skills they needed to even graduate from high school. We created and built out structured academic programs and began to focus on getting these kids up to speed and preparing them to pursue their education. At this time we also updated our mission statement to include that focus.

## Purpose

As our mission serves as the foundation of the organization, our purpose provides the framework for why we are doing what we do. It's our reason for being. The purpose of HOLA is to ensure that every child in the Rampart District has a chance. We aim to level the playing field so that every child can become successful in life and with that success transform their communities. Over the past several years, essential programs and services, including music and art classes and access to counseling, have

272

been significantly reduced or cut altogether from the schools our kids attend. These programs and services haven't been cut from independent schools or the public schools located just a couple of miles down the street from our campus in higher income neighborhoods. To level the playing field, we try to put back in what's been stripped out, to give our kids what they can't get anywhere else.

For instance, when we first began thinking about adding our orchestra program, we knew that in addition to providing intensive music education, we had to build into the structure of the program services that the students no longer had access to at school. We had to ensure that time was carved out for academic support and that there were sufficient opportunities for intervention for those kids who were really struggling. These essential pieces have helped to give the kids in the program the same advantages and opportunities that kids in other environments are getting.

## Primary Goals

An organization's primary goals serve as inspiration for the work to be done. While an organization's purpose is never really fully realized, the primary goals should be challenging, but require significant work to accomplish. These goals should be informed by the organization's purpose. Today, HOLA has three primary goals: (1) to see that 100 percent of the kids in our neighborhood are prepared to pursue post-secondary education; (2) to transform and revitalize our neighborhood so that it becomes safe for all kids who live and learn in it; and (3) to become a model campus of exceptional programs that provide roadmaps for social change.

HOLA has established a strong college-bound culture that permeates all of our programs. Each year we continue to make progress towards achieving the goal of ensuring that 100 percent of the kids in the neighborhood are prepared to pursue their post-secondary education, and each year more and more HOLA kids head off to college. But this lofty goal extends beyond HOLA to the entire community. To connect with the larger audience, we continually make efforts to extend our reach. For example, each year we hold an annual community graduation in the local park. Together with our partners at the Department of Recreation and Parks, we celebrate elementary, middle, high school, college, and graduate school graduates

273

from the entire community. Alumni are invited to sit on the dais and each alumnus/a is presented with a distinguished medal of honor.

HOLA is located in a crime-ridden neighborhood and it takes significant efforts to ensure that it becomes a safe place to live and learn. Toward that end, we have developed a number of partnerships and expanded our campus. With our partners, we are playing in public places, occupying more neighborhood buildings, and providing more adult supervision. Each of these activities helps to make the neighborhood a little bit safer for all of the community members.

The final goal – of becoming a model campus that provides road-maps for social change – permeates our programs. We work to strengthen the organization with partners and volunteers from a wide variety of fields. For example, the Longy School of Music of Bard College's Master of Art in Teaching program is housed on our campus and its students carry out some of their fieldwork in our music classes. This partnership provides access to talented graduate students who are in programs focused on fostering social change. In addition, we have a large volunteer pool, increasing the number and variety of programs we are able to offer and introducing our kids to professions they might not otherwise consider.

**Core Values**
Core values are fundamental beliefs that dictate the behavior of the organization and everyone who is a part of it. HOLA's core values of Respect, Responsibility, Positive Communication, and Support serve as the foundation of the HOLA culture. They guide our daily operations. All members of the community – staff, students, volunteers, parents, and partners – are held to the same standard, providing a framework for leading a large and growing organization.

**Vision**
The final piece of the structural framework of a strong organization is its vision of the future. HOLA's vision is of a place we continually strive to get to, but that place is always out of reach. Like our mission statement, our vision statement has also been revised and updated over the years as we have grown and developed as an organization. The vision still guides our steps forward. It is easy to be tempted to add programs that sound or feel

right, but it is essential to always keep our mission and vision at the core of all decision-making.

When we moved into our current location, the streets around HOLA were filled with gangsters, drug addicts, and drunks freely roaming the neighborhood. There is a park – La Fayette – directly across the street from our building and the park was the focus of most of this activity. It was a very dangerous place, and no one wanted to go near the park. This was very dispiriting, but when I closed my eyes, I envisioned a much brighter future. To work toward that vision, we formed a partnership with the Department of Recreation and Parks and began offering programs in the rec center located in La Fayette. We added an additional two buildings to our community campus and instead of serving kids from ten feeder schools, we now serve kids who attend over sixty different schools. We have added an El Sistema-inspired music program, a high-quality visual arts program, and a full STEM curriculum. Over the years, we have updated the vision statement to reflect the positive changes our presence in the neighborhood has had. While these changes have all contributed to the continued improvement in the safety of our neighborhood, we still have a long way to go. Our current vision statement describes our ideal future:

> Street corners once occupied by gangs and overrun by criminal activity are now safe for visiting artists, teachers, alumni, and volunteers. Drugs, weapons, and spray cans are replaced with instruments, books, sports gear, paintbrushes, and canvases. Everyone in the community is sharing lessons learned and the local schools and the surrounding neighborhoods are becoming strong foundations for fostering the next generation of productive and successful contributors. Heart of Los Angeles has become a beacon center of hope that unites partners with youth and their families to transform communities.

Every organization serves a number of participants, usually in a variety of groups. When picturing a future with your eyes closed, does your vision create a better environment for all of the participants? A good leader will keep asking this question and revising the picture.

**Modifying the Structure to Implement Our Mission**

Soon after my return to HOLA in 2003, it became very clear that we were not fully realizing our mission through the programming we had set up.

I remember that we were struggling to fill classes, attendance was wildly inconsistent, and the kids were barely getting through school. We had assumed that the primary concern of the parents was for their kids to be in a safe place with caring adults, away from the dangers of a gang-impacted neighborhood. Growing weary of the seeming indifference of the kids, we reached out to the parents and found that they craved structured, academic support for their kids. With this in mind, we expanded the scope of our academic programs and revamped the existing programs to create a more structured environment. We instituted an attendance policy and began collecting report cards. We involved the parents and held them accountable. We created a parent handbook and required attendance at parent meetings. The structure was met with resistance at first. Change is always difficult and staff and students questioned what we were doing as we began to implement the changes. It took a little while for everyone to understand what we were changing and why. By focusing on our purpose, goals, core values, and vision to create and continually modify the structure, we become a stronger organization.

## Students

The story of one of our current students, who I will call Marco, illustrates the effect the restructuring had on the entire organization. Many years back, long before we began our El Sistema-inspired orchestra, Marco participated in our music program, which consisted solely of private lessons and a small choral group that met once a week. Outside of the music classes, Marco was always getting into trouble at HOLA and at his elementary school. He was angry and struggled with ways to express the anger without resorting to fighting. He hung out with kids who were disruptive in class and always making mischief. Marco was really focused during his choral classes and enjoyed music, but the frequency of his altercations increased. Eventually, his music lessons weren't enough to protect him. Marco was suspended from school several times and ultimately from our programs as well. While he was away from HOLA, Marco made the transition to high school and continued to struggle. He was eventually kicked out of the traditional school he was attending and by his junior year, he found himself bouncing around between different continuing education schools.

At this point Marco was really struggling, and looking for a way back in.

He started to reflect on his life and where and when he last felt good about himself. That's when he returned to HOLA, a place he identified with feeling safe and successful. He returned during his junior year in high school, eager to participate in what was now a significantly larger and very different music program. When he came to visit, he didn't see just a few dozen students learning music, but hundreds of students of all ages, focused and excited about being a part of a very special team. He was struck by the mutual respect and positive communication between kids of all ages and their teachers. As I toured the rooms with Marco, I could see him respond, a transformation unfolding before my eyes. It didn't take long to see that Marco wanted "in." He saw this program as his opportunity to become reconnected to a pathway he'd strayed from, a pathway to success. Here was a situation that would provide the support and structure he craved. The program and the staff would be there for him every day of the week, with opportunities to play with great musicians and to share his own talents with hundreds of people both inside and outside his community. The director of the program felt the excitement too and recognized his potential. Marco was accepted into the program and since that day, he has taken his role very seriously. He is one of the oldest students and understands his responsibility as a role model for younger students. He has begun to excel in his school of continuing education and has taken the initiative to re-enroll in the high school he originally attended. He will go back in the fall and has set his sights on college.

The orchestra program did not exist the first time Marco attended HOLA. There was no "team" environment that provided the structure, frequency, and consistency he needed. This time, perhaps the right time for Marco, he was ready to take advantage of what was offered him. The program seemed built for him. What he hasn't quite figured out yet, but will soon discover: all humans crave some degree of consistency and to become part of a greater whole. The real question in our neighborhood becomes, what do the kids become a part of, a street gang, or a youth orchestra?

Marco and other kids like him who came through HOLA in the early days needed more than instruction alone to become successful. At that time, we didn't have enough of what they needed. We didn't have wraparound services that might have helped keep them on a clear path. We realized that we needed to add some level of mental health and/or family counseling services. Unlike providing free meals or providing housing, which clearly are outside the scope of our mission, these types of support services help ensure that our core values are lived out every day. Today, we have on staff both a licensed clinical social worker and a parent and community resource director. With these positions filled, we can now help kids like Marco, and if we can't, we can refer them to places that can provide the support they need.

It is true that in some situations where prolonged, intensive focus on one student would take away resources from the entire group, we have had to draw a line. It's not necessarily that we "can't" help a student, but that doing so could have a negative impact on achieving our overall purpose. For instance, helping a student navigate teen pregnancy or some form of addiction might be something that would overtax our own group, so we might choose to refer such students to places where they would be better served and our other students not suffer from a lack of attention.

## Staff

HOLA has only a handful of full-time staff members (administrators, development officers, and program directors), dozens of part-time staff members, and hundreds of volunteers. My job as the leader of the organization is to ensure that we operate as a cohesive unit. Doing so hasn't always been easy. The restructuring of our programs has taken time, patience, and perseverance, and there were staff members who challenged my approach along the way. There has never been an employee or volunteer who has walked through our doors who hasn't been passionate and committed about helping our kids, but there have been situations where I have had to make changes in order to successfully move forward.

A few years back we had a program director who was completely dedicated to the kids, but was unable to embrace our core values in engaging with the larger community, especially the police, board members, and established community partners. He interacted with his kids in a way that I felt was inappropriate and misguided. For instance, in an email to all of the students in his program, he characterized the police in a very negative way. His personal opinions were influencing his behavior, and the behavior of the kids, and he was taking the entire program down a road that strayed from our true mission.

In addition to exercising poor judgment with the students, the program director also failed to communicate positively with many long-time volunteers. Emails from board members would go unreturned, and offers of assistance from volunteers shunned. HOLA's core values apply to all audiences – kids, staff, and volunteers – and communication between the director and other members of the staff and volunteers was no longer positive; he was not taking full responsibility for his actions, and mutual respect among all of these groups was evaporating. When I sought to address these issues, some of my staff resisted. So I stripped the issue down to its most basic pieces: what was our mission and could we work effectively toward that mission without abiding by our core values? Putting it that way, I was able to build a consensus that the system had broken down and I needed to let the program director go.

Moving forward to replace him, I knew I needed someone who first and foremost embraced our core values. Today, the director of the program has worked hard to gain back the respect of the volunteers and return a structure to the program that had gone missing. She serves as a positive role model for the students, providing a renewed focus and direction to the program.

## Volunteers

Volunteers bring an additional set of challenges to an organization. They come through the door giving of themselves and their time, but they too must stay focused on the mission and core values. A couple of years ago, there was a very well-meaning volunteer who was mentoring some of our high school seniors. She had been volunteering for a number of years and each year established strong bonds with the kids she mentored. Many of these students encountered incredible obstacles in pursuing their dream of becoming the first in their families to go to college. She would often overstep her role and became very personally involved with some of the students, to the exclusion of others. The work she was doing, helping kids pursue their dreams of going to college, clearly was a goal of the organization, so initially we welcomed her support. However, over time the relationship soured. She often disagreed with the way we structured specific aspects of our program and she would express her disagreement in an inappropriate and disrespectful manner. She would publicly lambaste staff, roll her eyes, or mutter under her breath about advice that was being offered newer volunteers.

This volunteer's behavior raised a perplexing dilemma. Given the goal of this particular program – to see that first generation students made it into and through college – was this relationship one that was important to continue? Her mentees were benefiting from the quality of the individualized attention she was giving them, even if her behavior was beginning to affect the morale of the entire high school program staff. She was alienating the staff and the other mentors, volunteers who are vital to the success of the program. I was growing concerned that their passion and energy was beginning to wane, and I didn't want to forsake the good of the group for the work of one volunteer and a handful of students.

I called a meeting with the volunteer mentor and my high school staff. I found myself in a situation where I had to spell out for the mentor that her behavior was in direct opposition to our organizational core values. Though we shared common ground around why we were all here, our core values were an important foundation and needed to be respected. Throughout the conversation, the mentor refused to acknowledge or understand that her behavior was unacceptable. She could only focus on the end result – that she formed strong bonds with her mentees and guided them effectively in their search for the right college and provided continued support afterward. It didn't matter to her that her method of doing so was exclusionary and divisive.

It soon became clear that the conversation was going in circles. My staff was becoming very frustrated. I needed to find a way to explain to the volunteer why her method wasn't working for the organization as a whole. So I met with her privately and walked her through an analogy that I thought would illustrate the issue. While sitting in my small office around a big desk, I asked the volunteer to imagine that there were other staff and volunteers in my small office and that her "goal" was to get this big desk out of this small office. I then asked her to imagine herself dragging the big desk out by elbowing people as she pulled it through, knocking others out of the way, and getting bruised in the process. If she nonetheless succeeded in getting the desk through the tiny door, should she expect smiles and high fives from the people she had elbowed or knocked over? She answered "no," and it was clear that she had finally got the message: It wasn't just about getting the desk through the door, it was about "how" you got the desk through the door. Whatever the goals of a program, it is essential that everyone involved also embody the program's core values.

**Donors**

Donors too present their own sets of challenges. We operate on a very lean budget and we never want to have to turn down funds. But there have been times when a funder has asked us to move in a direction that would take us outside the scope of our mission. While it's tempting to do so, we have occasionally had to decline the opportunity to receive additional funding.

A situation with one funder in particular illustrates this point. This funder provided the financial backbone for our alumni program for a number of years. Recently, they made the decision to refocus their efforts to increase dramatically the number of kids and the geographic reach of their grant-making program. Instead of providing actual scholarship assistance, they decided to provide support for programs that assisted kids with their federal financial aid forms. This presented a difficult issue for us: Did we have the capacity and was it on mission to scale our program to fit the new requirements of the funder? I spent many hours with my staff discussing the pros and cons of scaling the program. While we would still be giving kids some tools to help them be successful, we would no longer be providing the quality of services that is at the core of our mission. We wouldn't be giving kids the combination of programs and services that would help at-risk kids pursue post-secondary educational opportunities. Additionally, we would have had to shift our college prep programs and services onto a school campus. Because we are a community-based organization, we have been able to extend a college-going culture into our park and the surrounding neighborhood, helping to transform the neighborhood and strengthen the community.

There is a very real need for the work that the foundation wanted to do and thousands of students would benefit, but the work would have taken our focus off of our purpose and stretched our reach way beyond our current service area. Ultimately, we decided not to alter our program to fit within the new guidelines of the funder. It was a very difficult decision, but one that we were comfortable with as we looked to how best to achieve our articulated mission.

**Leadership**

Besides a clearly articulated purpose, goals, core values, and vision, an organization must have someone who can bring all the pieces together into a unified whole. As the leader of a large organization, I often think about what it takes to be a strong leader. It is a constantly evolving process, but when I think about my leadership style, I realize that I live by the analogy of getting the big desk through the small door. Several times during the past couple of years, I have asked staff to create committees to make the decisions governing the development of new partnerships or projects. For instance, every summer we hold a staff retreat. Instead of dictating the day's activities, a committee of interested staff members is tasked with developing them. I provide two simple parameters: (1) the focus needs to be on outcomes (improved grades, maintaining above average high school graduation and post-secondary matriculation rates) and the development of non-cognitive skills, and (2) our core values must provide the foundation for all activities. In another situation when members of our community approached me about an increase in crime and gang activity in the neighborhood, I acknowledged the significance of the issue, but emphasized that it was one that we couldn't solve alone. Instead, I reached out to community members and staff to create a security committee that now meets every month with police officers, government officials, leaders of other local organizations, and businesses to address the situation. Everyone at the table has a voice, and we have been able to orchestrate noticeable change in the neighborhood.

At HOLA we reinforce our core values daily in large part by operating with a shared leadership model. We have nine different programs, each with its own director. There is no hierarchy. Each director is encouraged to develop the highest quality program she or he can envision. I am there to support and guide, but the directors have the freedom to dream big. As long as they stay true to our mission and our purpose of giving every child a chance to succeed, they are encouraged to craft programs as they see fit. This model fosters creativity and raises the quality of our programs beyond what would be achieved if I dictated how each program should be run. Positive communication is essential to make this model effective. If you are a leader who wants someone to feel as though they are being heard, be a good listener and communicate in a positive manner.

Our El Sistema-inspired orchestra program is a perfect example of the shared leadership style operating at a high level. What works in Venezuela wouldn't necessarily work in our neighborhood. When we started the program, I encouraged the director take a long, hard look at our community, to assess the particular needs and abilities of its members. She was building a program from the ground up in a community of high need. I was there to support and advise, but she was the one who understood best how to use the El Sistema philosophy to create a program that is adaptive and reactive to the needs and capabilities of our families. We started four years ago with young kids and as those kids get older, the program continues to grow alongside them.

The shared leadership model also allows me to elevate different types of people to senior staff positions. What works for one program or one type of kid is not always right for other programs or age groups. Someone who is great managing an elementary program might not be the right fit for high school kids and vice versa. Diverse leadership fosters a stronger team and allows us to better serve diverse kids with diverse needs. There are more voices around the table, a table where everyone's voice is given equal weight. When we stay true to our purpose, giving kids a chance, the conversation at that table is always lively, but always respectful.

All of the elements discussed in this chapter – purpose, goals, core values, and vision – are essential components to achieve success. When all are put together, they form our mission. My advice to anyone wanting to start an El Sistema program is: be intentional about developing these pieces before you do anything else. They will guide every step you take. Once these pieces are developed, it becomes much easier to craft a mission statement that can be shared and used as a tool for your own staff and volunteers.

CHAPTER 15

# Silence to Symphony: Steps for Building a System of Orchestras

*Dan Berkowitz*

*F*a fa sol la la sol fa mi re re mi fa fa mi mi*. The solfège of "Ode to Joy".
Beethoven's simple melody is a rite of passage for a new Youth
Orchestra Los Angeles (YOLA) program, and always brings a smile to
Gustavo Dudamel's face. In 2009, "Ode to Joy" was Los Angeles's
introduction to South LA's YOLA at EXPO when its students performed
the piece to a sold-out Hollywood Bowl crowd with Dudamel holding
the baton. In 2010, at the launch of the new YOLA at Heart of Los
Angeles (HOLA) location in LA's Rampart District, HOLA students
proudly introduced themselves to Dudamel as they sang "Ode to Joy".

On the morning of March 8, 2014, in a room in an East LA high school
that served as improvised concert hall for East LA's YOLA at Los Angeles
County High School for the Arts (LACHSA), "Ode to Joy" once again
became the triumphant centerpiece of a choral and orchestral presentation
for Dudamel, community leaders, public officials, and hundreds of proud
parents. Performance completed, the eighty nine-year-old string players
beamed as Dudamel hopped onto the podium and said, "What can I say?
This is wonderful. To make such progress in a short time, you should
be proud!" *

Just two months earlier, that room had been quiet after 4 p.m. every

---

* YOLA at EXPO, which began in 2007, is the first program of the Los Angeles Philhar-
monic's YOLA initiative – created in partnership with Harmony Project and the EXPO
Center, a City of Los Angeles Department of Recreation and Parks facility. YOLA at
HOLA, launched in 2010, is a partnership of the LA Phil and Heart of Los Angeles
(HOLA). YOLA at LACHSA began in January 2014 through a partnership of the LA Phil
and the Los Angeles County High School for the Arts (LACHSA).

284

weekday, and was empty on Saturday mornings. The students were strangers to their fellow students' families, and the community was unaware of the uniting power of an orchestra. This was an empty canvas in the middle of East LA – and an opportunity. Every great work of art begins like this – an empty space and a vision. For those of you starting El Sistema programs, the vision is somehow to weave the Venezuelan philosophy of *tocar y luchar* (to play and to strive) into every inch of your community in a nuanced manner.

Creating an El Sistema program can be an overwhelming imperative. This essay offers several steps to order your thinking, refine your approach, and provoke some experimentation. The steps involved in designing a system of orchestras within an El Sistema-inspired program are as follows: envision, create, refine, and expand. As you read the chapter that follows, consider how you might adapt concepts to your community and how those concepts might evolve over time. How might each step be different in your situation? How could you improve upon a concept to best serve students in your community? Each of us brings a unique set of skills to this work and will therefore create a new work of art.

## Step 1: Envision

Though there is no written formula for El Sistema-inspired programs, the overarching goal is clear: to create the highest quality musical and social experience for students and families. Experience like this develops the spirit and character that empowers a community – and stiffens its resistance to unwelcome experiences. *The orchestra must be able to compete with outside and sometimes negative influences . . . and win.* The orchestra has to be a place students want to be every day. Students in the top YOLA orchestras are playing concerts at the greatest venues in LA, going on international tours and spending summers at music camps. Those are great incentives, but the things that truly bring students back to programming every day are the camaraderie and friendships they have built through music. The orchestra should be a model of accessibility and pleasure – not because it is dictated, but because the community feels it. Once there is support, there will be a collective desire for the highest expectations.

To begin, start small: Identify community; engage partners; build a shared mission; hire teachers; recruit students; train staff; design the program; and begin. Throughout this process, always keep the perspective of a musician – as musicians are innately attuned to the elements integral to success. For musicians and program architects alike, the admirable attributes are quality, flexibility, resilience, commitment, diversity, a humble approach, and a strong appetite for risk. Let's take four of these admirable attributes and explore how strategic decisions at a program's beginning – at the point when the first orchestra is just forming – can have a long-term impact.

The first is *quality*. For all of us who teach music or have chosen a musician's life, we know that nothing replaces quality fundamentals. It can take years to repair bad habits, both physical and psychological. New programs have a tendency to consider quantity first, rather than building a culture of quality from day one. The long-term fallout can be devastating: a focus on quantity at the outset ultimately leads to a program that serves many students in a mediocre fashion, digging a difficult hole to get out of. Instead, focus on excellence from day one and build from there. Intentional growth will better serve your students and families down the road.

Next, *diversity*. Each student is a complex combination of personality, circumstance, and culture. Your program's offerings should be reflective of students' diverse needs. Consider ages, cultures, learning styles (auditory, visual, kinesthetic), academic needs, and intensity in your offerings if you want to reach each group of students in the most effective way. This can be challenging at the beginning, but over time it becomes the rationale for multiple orchestras based on levels of ability. Developing multiple level orchestras and different types of ensembles may be the best way of addressing the diverse backgrounds, interests, and capacities of your students. (We'll explore this in Step 2: Create.)

Complacency is our greatest enemy and *flexibility* our greatest ally. Throughout the history of El Sistema, its founders have identified the need for an orchestra and found resources to satisfy that need. Necessity is the driving force, but with so many variables, we must be both organic and opportunistic while pursuing solutions. Always keep an eye on your program design and question if your hypotheses remain correct – are your teachers and students excelling in this structure? If not, recognize and implement changes swiftly to keep the forward trajectory.

Finally, what is your tolerance for *risk*? Each program is an example of social innovation. With innovations come failures – large and small. Take the time to reflect; realize gains in program quality and investigate losses. In this difficult, often life-consuming work, the obstacles are plentiful. But the rewards balance the risks. And the greater community needs to observe results before an impact can reach beyond the classroom walls.

Stay focused on the process; it will tell the story through your humble beginnings. Each day, there should be progress musically or socially. An El Sistema-inspired program is an investment in the community. When nurtured, its benefits compound themselves over time. When you need to explain the program, use the *process of learning as the product of success*. Many third parties will visit your program looking for progress toward your ultimate vision. You do not need to show off a polished performance; each minute spent in the classroom is the product. Leverage the creative strengths of your teachers so that forward momentum is felt throughout the community. The students will feel this and want to strive together to reach your high expectations. Lastly, always keep your goal in mind. *Tocar y luchar . . . y sostener.* Once you engage community, you have committed to a long-term investment. It is your imperative to sustain it.

Eduardo Mendez, FundaMusical's executive director, explains El Sistema's goal as achieving a balance between the dream and reality; without that balance it will become a badly performed dream. You must take risks to achieve your dream, but you cannot promise a child, or a community, something you cannot deliver.

Now, let's take your vision and provide a contextual foundation to build upon.

## Step 2: Create

"Creating structure is not something you can do from an office." After hearing these words from Mr. Mendez in 2010, our inaugural class of Sistema Fellows from the New England Conservatory began its exploration of over twenty Venezuelan núcleos. In these programs, we commonly saw three orchestral environments for differentiated learning, a variety of music initiation tracks, folk ensembles, special needs programs, in-school residencies, and honors ensembles for excelling students. The núcleos were constantly evolving – maturing along with their student bodies.

This differentiated model reminded me of a common investment strategy: a core-satellite approach. When constructing a portfolio of investments, the goal is to gain broad exposure while limiting risk, cost, and volatility. The core elements represent the majority of a portfolio and generally contain passive investments that track the market as a whole (such as an S&P 500 Index). Satellites are smaller positions that are more risky, but provide exposure to interesting prospects not otherwise found in a passive portfolio. Because of this, they require more care and creativity. When combined, the core-satellite approach is successful because it has adventurous elements but is also diversified and therefore holds less risk.

As an architect of a núcleo, you are making an investment in a community. In the El Sistema context, diversification is also essential for sustainability. The core is the system of orchestras – sequential, integrated, and with multiple avenues for entry (or *initiation*). The satellite programs are add-ons that reflect the community's culture and social needs. They could include a folk ensemble or an in-school residency.

This approach complements stability (core) with room for experimentation and invention (satellite) to meet the specific needs of a community. Within each program component are unthreatening ways to entrust students with challenging situations, like teaching peers or basic fundraising. Assigning students this type of responsibility gives them an opportunity to develop maturity.

**Core Components**

Let's start with the core components of a "mature" program: three interwoven levels of orchestra with tracks for initiation. This structure supports a variety of learners: a safe place for *beginners* to experiment, a transitional group for *intermediate* students, and a cohort of *advanced* students to showcase publicly their musical achievement (and the associated value of your núcleo). Students in beginner and intermediate ensembles will aspire to reach the top group, and will drive their study accordingly. Advanced students become teachers and role models to inspire their less advanced peers. This cycle of aspiration enhances the quality of experience for each student. Each level of orchestra takes time to build. Be patient and intentional. Look for signals that it's time to grow (we will explore these below). Expansion points are never clean and clear, but there are always clues.

With that, let's start from scratch and set ourselves up for success. How do we get from zero students to 300 citizens?

First, we need an *initiation track* – courses that allow students with no previous musical experience or knowledge to enter the program to learn. Musicianship courses, choirs, and bucket drumming groups have all been used in the United States to immerse beginners in the language of music. In your first year, it is likely that every child who enters the program will be a fresh beginner and in need of a way to learn music from scratch.

For six-year-olds, a great initiation track component is the Paper Orchestra. This concept was developed by Josbel Puche at Núcleo La Rinconada in Caracas, Venezuela – initially out of need, since there were not enough instruments for each student in the orchestra. Mothers were therefore assigned to construct violins for their children using everyday materials. The ersatz violins evolved into an exceptional tool to introduce orchestral fundamentals like posture, instrument care, movement – as well as performance utilizing everyone's first instrument, the voice. To "graduate" from representative to real instruments, the paper orchestra members perform a selection of songs focused on teaching their community about the orchestra – thus beginning their orchestral experience as both teachers and learners.

As your El Sistema program matures, you will also need initiation courses that help beginners join a community of intermediate and advanced young musicians. In these future years, the intake should reflect the program's needs and resources. Student attrition, instrumentation, and funding frequently dictate the type of initiation course in any given year. For example, if you are trying to accelerate certain sections in the orchestra, your intake might be middle school students who will learn quickly and be able to catch up to a class of fourth-graders.

Thoughtful evaluation of your initiation courses at the end of each year will allow you to strengthen this track. Think about students' musical and social progress and develop your program's identity during the initiation process. Then, as soon as your program begins to stabilize, it is time to start your first orchestra.

*Orchestra #1: The Beginner Orchestra*
The first ensemble experience creates community "buy-in" for the students and families. It is, as Maestro Abreu said, "the only community that comes together with the fundamental objective of agreeing with itself. Therefore the person who plays in the orchestra begins to live the

experience of agreement." Here, students can put their musicianship into practice and strive together as a team.

The first orchestra is always a point of struggle. There is very little repertoire for a beginning youth orchestra, since so many school programs focus on separate wind ensembles and string orchestras. However, many teachers have identified creative ways to assemble an orchestra immediately. Play with unorthodox ensembles if you are not ready for a traditional orchestra. For example, try combining new wind players on recorder with strings, add Orff percussion or drumming to your ensemble to allow younger students to join in, arrange music to best fit your instrumentation, and use the instrument that everyone possesses – the voice – to fill in gaps as needed. The important point is to bring everyone together as a community of musicians as soon as students have instruments. Right away this will create a culture around the centrality of the orchestra. Over time, a traditional orchestra will form, and when it does students will already be familiar with rehearsal etiquette and peer support.

Over time, the first orchestra will become the foundational ensemble where your students can begin and grow. This is a safe place for students to come together and work as a team. Of course, certain sections of the orchestra may move faster musically than socially and vice versa. Create avenues for the students to mature in both ways. Each year, a new group of students tends to excel musically faster than they are maturing socially. Use your older students as an asset, and build programming to supplement for the deficits in student growth. Older and more advanced students, if prepared properly, can find great success in supporting younger sections both socially and musically.

To establish an orchestral culture, a beginner ensemble needs to meet no less than two times each week.

*Transition signals:* There are at least two routes to a second ensemble: programmatic tension and intake. Programmatic tension is the point where you experience consistent tension between ability levels: advanced students find the music boring and seek a new challenge while struggling students are frustrated as others progress beyond them. When this occurs, both over- and under-achieving students will begin to act out. This means it's time to add your next level.

Intake allows for a more elegant solution. As students are brought into the program each year, think about how you might anticipate the inherent problems in multi-level instruction. At YOLA's newest site, we are experimenting with alternating intake between winds/brass in one year, and strings the next year, allowing us to create a new orchestra every two years. In year one, we had intake of eighty string players. We will add forty winds/brass in year two, followed by a new group of forty to sixty strings in year three, forty to sixty winds/brass in year four, and so on. While the first few years will still experience programmatic tension, we hope to alleviate the scale of the inherent structural problem.

*Orchestra #2: The Intermediate Orchestra*
Committed students striving for higher levels of artistry who are achieving at a higher level can use this intermediate orchestra as their outlet. These students can also gain additional mentorship experience by frequently working with the beginner group.

For this level, refine your artistic goals and social expectations significantly compared to the goals and expectations of the Beginner Orchestra. Students respond to these challenges and create a culture of ambition and obligation. That obligation, of course, is to give back – to help students who know less than them. This creates a familial feel to the núcleo. Students are investing in one another for the greater cause. Ideally, each new orchestra should meet with more frequency than its predecessor to accelerate collective achievement.

This Intermediate Orchestra and all future orchestras should be held in high regard. Students who struggle with attendance, maturity, and/or musicianship can always return to the orchestra that preceded it, as leaders with incentives for growth and self-redemption.

Finally, this new orchestra allows for social and musical assessment. Auditions, essays, interviews, records of attendance, and assessments of motivation, effort, and leadership are all metrics by which to judge a student's readiness for the next level. They also give teachers and staff a clear grounding from which to explain and justify student progress, especially to parents who frequently require explanations for why their child is not progressing with their peers and what they can do to help.

*Orchestra #3: The Advanced Orchestra*
Once two orchestras have been formed, and the program again feels the tension between levels of musical and social achievement, it is time for a

291

third orchestra. This is the part of your program that will impress supporters on the outside and catalyze the investment of younger students on the inside. At first, you may find that your intermediate orchestra has only a very small number of exceptional students. For example, YOLA's first advanced orchestra emerged in exactly this way: as a chamber orchestra. There were only thirty-five students in this initial third orchestra, yet it was something for students to aspire to. Within a few years, the orchestra has grown to include seventy-five students.

| Initiation / Beginner Ensembles *Launch in Year 1* | Musical and Social Progress ➡ ⬅ Mentorship | Children's Orchestra (Beginner) *Launch in Year 1* | Musical and Social Progress ➡ ⬅ Mentorship | Youth Orchestra (Intermediate) *Launch in Year 2–4* | Musical and Social Progress ➡ ⬅ Mentorship | Symphony Orchestra (Advanced) *Launch in Year 4–6* |

This group of student leaders will shape the identity and dictate the culture of the program in the present and the future. Once this advanced orchestra begins, invest heavily in it through intensive retreats, large-scale performances, and more frequent rehearsals. As younger students see the musical and social transformation of the advanced group, they will want a similar path for themselves and will work harder accordingly. Additional opportunities are necessary for students at this level; these opportunities include chamber music, advanced theory, conducting, and leadership committees.

★  ★  ★

This multi-tiered, integrated system of orchestras is the core núcleo structure. Could more levels be needed for a larger group of students? Absolutely. The El Sistema approach is inherently dynamic, adapting to change each day.

At the same time, many programs struggle to find their stride at the beginning for lack of looking ahead. It can seem overwhelming to plan more than one year in advance, but you must always be forward-looking, self-aware, and introspective, and have a big-picture focus. What instrumentation and age group will be best for my intake next year? How can I leverage assets (teachers, space, time) to give students a better experience?

Remember, this program is being constructed *with* the community, not *for* it. That is what makes each of these programs look so different in practice. The goal is to create an all-encompassing society within the núcleo. Once you've established your foundation you are ready, as Maestro Abreu has said, to "grow without fear."

## Satellite components

El Sistema programs in the United States should strive to build on a community's identity and support it where it is weak. Some examples that have been seen around the globe include: special needs programs, folk music ensembles, parent ensembles, in-school residencies, solo competitions, intensive chamber music, academic support, choir, college preparation workshops, and leadership committees. These can be implemented from the program's outset to engage the families or initiated organically once the core components begin to mature.

Use flexible times like the summer to pilot these elements. This way you can gauge the student interest and refine this element.

## Step 3: Refine and Expand

Everyone loves the concept of expansion – after all, we all strive to serve more students. That said, it is essential to maintain the quality and integrity of the program in the process of expanding to new sites. Maintaining quality while growing means identifying exceptional community partners, training new faculty, and adapting to a community's needs. It is one thing to create a culture; it is another to sustain it.

Another consideration is the growth capacity of the individual sites. At the beginning, focus on depth over breadth, so that you can be intentional about growth. As you roll out a new program, take everything that is known about El Sistema philosophically and adapt it to a new community of students, teachers, family members, and institutions. There will always be new challenges and therefore new opportunities. Maestro Abreu's advice to "start small and think big" is relevant on both the programmatic and institutional level.

As you grow, remember that with more sites, there are more places to experiment, a larger staff of creative people and, of course, more students. Little innovations accelerate learning as an initiative and help with the overall evolution of José Antonio Abreu's vision. First pilot new program elements for various age groups and demographics within existing programs. Then, take that learning and apply it to other sites. Each site will be structured differently to meet the needs of the specific neighborhood or community, but philosophy and artistic direction should remain the same. When considering expansion into multiple locations, quality should remain the driver for all decisions. Ask yourself, "do I have enough teachers who understand the mission? Is there enough administrative capacity to ensure that students are served in an exceptional way? What can this program learn from location to location and how can it collaborate?" These are not new questions, but this kind of productive introspection is your insurance policy at each juncture.

Also, continue to be mindful about the lifecycle. El Sistema-inspired programs will experience infancy, adolescence, and relative maturity, just as humans do. As with the human lifecycle, healthy living during infancy, adolescence, and young adulthood often predicts a long and healthy life. Each phase has its own nuance and character. You will experience a difficult transition between each. At these transitional moments you should focus on the process itself. This "product" will feed the community's vision of what is possible.

Unlike humans, programs are often reborn, therefore avoiding mortality. *Design* new elements, *assess* regardless of outcomes, and *refine* your "system." Be opportunistic – you do not need permission to make a change in structure, host a workshop, or bring together hundreds of students to perform Tchaikovsky. If things ever feel settled, take that as a cue to restart, redesign, and re-imagine your program(s). This is how El Sistema evolves and, in the long run, survives.

CHAPTER 16

# El Sistema Connectors: Bringing People Together

*Alvaro Rodas*

IN 2001, Dr. José Antonio Abreu was interviewed on CBS's *60 Minutes*, the first report on El Sistema widely seen in the United States. When he was asked about the future of El Sistema, he said "I am dreaming now of a worldwide system of youth orchestras." Back then, the El Sistema movement was already spreading throughout Latin America, but little of it was known in the classical music worlds of the United States, Europe, and Asia. In Venezuela, what had started in 1974 as a national movement of youth orchestras (also referred to as "social action through music"), was already receiving a high level of attention from the state. Abreu had conceived a state foundation to support and oversee this countrywide system of youth and children's orchestras. The State Foundation for the National System of Youth and Children's Orchestras of Venezuela (FESNOJIV, now called Fundación Musical Simón Bolívar, or FundaMusical) was established in 1979. Despite this state sponsorship, the guerrilla style of music education entrepreneurship that gave birth to the movement was still alive there and spreading throughout the rest of Latin America. In the years after this *60 Minutes* report, new social action through music initiatives inspired by the Venezuelan model started to emerge in the rest of the world, including the United States.

I first heard of El Sistema when I participated in the Youth Symphony Orchestras of the Americas Festival in Puerto Rico in 1989. There, I was roommate with Tarcisio Barreto, now one of the leaders of Venezuela's Barquisimeto núcleo, where Gustavo Dudamel grew up. Tarcisio told me about the dozens of orchestras that were part of the movement. The idea of the Venezuelan orchestra movement – "*el movimiento*," as he kept referring to it – got stuck in my imagination. It was a new, out-of-the-box idea that I could only dream of seeing implemented in my home country, Guatemala. It took nearly one decade to see that dream come true. The replication of El Sistema in Guatemala that started in 1996 raised many questions about organizational models and leadership in the context of an arts education organization with a mission of social change. These questions drove me to come to New York to study arts administration in 2004 on a Fulbright scholarship, with "*el movimiento*" still in my mind. During that time in New York City I also came up with the idea of a núcleo to serve the Guatemalan immigrant population here. So when I was admitted to the first class of the El Sistema Fellows (formerly Abreu Fellows) at the New England Conservatory in 2009, I had my mind set on starting a new núcleo in the Queens neighborhood of Corona. The Corona Youth Music Project was launched in the summer of 2010 and since then has grown to over 200 students, two orchestras, a children's choir, and an orchestral initiation program.

The notion that El Sistema is a *social movement* rather than a *system* that can be learned and transplanted is very relevant in this stage of its development in the United States. Programs across this country (and around the world) are currently raising valid questions about El Sistema pedagogy and organizational structure, leadership models, and local or national control. Social theorist Herbert Blumer defines social movements as collective efforts to attain social change: "They have their inception in the condition of unrest, and derive their motive power on one hand from dissatisfaction with the current form of life, and on the other hand, from wishes and hopes for a new scheme or system of living."[*] More recently, social movement theorist Sydney Tarrow points out that while social movements are defined by collective challenges and driven by common causes, they are actually "in sustained interaction with elites, opponents and authorities."[†]

To see the El Sistema-inspired initiatives as components of a social

---

[*] Bumer, Herbert. "Collective Behavior." In *An Outline of the Principles of Sociology*, Robert E. Parks, ed., 199. New York: Barnes and Noble, 1939.
[†] Tarrow, Sydney. *Power in Movement: Social Movements, Collective Action, and Politics*, 4. Cambridge: Cambridge University Press, 1994.

movement is to allow them to raise questions locally or nationally, and to implement possible solutions with independence, while taking advantage of any opportunity, even with organizations or structures that would oppose any non-traditional approach to music education, youth development and even poverty – and as a result, fostering social action through music across the board.

Social action through music, simply put, means to aim for social change using music as the vehicle. This on one hand, contradicts the conventional perceptions of social action as being a protest, a demonstration, or even a strike, and on the other hand, debunks the idea of arts for arts sake, which sees the notion of "arts as a social cure" with disdain. First, instead of protests, there is intensive music training, followed by luscious concerts. Second, the results of this intensive music training and the luscious concerts go beyond the aesthetic: they show that music education made accessible to everyone has a deep positive impact on whole communities.

While its effort to reach high levels of music excellence is one of the main attributes of El Sistema, at least three more attributes have been key to its success as a movement: (1) Its participants are always trying to grow the movement, to multiply the number of individuals and organizations that are part of it. "The idea is to add, not to subtract," a Venezuelan teaching artist in Guatemala once told me when I asked if a forty-something percussion student could join the new youth orchestra in 1996; (2) There's a deliberate curricular flexibility. Teaching methods are a result of the constant professional development of the teachers, informed by whatever new information they can get their hands on, and in response to the particular challenges their orchestras and programs are facing at any given moment, without the dictate of a central pedagogical method; (3) It thrives on connectedness: information and knowledge is shared though informal networks, and organizations take on the role of network facilitators, rather than that of supervisors or controllers of the information and knowledge that passes through them.

The existence of the El Sistema movement depends on its constant growth: to keep adding new individuals (teachers and students, who are also the "activists" in this movement), and new organizations that identify with El Sistema. Big numbers, as well as big artistic results, give the cause political weight. The more children, families and communities participate in the movement, the more relevant music education and artistic excellence in music turns out to be. Many El Sistema anecdotes heard during the late 1990s were not only about the high musical standards, but about the big number of participants – how mayors, governors, and even presidents had no choice but to pay attention and commit to support the orchestra and music education. Its priority on expansion and growth – by establishing new programs, or núcleos, and the inclusion of more children with different needs and challenges – is key to its sustainability.

Therefore El Sistema must also remain boundless and flexible: a movement that is in a permanent state of "not being there yet," or "ser no ser todavía," as Dr. Abreu put it in 2009. Here lies a key difference between the development of El Sistema in Venezuela and the rest of the world. While a common organizational structure was adopted in Venezuela for operational and legal advantages, in other countries many different organizational structures have been tried out. During these initial stages of the internationalization of the El Sistema movement, new programs and initiatives keep emerging from the many different circumstances, challenges, and opportunities; organizations and partnerships are established to secure financial and legal standing. These new programs keep evolving in response to their own growth and changes in their environments. The result: many different types of organizations abiding by a diversity of local or national policies and mandates.

But doesn't the creation of national associations or local non-profits contradict the "ser no ser todavía" nature of El Sistema? If El Sistema is a free-growing social movement, doesn't the stiffness of organizations "choke" it? Not really, since the main goal of an organization, whether local, regional, or national, is to secure financial support and to provide legal structure to the programs. True, regional or national organizations can become qualifying (and disqualifying) bodies that discourage innovation and evolution within the movement. However, small, independent non-profits have the capacity to pursue innovative strategies and practices that attain the same goals of the movement. In sum, the movement is one of flexible, ever-changing organizations and the individuals that participate in them, all connected by a common cause.

In Venezuela FundaMusical, the state foundation established to oversee and support the national system is actually a big network of regional and local organizations. Around 90 percent of FundaMusical's income comes from many different branches of the government. A large part of these funds pay the salaries of artists and teachers in local and regional El Sistema organizations. In exchange these organizations raise funds (mostly from other local and regional branches of the government) to support their operations and special projects. This way, the social movement nature of El Sistema stays alive nationwide, while support for its human resources is guaranteed.

The Venezuela model may not be directly replicable in the United States and other countries, but it highlights the importance of flexibility and connectedness essential to the growth of the movement. The local, regional, and national organizations and initiatives provide the space for exchanging information and knowledge. Their role, if not to provide funding for human resources as they do in Venezuela, is to weave together the many interlacing networks of people – teachers, students, administrators, and leaders. However, since these networks emerge from needs on the ground, the existing El Sistema-inspired programs must create "connectors" in response to particular needs, challenges, and opportunities. Venezuela has created many "connectors" that have produced amazing results and can serve as models in their inventiveness and resourcefulness, while also inspiring new ideas appropriate to different circumstances.

The concept of "connectors" harks back to the idea of El Sistema as a social movement, since these "connectors" are collective actions equivalent, in a peacefully transformative way, to the protests and demonstrations of traditional social movements. In El Sistema's case, these activities result in highly energetic public performances that are the actual public expression of the cause. They can be of many types and sizes. Some are showcase concerts and performances at public events involving elected officials. Some involve large ensembles of children playing at a public event – in no way politically charged, but with the clear goal of demanding support for the El Sistema cause.

In 2010, the Corona Youth Music Project, in Queens, NY, launched with a two-week chorus camp that included 100 children. Elected officials were invited to the final concert, a performance that was the most eloquent way to present the project and its goals. Support from the local government has since been continuous. This public performance strategy has been used in Venezuela since the 1970s and continues even today: in July 2013, a "mega-concert" was organized in Anzoátegui State in Venezuela that included 2,000 children.

Essentially, the main role of these connectors is to provide more educational opportunities for more students. But their connecting nature should not be taken for granted: they bring together many people from different regions, different ages, and different stages in their music education. It gives all of them awareness of being part of a movement, and creates the links for the many networks that shape the movement. Some of these connectors, such as the "seminario," have already received a lot of international attention. But other models from Venezuela can be adapted to particular circumstances and put into practice elsewhere. These include the conservatory in its many variations (itinerant conservatories and conservatory extensions), núcleo "modules," and national instrument academies.

### The Seminario

Jesús Morín, regional director of orchestras in Guárico State in Venezuela, spoke on the topic of the seminarios at the 2014 Take a Stand Symposium in Los Angeles. According to Morín, a seminario is a way to "compress the work of many months into a shorter period of consecutive days of intensive work." He explained that during the seminarios students are pushed to do more than they are used to – to play much more difficult repertoire – rather than to intellectualize about music and technique. Through this intensive work, students end up accomplishing much more than they realized they could. As a result they come out empowered and with more confidence about their potential as individuals. The end results also foster collective pride in their orchestra. Finally, and relevant to the subject of this essay, students at these regionwide seminarios get a better sense of being connected with each other and with a larger movement.

A seminario of intensive work toward a specific goal (a full concert program or especially difficult parts of a program) can vary in duration from a long weekend to two weeks. Seminarios are often organized to prepare a large ensemble, but there are also instrument-specific seminarios. In April 2014, the Corona Youth Music Project (CYMP) Orchestra and Upbeat NYC from the South Bronx brought together their youth orchestras for a three-day seminario, part of the preparation for a large showcase concert three months later. The goal of the seminario was to read through a piece to make sure that both orchestras were on the same page in the learning process of this piece in particular.

But seminarios do not necessarily bring together students from different programs. A program can organize a very successful seminario by itself, as long as it accomplishes in a few days of intensive work musical results that would otherwise take months to accomplish. In February 2014, CYMP organized a student-led seminario in which members of the youth orchestra (ages seven to fifteen) mentored and coached the children's orchestra (ages four to ten) in learning from scratch a new piece.

Seminarios can have their own risks, however, according to Morín: Programs can fall into a bad habit he called "seminarismo" in which leaders tend to implement seminarios constantly, one after the other, without paying attention to the slow, methodical follow-up work needed to intellectualize music and to reinforce technical skills. A seminario is not a substitute for that. In fact one could say that an effective seminario reverses the steps of the learning process: first students play the music almost to perfection, so that their bodies understand the energy this level of musicianship demands, and afterward they go back to the classroom to study the new repertoire's theoretical foundation in depth, and to their instruments to refine the technique the repertoire requires.

## Venezuelan Conservatory Models

El Sistema in Venezuela offers recurring advanced instruction through several different programs. As long as they focus on in-depth technical skills and musicianship, they are referred to as conservatories. The three distinctive conservatory models are the traditional conservatory (like the Simón Bolívar Conservatory in Caracas), the conservatory extension, and the "itinerant" conservatories. These models emerged from the immediate need to provide more students in many regions the opportunity to advance in their education, build networks, and be exposed to new situations that foster personal growth.

A conservatory extension, such as the one in Calabozo in Guárico State, is one of these El Sistema solutions to immediate needs. Conservatory extensions take place for short periods of time on a regular basis – one full weekend every month – in the same location. They gather master teachers from everywhere in the country and selected students from a larger region for intensive learning. This way, students in remote areas have the opportunity to receive advanced training from some of the best teachers in the country, without having to leave their own communities. The level of instruction is such that upon their return these students immediately spread the new knowledge and help train newer generations of local musicians. In Calabozo, the conservatory is managed locally as a stand-alone organization, although all of its teachers belong to the central FundaMusical roster. Students are chosen by their commitment and potential to become teachers and leaders.

In the same way, missions of Venezuelans have traveled abroad to impart lessons in what they call "itinerant conservatories." One such mission, an initiative of the Andean Promotion Corporation (CAF), made extended visits to several Andean countries including Bolivia, Ecuador, and Peru. Groups of master teachers went to several cities in these countries on a regular basis to teach the same core group of students for short periods of time. Indeed this concept of a "mission" leading seminarios, itinerant conservatories, and conservatory extensions has been an essential feature of El Sistema throughout Venezuela and Latin America.

Venezuelan missions to other Latin American countries in the 1990s were part of the vast strategy that Abreu led to expand the movement internationally. His strategy also involved extensive research to identify key players and build both diplomatic and academic relations with individuals who could be potential leaders in expanding the movement. Here is an example of how they did this in Guatemala: In the fall of 1996, a small Guatemalan university organized the first-ever music festival of student ensembles from all over the country. Few such ensembles were in place in Guatemala back then: a few chamber groups from the conservatory and other music schools; a high school marching band; and a military school band. But the main attraction of the festival was a ninety-member youth orchestra that flew in directly from the Venezuelan countryside. The Cumaná Youth Orchestra (Mérida State) arrived unassumingly in a military plane, and its young members stayed in bunks at a military base outside of Guatemala City. Without much media fanfare, this orchestra presented repertoire not usually heard in Guatemala in two of the most amazing concerts in the recent history of the country – playing with the exuberance that the Venezuelan orchestras are now widely known for.

Among the orchestra's entourage was a professional musician who had come on a diplomatic mission, namely to introduce "el movimiento" to the committee that was helping with the university's festival, of which I was part. Armed with a grainy VHS video of the Venezuela National Children's Orchestra playing Tchaikovsky's Fourth at the speed of light, he proposed that they help us accomplish something similar in our country. He had to counter our skeptical arguments that such a level of musicianship couldn't possibly be reached in Guatemala. Eventually he persuaded us to take on this challenge.

We started the following spring, in 1997, when a mission of ten Venezuelan teachers arrived to lead a ten-day *seminario*. In preparation, we assembled for the first time ever a 100-member orchestra. Some of us remained skeptical about what this group could accomplish: the orchestra was made up of students from different walks of life, and many of them had never played in an orchestra before. The *seminario* welcomed students as young as eleven and as old as forty, although most were young teenagers.

At the end of ten days this orchestra played two movements of Beethoven's Fifth Symphony, Mozart's Overture from *The Abduction from the Seraglio*, and a Vivaldi violin concerto. No youth orchestra had played like that in Guatemala before. Even after all the intensive work of ten days – rehearsals and workshops would start at 8 a.m. and end at 8 p.m. – you could feel the Venezuelan-like exuberance during the final concert by the young Guatemalan musicians.

In the 1990s many Venezuelan musicians went on such missions in an attempt to replicate in other Latin American countries (Uruguay, Colombia, Brazil, Ecuador, Peru, Bolivia, etc.) the Venezuelan experience. In a way they were a replay of the first years of the El Sistema movement in Venezuela, when young musicians had to travel back and forth from Caracas to their hometowns where they had limited time to teach and give back to their communities. Knowledge, ideas, and the *tocar y luchar* spirit spread all over Venezuela this way.

## Núcleo Modules

In Guárico State, distances between núcleos were so great that many areas were being left out of the movement. There were not enough teachers to start new núcleos in those "in-between" areas, and students didn't have the resources to travel to the closest núcleo on a regular basis. In response, some núcleos started sending one of their teachers on a regular basis to one of these remote areas to initiate a group of young children into music. With time, the most committed of these "remote" students would make an extra effort to travel to the central núcleo to further their education. In 2004, some núcleos had up to four of these remote classrooms or "modules." Some modules were not so distant, some operated out of the living room of one of the students and one was in an open-air basketball court, but many started taking place in schools during the school day.

In Corona, Queens, we found in the idea of the modules the solution to a very real challenge: namely that, especially in winter, many families would not travel more than a few blocks to bring their young children (and their even younger siblings) to music class. Our solution was to provide two closer locations for these families. In 2014 we operated four orchestral initiation modules in three different locations, and next year we plan to open two more. Through these modules, smaller groups of children receive their first instruction by a core group of teachers, with the goal of preparing them to take on an orchestral instrument. Eventually, each module could house a full orchestra.

**National Academies**

The most advanced students in Venezuela can apply to be part of the national academy of their respective instrument. The Venezuelan El Sistema Violin National Academy is now famous throughout Latin America for setting standards in performance and technique. When accepted into the academy, the student has access to even higher training in their instrument, but also higher responsibility for further teaching. Students in the national academies usually have more access to master classes and workshops by world-renowned teachers. Needless to say, being part of a national academy provides an extra opportunity to connect with a network of advanced students in each particular instrument.

**A Culture of Connectedness**

The development of an El Sistema common culture depends on the connectedness of many organizations, ensembles, initiatives, and individuals working toward the same goals. As the movement grows internationally, three connecting characteristics remain common in every new initiative. The first is this now famous *tocar y luchar* spirit in El Sistema: to play and to strive or to fight. But strive or fight against what? It could be a fight against

304

adverse conditions: to keep playing no matter what. Or it could be a fight against a system that prevents wide access to music education.

A second connecting characteristic is the movement's collective identity. El Sistema embraces a common identity across organizations and participants. It is a well-known brand whose cause is universal: music education in the context of an orchestra or choir is a powerful tool for social change and should be accessible to everyone, especially those who have fewer opportunities because of economical, social, or personal circumstances. Building this global common identity while keeping it connected to the original Venezuelan movement must involve all current and future students, who need to be informed about the ethos and history of El Sistema through stories, anecdotes, movies, etc.

The last common characteristic of the El Sistema movement is the networks it relies upon. In the 1980s and 1990s, at the initial stages of the expansion of El Sistema throughout Latin America, Dr. Abreu would offer training opportunities for young conductors on the condition that they work on replicating the movement in their home countries. This was the start of the first international El Sistema network. Later networks were built around student exchanges and international and regional orchestra festivals. Since then, the emphasis has been on programming those connectors so that students can build their own networks.

In 2012, four El Sistema-inspired programs in the New York City metropolitan area – the Corona Youth Music Project, the Union City Music Project, the Upbeat NYC program, and the Washington Heights-Inwood Music Project – started presenting annual showcase concerts for both their orchestras and choruses. Since then, the network has grown to gather students from six programs. Many of these programs have organized gatherings in which students from two or more orchestras read new repertoire, or even work together in seminarios like the ones mentioned above. Significantly, the emphasis of all these connectors is on the students. Rather than organizing lofty gatherings of pedagogues and managers discussing endlessly how El Sistema trusts young people or how teachers can improve their skills, El Sistema connectors put students at the core, expecting them to attain higher goals, to be accountable for their individual work, but also for the collective performance of the ensemble. They are treated as professionals, and are pushed to find solutions to their own challenges.

Through this focus on students' agency in the movement – by thinking of them, in other words, as more than just music students – the movement secures a new generation of well-trained and well-connected leaders who have a deep understanding of the big picture. Take for instance, Rodrigo Cedeño, from Calabozo, a little town in Guárico State. Cedeño started as a cello student. He became a member of the Venezuela Children's Orchestra, now the Simón Bolívar Orchestra. Later, he left the orchestra to become director of the Guárico Conservatory's extension of the Simón Bolívar Conservatory in Calabozo, and he also serves as the regional music director for the whole state and as a teacher for the National Children's Orchestra of Venezuela. His seemingly long career within El Sistema (he was in is mid-twenties when we met) is a result of the emphasis on making children and youth accountable for the advancement of the movement.

## Risks in Losing the Social Movement Spirit Early in the Game

El Sistema in Venezuela is a complex system of organizations and people connected through an intricate network of formal and informal links that have been built through many connectors. To many, this system of organizations appears to be a simple pyramidal structure, but it's not. FundaMusical doesn't oversee the operations of each organization in the national system, and there is no exclusive top-down control over programming, or music teaching standards. Local organizations are still flexible to mold their operations and curriculum to their particular needs, and to raise funds to accomplish their own particular artistic and organizational goals. Take the paper violin program in La Rinconada, in Caracas. Many in the United States have the impression that this is a broadly-used program in Venezuela. However, many teachers in Venezuela don't use cardboard violins and are not even familiar with the program. Many initiatives emerge from any part of the country and gain popularity when stories of their success travel through these informal networks of teachers and students. However, their success and popularity doesn't lead FundaMusical to turn them into mandatory components of a national curriculum. With this, the movement is allowed to continue evolving organically and allow room for new ideas and initiatives to emerge.

When countries in Latin America tried to replicate the Venezuelan model of a national system, something interesting happened: many perceived the model to be the familiar and simple pyramidal structure and adopted such a model: a leader on the top – hopefully an Abreu-like, charismatic leader, but sometimes the leader turned out to be a politically appointed government official. Students and teachers remained on the bottom of the pyramid, supporting the movement from the ground up. They were content with their role within this structure, until one or two of them were not. So they decided to start their own system, which they would lead. This resulted in more than one pyramid-shaped national organization in the same country. In a small country like Guatemala, more than two organizations emerged like that in the 2000s. With scarce resources, especially qualified teachers, the bottom of these pyramids inevitably overlapped. These teachers – the most essential assets of the movement – had to work for two or three different El Sistema-inspired organizations. In other words, the core agents of the movement were the same, but the leaders and their priorities were different and often competing against each other. They would fight for the scarce resources, which included mostly government support, some private funding, and media attention (not to mention their competition to get the few good teachers, who had to negotiate their time with several organizations, while fighting for the same cause). Challenges similar to this appeared in many Latin American countries.

In the United States, there exists the potential for a proliferation of multiple regional or national pyramid structures and leaders. While such a multiplicity poses many questions, the risk of centralized control over a national movement so early in the game has already led to the formation of some apparently competing interests. Yet this same process has also opened a space for a valuable conversation about the growth and flexibility of the movement in the United States. Many of the questions that have come from this conversation have already been discussed at length in other contexts. For instance, the risk of public funding in the arts becoming a tool of cultural domination by the government has been debated for years – ever since the creation of the National Endowment for the Arts and other state and city arts funding agencies. As a result, the United States is one of the few countries (if not the only one) that has never produced specific, clear-cut arts policies. However, many federal, state, and city regulations such as tax exemptions, zone regulations, etc., constitute de facto arts policies; yet few legislatures have dedicated time to produce laws that specifically regulate the arts.

For El Sistema to stay in this permanent state of "not being there yet," especially at this early stage of the movement, it is urgent to create many different ways to facilitate networks and to foster an open-source common culture among leaders and teachers — but most importantly among students. Many cities and programs are already doing so. These initiatives are evidence that the movement is aiming to strengthen participation and commitment, especially of the younger generations of El Sistema participants.

# Resources and Further Reading

In an effort to keep this manuscript evolving and expanding beyond its printed form, a website has been created as a companion to the text. Please find the site at:

adaptingelsistema.com

Readers can find here further readings, resources, and the most recent content to explore. The types of materials surveyed on the site will include updates from programs and contributors to the book; suggestions, ideas, and information from El Sistema students, parents, teachers, and leaders from across the globe and from experts in related fields; sample documents, curriculums, and videos from and for teachers and leaders; and links to other websites and blogs relevant to the topic of El Sistema.

## Selected Reading List

Booth, Eric. *The Music Teaching Artist's Bible: Becoming a Virtuoso Educator*. New York: Oxford University Press, 2009.

Borzacchini, Chefi. *Venezuela en El Cielo de los Escenarios*. Caracas: Fundación Bancaribe, 2010.

Boyle, Gregory. *Tattoos on the Heart: The Power of Boundless Compassion*. New York: Free Press, 2010.

Crutcherfield, Leslie and Heather Mcleod Grant. *Forces for Good: The Six Practices of High-impact Nonprofits*. 2nd edition. San Francisco: Jossey-Bass, 2012.

Duke, Robert. *Intelligent Music Teaching: Essays on the Core Principles of Effective Instruction*. Austin, TX: Learning and Behavior Resources, 2005.

Jensen, Eric. *Teaching with Poverty in Mind: What Being Poor Does to Kids' Brains and What Schools Can Do About It*. Alexandria, VA: Association for Supervision and Curriculum Development, 2009.

Levitin, Daniel J. *This Is Your Brain on Music: The Science of a Human Obsession*. New York: Penguin, 2006.

Madsen, William C. *Collaborative Therapy with Multi-Stressed Families.* 2nd edition. New York: The Guilford Press, 2007.

McGoldrick, Monica. *Re-Visioning Family Therapy: Race, Culture, and Gender in Clinical Practice.* 2nd edition. New York. The Guilford Press, 2008.

Ries, Eric. *The Lean Startup: How Today's Entrepreneurs Use Continuous Innovation to Create Radically Successful Businesses.* New York: Crown Publishing, 2011.

Rohnke, Karl and Butler, Steve. *Quicksilver: Adventure Games, Initiative Problems, Trust Activities and a Guide to Effective Leadership.* Dubuque, IA: Kendall Hunt Publishing, 1995.

Tarrow, Sydney. *Power in Movement: Social Movements, Collective Action and Politics.* Cambridge: Cambridge University Press, 1994.

Tough, Paul. *How Children Succeed: Grit, Curiosity, and the Hidden Power of Character.* New York: Houghton Mifflin Harcourt, 2012.

Tunstall, Tricia. *Changing Lives: Gustavo Dudamel, El Sistema, and the Transformative Power of Music.* New York: W. W. Norton, 2012.

# About the Editor

## Christine Witkowski
### *Founding Director, YOLA at HOLA*

Christine Witkowski is a musician, educator, and youth advocate special-izing in community-centered arts education. As the founding director of YOLA at the Heart of Los Angeles (HOLA), Christine designed and implemented one of the nation's premier El Sistema-inspired programs, which now serves hundreds of children and families in LA's Rampart District with intensive music education, leadership training, and social services.

Growing up in the Detroit area, Christine was fortunate to begin her musical studies at the age of fourteen with Motown studio horn player Joe Buono. She pursued her dual passions of music and youth development in Chicago, studying Music at Northwestern University and working as a Program Coordinator for the youth development agency Youth Organizations Umbrella, Inc.

Christine earned her Master of Music degree from McGill University in Montreal, QC, and was awarded a fellowship at the Aspen Music Festival and School in Colorado. In 2009, she was chosen as one of ten fellows to participate in the inaugural "Sistema Fellows Program" at the New England Conservatory of Music in Boston. She is now a leader in the ever-expanding network of El Sistema-inspired programs, mentoring and training initiatives across the United States and also abroad. Recognizing that El Sistema work requires skills beyond music education and admin-istration, Christine furthered her studies at the Southern California Counseling Center and holds a Certification in Community Counseling.

# Notes on the Contributors

### Dr. José Antonio Abreu
*Founder, El Sistema  (Fundación Musical Simón Bolívar)*
Four decades ago, visionary musician, economist, and politician Dr. José Antonio Abreu founded El Sistema in Venezuela. Today, El Sistema – the National System of Youth and Children's Orchestras and Choirs of Venezuela – has provided millions of children in Venezuela and around the globe with access to free music education.

Abreu began studying music at the age of nine with pianist Doralisa Jiménez de Medina in Barquisimeto. In 1957, he attended the Caracas Musical Declamation Academy, where he studied piano, organ, harpsichord, and composition. Abreu obtained a PhD in petroleum economics at the Universidad Católica Andrés Bello in 1961, where he would later return as a professor of economics and law in addition to his faculty position at the Universidad Simón Bolivar. As a politician, Abreu served as a Deputy at the Chamber of Deputies in the Congress of Venezuela and as the Minister of Culture and president of the National Council of Culture.

In 1975, Abreu began El Sistema with eleven students in a parking garage and a belief that art could be used as a vehicle for social justice. Twenty years later, Abreu's vision and leadership led to the creation of a new state foundation – Fundación Musical Simón Bolívar (formerly FENOJIV) – to ensure the sustainability of El Sistema in Venezuela. Since its inception, El Sistema has touched the lives of millions of children around the globe. Abreu has been internationally recognized for this success: in 1998, he was designated a UNESCO Ambassador for Peace. That same year, he received the Légion d'honneur of France. In 2001, he was awarded the Right Livelihood Award and in 2009 the TED Prize award.

# Malin Aghed
## *El Sistema Gothenburg*
Malin Aghed and the Swedish El Sistema team coordinate more than twenty núcleos in Sweden; in 2012, they and five other organizations formed Sistema Europe, a network that today includes groups from almost twenty European countries meeting on a regular basis. Malin was brought up in a small town in the south of Sweden, playing first the flute and then the trombone in a local orchestra, as well as singing in different choirs. In 1994, she moved to Gothenburg to become a theater teacher, and later also taught in Tanzania and Ethiopia. Malin continued to combine teaching in different art subjects with different kinds of social work in Sweden as well as in Ethiopia. After finishing her music teacher education she worked at the University of Music and Drama and at one of the municipal schools of fine arts of Gothenburg. In 2009, the idea of launching an El Sistema program in Sweden was born after a local concert in her neighborhood featured the Gothenburg Symphonic Orchestra and Maestro Gustavo Dudamel. Malin is now the coordinator of twenty El Sistema núcleos in six different Swedish cities, and is developing some fifteen new núcleos by the end of 2015.

# Dan Berkowitz
## *Manager, Youth Orchestra Los Angeles, Los Angeles Philharmonic*
Named one of Forbes 30 Under 30 for Education in 2014, Dan Berkowitz is using music as a vehicle for social change. A musician and educator with degrees in economics and trombone performance from Northwestern University, Dan began his economics career with Morningstar Inc., soon moving to London to start up their European fund research endeavor. In 2009, he was chosen as an inaugural Sistema Fellow at the New England Conservatory. After graduation, he moved to Los Angeles to build Youth Orchestra Los Angeles (YOLA), one of the nation's most robust El Sistema programs. With the support of the LA Philharmonic, Gustavo Dudamel, and community partners, Dan has grown YOLA to over 600 students – each receiving twelve to fifteen hours of free programming each week. Internationally, Dan designs symposiums that explore the intersection of music and social innovation for the LA Phil and its institutional partners. He also advises organizations worldwide through various stages

of development, including residencies at El Sistema Japan and Sistema Taiwan.

## Leni Boorstin

*Director, Community and Government Affairs, Los Angeles Philharmonic*
As director of community and government affairs for the Los Angeles Philharmonic Association, Leni Boorstin is responsible for Neighborhood Concerts and other community programs, including those that opened Walt Disney Concert Hall, celebrated its fifth and tenth anniversaries, and welcomed Gustavo Dudamel to Los Angeles as the LA Philharmonic's music director. She worked with a coalition of stakeholders to introduce El Sistema-influenced programs to Los Angeles, and helped develop the partnerships that have resulted in the robust Youth Orchestra Los Angeles (YOLA) programs in three sites, currently serving over 600 students. Leni's previous experience in arts management was at KPFK-FM and San Francisco's Exploratorium Museum. As a graduate student she was a Public Affairs and the Arts Fellow with the CORO Foundation. Leni has served three mayors as a City of Los Angeles human relations commissioner. She is a founding board member and chair emeritus of Arts for LA.

## Eric Booth

*Arts Learning Consultant*
In addition to careers as a Broadway actor, successful entrepreneur, author, and teacher, Eric Booth has been described by the press as "the father of teaching artistry" and "one of the twenty-five most important arts educators in the U.S." On the faculty of Juilliard (twelve years), Lincoln Center Education (twenty-six years), and the Kennedy Center (fourteen years), he now consults with many arts organizations, including six of the ten largest orchestras in the United States, and five national service organizations. Author of five books (including *The Music Teaching Artist's Bible*), he founded *Teaching Artist Journal* and two international teaching artist conferences and has written many essays on El Sistema. He was asked to do the closing keynote speech at UNESCO's first world arts education conference in Lisbon (2006), and to give the opening keynote at the organization's 2014 world conference in Seoul. He is one of the world's leading consultants on El Sistema programs.

## Deborah Borda

### *President and CEO, Los Angeles Philharmonic*

Throughout her career, Deborah Borda has extended the boundaries of the American symphonic world. Prior to becoming president and CEO of the Los Angeles Philharmonic in 2000, she was executive director of the New York Philharmonic, general manager of the San Francisco Symphony, and president of the Saint Paul Chamber Orchestra and Detroit Symphony Orchestra. During a decade in LA she implemented an acclaimed artistic and business plan, oversaw the construction of Walt Disney Concert Hall, restored the orchestra to fiscal health, and spearheaded the appointment of Gustavo Dudamel as music director. Under Deborah 's leadership, the orchestra has gained international acclaim for its peerless commitment to new music and imaginative interpretations of classic works, such as the Mozart/DaPonte Trilogy designed by leading architects and couturiers. Recognizing the social, as well as artistic, imperative of the orchestra, Deborah has ushered in an era of increased community engagement through such influential programs as Youth Orchestra Los Angeles (YOLA). While serving local audiences through its artistic and educational efforts, the LA Phil continues to broaden its reach by touring, offering an extensive catalog of recorded music, and with radio, television, and theater broadcasts.

## Leon Botstein

### *President and Leon Levy Professor in the Arts of Bard College*

Leon Botstein is an important American conductor and leading academic known for his innovative programming and interest in contemporary and neglected repertory. Botstein is President and Leon Levy Professor in the Arts of Bard College, the author of several books, and the editor of *The Compleat Brahms* (1999) and *The Musical Quarterly*. He is currently working on a sequel to *Jefferson's Children*, about the American education system. The music director of the American Symphony Orchestra for nearly a quarter century, he is also conductor laureate of the Jerusalem Symphony Orchestra, where he served as music director from 2003–2011. Botstein can be heard on numerous recordings with the London Symphony, the London Philharmonic, NDR-Hamburg, and the Jerusalem Symphony Orchestra. Recently, he conducted the Sinfónica Juvenil de

Caracas in Venezuela and Japan, the first non-Venezuelan conductor invited by El Sistema to conduct on a tour. Botstein holds a BA from the University of Chicago and an MA and PhD from Harvard University. For his contributions to music, he has received the award of the American Academy of Arts and Letters and Harvard University's prestigious Centennial Award, as well as the Cross of Honor, First Class from the government of Austria.

## Tony Brown
*Executive Director, Heart of Los Angeles (HOLA)*
Tony Brown has been the Executive Director of Heart of Los Angeles (HOLA) since 2007. He is a graduate of Loyola Marymount University and received a master's degree from the University of Tennessee in sports management/marketing. After working at HOLA in the 1990s, Tony worked for several years as a teacher and served as the athletic director and a coach for private schools while owning and managing several successful camp programs. Tony is a Stanford University Graduate School of Business Center for Social Innovation Fellow and serves on the dean's board of advisors of the University of Tennessee's College of Education, Health, and Human Sciences. Tony has been acknowledged by Loyola Marymount with the Distinguished Alumni Award, by Bank of America with the Local Hero Award, and by KTLA as a Hometown Hero. Most recently, he received the Leadership Excellence Award from the *Los Angeles Business Journal*.

## Marianne Diaz
*Director of Outreach Services, Southern California Counseling Center; Founder, Clean Slate Inc.*
Marianne Diaz is a therapist in Los Angeles, where she works with numerous organizations to support young people and train counselors from all backgrounds. After becoming a gang member at the age of thirteen, Marianne learned that the violence she experienced at home was just a symptom of the way people with social and financial power treat those without. Gangs, she realized, were a means of equalizing the power balance in her community, where the currency was intimidation, violence, and control. Since her release from prison in 1982, Marianne has focused her work on the reasons that communities continue to turn their rage

317

against themselves. Through her programs, which focus on those on the receiving end of racism, sexism, poverty, social injustice, and inequality, Marianne opens up conversations with those who are in the best positions to turn a lens toward the reality of the natural consequences of oppression.

## Gustavo Dudamel

*Music & Artistic Director, Los Angeles Philharmonic*

Gustavo Dudamel is defined by his untiring advocacy of access to music for all. As a symphonic and operatic conductor, his music making on four continents continues to inspire audiences of all ages. He is currently serving as Music & Artistic Director of the Los Angeles Philharmonic and Music Director of the Simón Bolívar Symphony Orchestra of Venezuela, and the impact of his musical leadership is felt internationally. While his commitment to these posts accounts for the major portion of his yearly schedule, Dudamel also guest conducts regularly with some of the world's greatest musical institutions, including the Berlin Philharmonic and the Vienna Philharmonic.

Grammy-winner Gustavo Dudamel has numerous recordings on the Deutsche Grammophon label, as well as many video/DVD releases that capture the excitement of significant moments of his musical life.

One of the most decorated conductors of his generation, recent distinctions include the 2014 Leonard Bernstein Lifetime Achievement Award for the Elevation of Music in Society from the Longy School, 2013 Musical America's Musician of the Year and induction into Gramophone Hall of Fame, 2010 Eugene McDermott Award in the Arts at MIT, 2009 Chevalier de l'Ordre des Arts et des Lettres and one of *TIME* Magazine's 100 most influential people, and 2008 "Q" Prize from Harvard, along with several honorary doctorates.

Born in 1981 in Venezuela, access to music for all has been the cornerstone of Gustavo's philosophy both professionally and philanthropically.

## Loralie Heagy

*Founder, Juneau, Alaska Music Matters; Music Teacher, Glacier Valley Elementary School*

Loralie "Lorrie" Heagy is a music teacher and program director of Juneau Alaska Music Matters (JAMM), an El Sistema-inspired program that provides string instruction for over 500 students. In 2009, Lorrie was selected as a Sistema Fellow at the New England Conservatory. She has eighteen years' experience in the classroom and has provided teacher training for El Sistema initiatives across the country, focusing on early childhood practices, brain-based learning, and student engagement. Lorrie holds three master's degrees in education: elementary, music, and library education. She is pursuing a Ph.D. in education with a specialization in instruction, learning, and innovation. She is honored to have represented Alaska's teachers as the 2011 Alaska Teacher of the Year.

## Shirley Brice Heath
*American Linguistic Anthropologist, Stanford University, Brown University*
Shirley Brice Heath, linguistic anthropologist, studies learners across the lifespan in non-formal environments of learning. She is the author of *Words at Work and Play: Three Decades in Families and Communities* (2012) and the classic *Ways with Words: Language, Life, and Work in Communities* and *Classrooms* (Cambridge University Press, 1983/1996). Heath has taught at universities throughout the world, most notably Stanford University and Brown University, and as visiting research professor at King's College, University of London. Of particular note are Heath's publications written for community advocates about creating environments in which the arts and sciences are both viewed as essential for effective learning. In 2004, she published with Shelby Wolf a series on "visual learning" for teachers and arts practitioners; in 2005, a similar series on learning through drama and in arts and science project–based work was published. She has studied youth-based community organizations in several nations. Her resource guide and prize-winning documentary, *ArtShow* (2000), features young leaders in four interracial and cross-class community arts organizations in the United States. She also directed and produced two short documentaries on youth organizations dedicated to sustainable agriculture and environmental architecture.

## Yutaka Kikugawa
*Executive Director/CEO, Friends of El Sistema Japan*
Yutaka Kikugawa was born in Kobe in 1971 and holds a bachelor's degree in geography from University College London, as well as a master's in policy studies from the Institute of Education, University of London. He

joined UNESCO in 1998 as program officer in education after working with the Institute for Social Engineering, Inc. In 2000, he joined UNICEF as an adolescent and youth development officer in Lesotho (2003) and HIV/AIDS coordinator in Eritrea (2007). He moved to the Japan Committee for UNICEF to take on the responsibilities of Junior 8 Summit program coordinator (2008); manager, Group and Organizational Relation Division (2011), and chief coordinator, East Japan Earthquake and Tsunami Emergency and Recovery Operation (2012).

## Dr. Isaiah "Ike" McKinnon

*Deputy Mayor, City of Detroit*

Isaiah "Ike" McKinnon is currently the deputy mayor of the city of Detroit and an associate professor of education at the University of Detroit Mercy. After joining the Detroit Police Department in 1965, Isaiah McKinnon rose through the ranks to become police chief under Mayor Dennis Archer from 1994–1998. He graduated from the FBI Academy in Quantico, Virginia, and holds a doctorate in higher education administration from Michigan State University, a master's degree in criminal justice from Mercy College of Detroit, and a bachelor's degree in history and law enforcement from the University of Detroit. Ike has authored or co-authored three books and numerous articles on crime, won an Emmy Award for his work as "Detroit's Safety Consultant" on NBC News/WDIV-TV, and has been interviewed on the *Today Show*, *Oprah*, *Good Morning America*, *Rivera Live*, and the History Channel. Ike also works as a national motivational/inspirational speaker to Fortune 500 companies and schools.

## Gretchen Nielsen

*Director of Educational Initiatives, Los Angeles Philharmonic*

Gretchen Nielsen leads the Los Angeles Philharmonic's education programming. Since 2007, Gretchen has designed, implemented, and supervised an integrated set of education programs that annually reach more than 150,000 schoolchildren, teachers, families, young musicians, and concertgoers. In 2007, Gretchen launched Youth Orchestra Los Angeles (YOLA), Gustavo Dudamel's signature program based on El Sistema. Since that time she has worked to expand YOLA locally, and broaden its reach nationally by helping to form the Take a Stand partnership with the LA Phil and Longy School of Music of Bard College. Internationally, Gretchen is connecting the social and artistic imperatives of the Los Angeles Philharmonic by leading LA Phil education projects with the Barbican Centre in London and El Sistema in Venezuela. Gretchen is a former management fellow of the Opera America Fellowship Program, a current member of 24th Street Theatre's board of directors, and a proud mentor of YOLA students.

## Paloma Udovic Ramos
*YOLA at EXPO Program Manager, Harmony Project*
A violinist since age three, Paloma Udovic Ramos has spent her life making music and pursuing a strong passion for social justice. Paloma received her bachelor of arts degree from Northwestern University in anthropology, with a focus on ethnomusicology and Latin American studies. She moved to Los Angeles in 2004, where she began performing and teaching. Paloma joined Harmony Project in 2008 to oversee and manage their YOLA EXPO site. Under her direction the program has tripled in size and depth, and now includes three full orchestras and 300 students.

## Alvaro Rodas
*Founder/Executive Director, Corona Youth Music Project*
In 1997, Alvaro F. Rodas was in the leadership team that hosted the first replication of El Sistema in Guatemala, his native country. He worked as a teacher and mentor of young musicians in Guatemala until 2004. There, he also taught percussion at the National Conservatory, and was the principal percussionist at the National Symphony. His interest in leadership and administration related to El Sistema earned him a Fulbright scholarship to complete a master of arts in arts administration at Columbia University in 2006. In 2009, he was selected as part of the inaugural class of the El Sistema Fellows at the New England Conservatory. A direct result of this fellowship was the creation in 2010 of the Corona Youth Music Project. That year, Alvaro was also a consultant for the government of El Salvador to develop the plan for El Sistema in that country.

## Ariadna Sanchez

### *Proyecto LEA Founder; YOLA at HOLA Parent*

Ariadna Sánchez was born in Oaxaca, Mexico and has lived in Los Angeles since December of 2003. She was studying her bachelor of arts in business and tourism before she decided to emigrate to the United States with her husband. In 2010, she earned her high school diploma from Metropolitan Skills Center and decided to enroll at Los Angeles Community College, where she currently pursues an AA degree in liberal arts. Ariadna is the director of Proyecto LEA (Líderes En Acción), a community group that promotes reading in the community by storytelling at local events. Since May 2013, Ariadna has been a weekly contributor for *Los Bloguitos*, a Spanish children's blog, and beginning October 2013 for *La Bloga*, a Latino literacy blog. She is also a monthly contributor for *Oaxaca Profundo* magazine and this fall will make her first contribution to *Iguana*, a prestigious Spanish language children's magazine. Ariadna is the proud mother of two of YOLA at HOLA's young musicians, Carlos and Mateo.

## Nikki Shorts

### *String Specialist and Children's Orchestra Conductor, YOLA at HOLA*

Nikki is a freelance performer and teacher throughout southern California who believes in making music available to all people, especially within underserved communities. She received her master's in viola performance from Northwestern University in 2007, and her bachelor's of music in viola performance from California State University Long Beach in 2004. She is a member of the Kroma Quartet and has performed with the Southeast Symphony, Camarata of Los Angeles, Marina del Rey Symphony, Culver City Symphony, Santa Monica Symphony, and Downey Symphony. She also performs with Multi Ethnic Star Orchestra (MESTO) which is known for its performance of orchestral transcriptions of traditional Middle Eastern music. Nikki is also a recording artist, working with such artists as Tyrone Wells, Rihanna, and the Trans Siberian Orchestra. Besides her work at YOLA at HOLA, she is a curriculum writer and teaching artist with the Los Angeles Philharmonic's School Partners Programs and a mentor teacher for the Longy/Bard Master of Arts in Teaching program.

# Rebecca Reid Sigel

*YOLA Coordinator, Los Angeles Philharmonic*

With a background in music and outdoor education, Rebecca is committed to comprehensive approaches to community building and student leadership development. While working toward a bachelor of arts in music (ethnomusicology) at Brown University, Rebecca worked with linguistic anthropologist Shirley Brice Heath as a researcher and participant/observer with youth-based arts programs, while also coordinating seminar retreats for young people engaged in upstart social entrepreneurship initiatives. Experience with the National Outdoor Leadership School (NOLS) led Rebecca to years spent as a campcraft counselor, backpacking trip leader, and ski instructor. In 2012, Rebecca came to Los Angeles to serve as the Los Angeles Philharmonic's YOLA Coordinator. With YOLA, she produces large-scale events, organizes evaluation efforts, and designed this year's Leadership Forum for Young Musicians.

# Dalouge Smith

*President and CEO, San Diego Youth Symphony and Conservatory*

Dalouge Smith is in his tenth season leading San Diego Youth Symphony (SDYS) and Conservatory. He has overseen development of SDYS's vision to "make music education accessible and affordable for all students." In pursuit of this vision, Dalouge has transformed SDYS into a community instigator for restoring and strengthening music education in schools as SDYS has expanded its work beyond music programs to include measurement, partnerships, community awareness, and community action. Along with using its flagship orchestras and ensembles in pursuit of its vision, in 2010, SDYS launched its first community music program inspired by Venezuela's El Sistema. In early 2013, SDYS's school district partner, Chula Vista Elementary School District, announced its commitment to return music education to all forty-five of its campuses and all 29,000 of its students. At the beginning of 2014, the district was one of only two districts nationwide to become a new VH1 Save the Music Foundation grantee.

# Tricia Tunstall

*Independent Writer, Speaker, Music Educator*

Tricia Tunstall is the author of *Changing Lives: Gustavo Dudamel, El*

*Sistema, and the Transformative Power of Music* (W.W. Norton, 2012), which won ASCAP's 2013 Deems Taylor Award. A leading speaker, writer, and consultant in the field of El Sistema and music education for social change, she is an advocate for the El Sistema vision in forums including London's Southbank Centre, Tokyo's El Sistema symposium, Berkeley's Cal Performances, the Los Angeles ALOUD program, and Carnegie Hall's Academy Program. Tricia is currently working on a new book about the international El Sistema movement, to be co-authored with Eric Booth (W.W. Norton, projected publication fall 2015). She is also the author of a musical memoir, *Note by Note: A Celebration of the Piano Lesson* (Simon & Schuster, 2008), and maintains a very active piano studio in the New York metropolitan area.

## Monika Vischer

### Board President, El Sistema Colorado

Monika Vischer is the classical program director at Colorado Public Radio where she's been an on-air host for twenty-four years. Among the classical music luminaries Monika has interviewed have been El Sistema founder José Antonio Abreu and Los Angeles Philharmonic music director Gustavo Dudamel. Outside of her radio work, she felt personally impassioned to see Denver's underprivileged children benefit from El Sistema's riches, co-founding El Sistema Colorado in 2011 with Denver business owner Susan Probeck and pianist/New England College graduate Carol Rankin.

## Ines Williams

### Union City Music Project Parent

Ines Williams-Gonzalez was born in Santo Domingo, Dominican Republic, and raised in the province of Salcedo. She arrived in the United States in 1998 and has been living in Union City, New Jersey since 2008. She earned a degree in engineering and computer science at Universidad Tecnológica de Santiago, Moca campus, where she was also director of the university English center during the fall of 1998. In 2010, Mrs. Williams earned a bachelor of arts, cum laude, and in 2012, a master of arts, both from New Jersey City University. In her native country, Ines was a reporter for TV 12, TELEINCA for two years, as well as producer and host for the local TV show *Acontecer Salcedence*. For the last three years, she was the leader of the Girls Ministries at the local Evangelic Pentecostal Church and has served as a parent volunteer at the Union City Music Project since 2012. She lives with her husband Wilber Gonzalez, and they are the proud parents of Ashley, 11, violin concertmaster; Breanna, 8, first cello; and Shiloh, 6, violin.

## Dr. Michael Witkowski
*Associate Professor of Criminal Justice, University of Detroit Mercy*

Dr. Michael J. Witkowski, CPP is a tenured associate professor of criminal justice and director of the graduate program in security administration at the University of Detroit Mercy. Michael is a nationally known security litigation expert with many years of experience handling civil litigation involving premises liability issues and crime by street gangs. He has researched gang activity occurring in a number of venues including public housing, Section 8 apartments, schools, casinos, nightclubs, concerts, fast-food restaurants, shopping centers, sporting venues, convenience stores, and entertainment centers. He is a member of the Detroit Chapter of the American Society of Industrial Security (ASIS), the Crime Prevention Association of Michigan, and the Downtown Detroit Executive Security Council. He is also a Certified Protection Professional (CPP) by examination and is considered a board-certified security consultant by ASIS, and is also a member of the Midwest Criminal Justice Association, and the American Society of Criminology. He has been awarded the Frederich Milton Thrasher award for excellence in gang research three times by the National Gang Crime Research Center.

## Karen Zorn
*President, Longy School of Music of Bard College*

Karen Zorn has been president of Longy School of Music of Bard College since 2007 and a vice president of Bard College since 2012. In the seven years since her arrival, Zorn has led Longy through a process of radical change unprecedented in its nearly 100-year history. A fearless educational entrepreneur, she has balanced the budget, boosted enrollment, executed a merger with Bard College, and established partnerships with the Los Angeles Philharmonic and Fundación Musical Simón Bolívar (El Sistema in Venezuela) to launch innovative programs of study and community engagement. These include the recently launched Take a Stand program and new Master of Arts in Teaching (MAT) in Music program based in Los Angeles, as well as initiatives that embed Longy Conservatory students as teaching assistants in public schools, community centers, prisons, shelters, and other external venues where the traditions of music education can contribute to public life. Karen is herself a classically trained musician, having been educated as a pianist in the United States and Germany. Prior to her tenure at Longy, Karen served as associate provost at Berklee College of Music and acting director and director of instruction at MacPhail Center for the Arts in Minneapolis. She has taught as a member of the faculties of Berklee, MacPhail, and the University of Missouri, Kansas City.